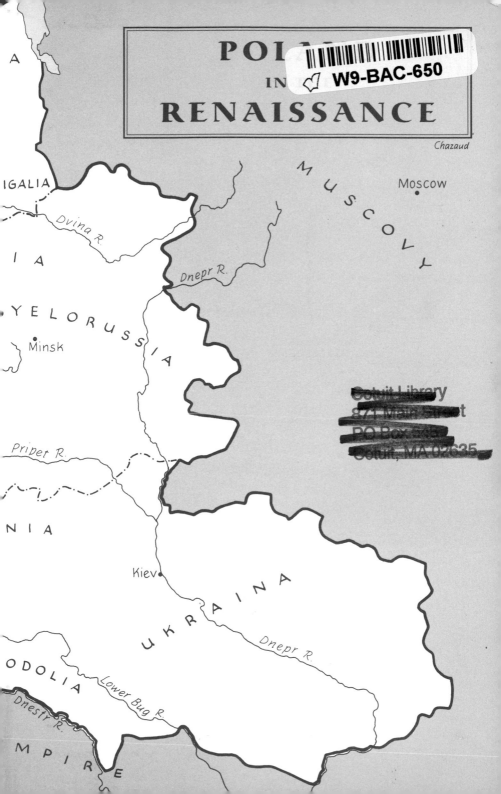

POL...
IN...
RENAISSANCE

Chazaud

MUSCOVY

Moscow

IGALIA

Dvina R.

Dnepr R.

IA

YELORUSSIA

Minsk

Pripet R.

NIA

Kiev

UKRAINA

Dnepr R.

ODOLIA

Lower Bug R.

Dnestr R.

MPIRE

Shtetl

Shtetl

THE LIFE

AND DEATH

OF A SMALL TOWN

AND THE WORLD OF POLISH JEWS

Eva Hoffman

HOUGHTON MIFFLIN COMPANY

BOSTON NEW YORK 1997

Copyright © 1997 by Eva Hoffman

For information about permission to reproduce selections from
this book, write to Permissions, Houghton Mifflin Company,
215 Park·Avenue South, New York, New York 10003.

Library of Congress Cataloging-in-Publication Data
Hoffman, Eva.
    Shtetl : the life and death of a small town and the world of Polish Jews /
Eva Hoffman.
        p.   cm.
    Includes bibliographical references.
    ISBN 0-395-82295-5
    1. Jews — Poland — Brańsk — History.   2. Holocaust, Jewish
(1939–1945) — Poland — Brańsk.   3. Brańsk (Poland) — Ethnic relations.
I. Title.
DS135.P62B694 1997   943.8'3 — dc21   97-2615   CIP   r97

Book design by Anne Chalmers; maps by Jacques Chazaud
Typeface: Stempel Garamond by Linotype-Hell

Printed in the United States of America

QUM 10 9 8 7 6 5 4 3 2 1

The drawings that appear at the ends of chapters are of Brańsk synagogues that
were destroyed during World War II. (From *Synagogues and Jewish Communities
in the Białystok Region* by Tomasz Wiśniewski; reprinted by permission of the
author)

TO

MARIA AND BORIS,

WHO SURVIVED THAT TIME

WITH THE HELP OF OTHERS

AND IN MEMORY OF BORIS,

WHO DIED IN 1995

This book was inspired in part

by Marian Marzynski's documentary *Shtetl,*

which aired on PBS's *Frontline* series in April 1996.

Acknowledgments ౨

My first debt of gratitude goes to Marian Marzynski, the director of the film *Shtetl*, and to *Frontline* and WGBH in Boston, which coproduced and aired the documentary. The book arose out of the film and to some extent covers the same geographic and thematic territory. I am therefore especially mindful of Mr. Marzynski's considerateness in allowing my text to take its own shape and direction, even if it sometimes departs from his film's. He has been generous in sharing information and indispensable primary sources with me, including the Polish translation of the Brańsk Yizkor Book. His energy and support have been important in instigating the project and maintaining its momentum. Marrie Campbell at WGBH was also most helpful in the initial stages of the undertaking.

In the course of researching and writing a book like this, one is dependent on the goodwill and openness of many people. My particular thanks go to the present and former inhabitants of Brańsk, who gave their time, thoughts, and memories so unstintingly. On the Polish side, the pioneering research of Zbigniew Romaniuk permeates the entire manuscript. The text gives evidence of this, but I would also like to thank him and his wife, Yolanda Romaniuk, for inviting me into their small apartment and treating me with such warmth and hospitality during my stay. The interviews with Irena Jabłonowska and Anna Woińska were invaluable; in addition, I would like to mention Mieczysław Korzeniewski, who contributed his time and labor to the creation of the Jewish memorial cemetery in Brańsk and whose remarks during our talk were genial and informative. In Warsaw, Helena Luczywo and Wanda Rapaczynska put me up and put up with me during my travels; for their sustaining wit and friendship, these are just small thanks.

In Baltimore, Jack Rubin was tireless, at a difficult time, in recounting his story and responding to my many, undoubtedly tiresome questions. His wife, Sonya Rubin, also a former inhabitant of Brańsk, was tolerant of my intrusions and contributed informative comments. I profited greatly from conversations with Minnie Shapiro and Bluma Shapiro. My special thanks to Rubin Roy Cobb for his time and willingness to help, especially in gathering important materials. I appreciate the kindness of Evelyn Iteld Silverboard in making available her rare photographs.

I am grateful to Joanna Michlic-Coren, who assisted me at all stages of work on this book. Her knowledge of Polish-Jewish history was a steady resource; her skills in providing pertinent materials and making her way through thickets of information were consistently reliable.

Conversations with many friends have enriched my understanding of my subject. In New York, I have repeatedly sounded out Marta Petrusewicz about various historical issues, in the trust that I would neither wear out her patience nor exhaust her intelligence. In London, I have been edified and entertained by discussions with Felix Scharf, whose amazing powers of recall and eloquence in several languages brought the world of prewar Polish Jewry alive for me. His perceptions and moral sense inform many pages of my book.

I would like to thank Tomasz Wiśniewski in Białystok,

Dorota Dec at the Czartoryski Museum in Cracow, and Urszula Fuks at the Jewish Historical Institute in Warsaw for their kindness in pursuing illustrations and making them available. Marek Web and Krystyna Fisher at the YIVO Institute in New York were gracious in giving me their time and guidance.

Finally, I want to express more than formal appreciation to Steve Fraser at Houghton Mifflin for his faith in this project and for nurturing it with tact and intelligence in every phase of development. His assistant, Lenora Todaro, was not only helpful but retained her amiability throughout. To Georges Borchardt and his stalwart staff, for their always reliable and sensitive support, my thanks, as ever.

Contents ᘒ

Shtetl

Introduction ✷

Gone now are those little towns where the shoemaker was
    a poet,
The watchmaker a philosopher, the barber a troubadour.
Gone now are those little towns where the wind joined
Biblical songs with Polish tunes and Slavic rue,
Where old Jews in orchards in the shade of cherry trees
Lamented for the holy walls of Jerusalem.
Gone now are those little towns, though the poetic mists,
The moons, winds, ponds, and stars above them
Have recorded in the blood of centuries the tragic tales,
The histories of the two saddest nations on earth.

      — Antoni Słonimski, "Elegy for the Jewish Villages"

WHAT REMAINS of the Jews of Poland? Mostly traces, echoes, and a few monuments; and also sorrow, rage, guilt, and denial. There are a few thousand Jews left in Poland today, but the communities they inhabited, their characteristic culture and society, were all destroyed during World War II. Because the extent of the loss was so great — so total — the act of remembering the vanished world has become fraught with painful and still acute emotions.

The destruction was nowhere more complete than in the numberless Polish shtetls, those villages and small towns that dotted the Polish landscape and that were sometimes partly, sometimes preponderantly, Jewish. The villages are still there, many of them lovely enough to justify geographic longing; the towns can be found, often transformed into bleakness by postwar poverty and socialist architecture. A few synagogues still stand, some of them crumbling from neglect and disuse, others preserved and restored to their former dignity. Occasionally, outside the borders of a village, there is a small Jewish cemetery, with weeds and vegetation climbing up the crooked headstones. A Polish farmer will point out a copse where the Jews were rounded up by the Nazis and shot; in a few places, modest monuments have been erected to those who perished. Relics, scattered and enigmatic, as of a lost ancient civilization. But the pulsing Jewish world that was here, the small shops and stalls, the bustle of people, carts, horses, the sounds of Yiddish and Hebrew — these are no more. The Jews, a Polish poet wrote, "were captured in the hot act of life." That life can almost be intuited beyond the curtain of abrupt absence. We think we can almost cross the curtain; but we cannot.

In post-Holocaust memory, Poland holds an exceptional place: that was where most of the world's Jewish population lived before the war, and that was where the extermination of European Jewry took place. At the beginning of the war, there were three million Jews in Poland; at the end, between 240,000 and 300,000 remained. Most of the Nazi concentration camps were built in Poland, and it is often said that the Nazis counted on the collusion of the Poles in their project of extermination. Such an explanation has been repeatedly and convincingly refuted. It is much more likely that the camps were placed in Poland for logistical reasons: Poland was where most of the people targeted for extermination were located.

Fifty years after the cataclysmic events, there is perhaps no past as powerfully contested as that of the Polish Jews. The Holocaust in Poland, and all of Polish-Jewish history, continues to be the embattled terrain of three different and sometimes bitterly competing sets of collective memory: Jewish memory, Polish memory, and the memory of the West.

In postwar Jewish memory, in the minds of many Holocaust survivors and their descendants, Poland has come to figure as the very heart of darkness, the central symbol of the inferno. Our psyches are associative: because the Holocaust happened there, because so many people were tortured and murdered on its soil, Poland became scorched earth, contaminated ground. What is remembered most vividly is the suffering; what remains lodged most sharply in the heart are the shards of rejection and betrayal. On the individual level, the accounts of Polish indifference or criminality are rarely an exaggeration in a realm where, in a sense, no exaggeration is possible. But taken collectively, the linking of Poland with the genocide involves a form of partial memory, which has enormously increased Polish defensiveness and rancor.

Unfortunately, the Polish response to the Holocaust in the aftermath of the war only added to the Jewish survivors' anger and hurt. There were horrible episodes of violence and murder. But there was also — after a brief initial period of commemoration and documentation — the wider pathology of silence. During the postwar decades, the specific history of the Holocaust, the Jewish aspects of prewar Polish culture, even the Jews themselves, became untouchable, and gradually forgotten, subjects. The amnesia was undoubtedly caused in part by the extremely disturbing nature of what needed to be remembered, by incomprehension, psychological numbing, and guilt. But the repression of memory was greatly aided and abetted by the falsifications of Communist history and by the fact that under its aegis, discussion of many politically charged issues was stifled. The fate of the Jews during the war, as well as the Polish role in witnessing and sometimes participating in their destruction, were among those issues. So, incidentally, was the role of the non-Communist Polish resistance in opposing the Nazis. The reasons for such distortions varied but were always part of a larger Communist agenda, and it suited that agenda to subsume Jewish victims of the Holocaust under the national categories of Poles, Czechs, Hungarians, and so on. It is no accident that these repressed themes began to be examined publicly again once the Iron Curtain was lifted in 1989. In Poland, painful and still halting discussions of anti-Semitism have begun. But the previous deletions and denials immensely augmented Jewish frustration at what was in effect an erasure of their tragedy from their former countrymen's consciousness.

The Western perspective added more layers of grievance and misunderstanding. In the West, knowledge of what happened in Poland during World War II was simplified to begin with, and clouded by Communist propaganda to boot. Moreover, instead of being modified by time and change, the bleak images of Poland were calcified by the Cold War. The Iron Curtain was a force of and for reductiveness. The countries behind that divide became relegated, even more strongly than before, to a category of Otherness, a realm of leaden, monolithic oppression. While the Western public was aware of the revisions of mood and opinion in West Germany, for example, Poland as a real entity was supplanted by static abstractions. West Germany, with its new democracy and economic prosperity, came to be seen as one of "us," while Poland and the rest of Eastern Europe grew more alien, and therefore susceptible to Western projections. And so, while it became increasingly unfashionable to talk about "German anti-Semitism" as if it were a national trait, or to confuse the German nation with the Nazi phenomenon, it remained quite possible to speak about Polish anti-Semitism, as if that attitude were an essential and unchangeable feature of Polish character. This in turn increased Polish resentment of the exaggerated charges and at the world's forgetfulness of Poland's own struggle for survival during the war, and its immense losses. The incompatible interpretations have deepened the ruts of prejudice and hostility.

It might be said that my argument in the following pages stands in a kind of counterpoint to Daniel Goldhagen's thesis in his hotly debated work, *Hitler's Willing Executioners,* although my book is in no way intended as a riposte to his. In trying to demonstrate that Nazi anti-Semitism had deep roots in a history of German anti-Semitism, Mr. Goldhagen was, in effect, revising what had become the received liberal opinion: that Nazism had nothing to do with the German mentality and that ordinary Germans should in no way be held accountable for the Holocaust, which had arisen from specifically political policies. This book is an effort to counter what I see as the reverse distortion: the notion that ordinary Poles were naturally inclined, by virtue of their congenital anti-Semitism, to participate in the genocide, and that Poles even today must be viewed with extreme suspicion or condemned as guilty for the fate of the Jews in their country. My aim is not to absolve any more than it is to condemn, but it is, at the very least, to complicate and historicize this picture.

Family knowledge can be useful in making abstract history concrete, and from the stories of my own family, I know just how terribly tangled things could become in the untenable conditions created by the war. My parents lived through that period in a region of the Ukraine that belonged to Poland before the war and became Soviet immediately thereafter. On several occasions they had to escape hostile local peasants who might have given them away to the Nazi authorities. But my parents were also repeatedly helped by people who gave them food and temporary shelter, and by a peasant who hid them for nearly two years, with the full knowledge that he was thereby risking death for himself and his sons. The other awful aspect of my family story was that two relatives died because of an act of betrayal committed by a fellow Jew — a man who, in the hope of ensuring his own survival, led the Germans to a hiding place.

The only reason to record such wrenching facts is because I believe that if we are to understand what happened in Poland during the war, we must begin by acknowledging, from within each memory, the terrible complexity of everyone's circumstances and behavior. The instances of Polish complicity in Nazi murderousness cannot be excused or explained away, and yet it would be an unjust distortion not to see even these most distressing phenomena as part of a more complete picture.

In the maelstrom of war, Poland was probably the zone of highest pressure and of almost unbearable tensions. At the outset, the country found itself invaded by two powers, Germany and the Soviet Union. For six years, Poles were engaged in massive resistance against both invaders. The Soviet conquest created new enmities between Poles and Jews, as the latter often welcomed, for their own entirely comprehensible reasons, the armies of Poland's traditional enemy. The Nazi occupation of the country was, even by the brutal standards of the time, exceptionally ruthless. The Poles, in the Nazi hierarchy, were next only to Jews and Gypsies in the order of inferior races — slated for complete subjugation and, in the more visionary Nazi plans, for eventual extermination. The Poles, then, were fighting against just about hopeless odds, while the Jews in their midst were being exterminated with no odds on their side at all.

It is undeniable that during that time a portion of the Polish population were willing to turn a blind eye to the horrors perpetrated on their far more vulnerable countrymen. There were Poles who watched the roundups of their Jewish neighbors with indifference or even gratification; there were those who informed or gave Jews away to the Nazi authorities. But every Polish Jew who survived in occupied Poland (rather than in the Soviet Union) did so with the help of individual Poles and of organizations set up for the purpose of aiding Jews. This was help offered at enormous risk, since sheltering Jews carried with it the penalty of death. Under the immense, fearful stresses of the time, both cowardice and courage were magnified; both meanness and mercy reached new proportions.

ᴔ   ᴔ   ᴔ

The shadow of the Holocaust is long, and it extends backward as well as forward. Our readings of the prewar Polish-Jewish past have been burdened retroactively by our knowledge of what came at the end. For some descendants of Eastern European Jews, the lost world of their parents and grandparents has become idealized, sequestered in the imagination as a quaint realm of "before." For others, the whole Polish past is seen in darkened hues, as nothing but a prelude and a prefiguring of the catastrophe.

The retroactive revisions are understandable: the meaning of every story is crucially affected by its conclusion, and the story of Polish Jews has become shaped in our minds by what was, for so many, the final act. And yet history isn't exactly like story; it isn't shaped by an author who is leading up to a preconceived finale from the outset, or who can at least invent an appropriate ending to fit the narrative's shape. History doesn't unfold that logically or purposefully, and the history of Polish

Jews wasn't a tale that led inevitably to its tragic denouement. Before the destruction, there was multifarious, vibrant life. There had been several centuries of collective existence and coexistence, periods of greater and lesser prosperity, episodes of violent hostility and inspiring cooperation, intervals of turmoil and peace.

If we denude this past of its variety, we deprive ourselves of a wonderfully interesting heritage and a rich lode of knowledge and self-knowledge. After all, for about six hundred years Poland was one of the most important centers of Jewish life in the world. The Jews first started settling there as early as the eleventh century, and they started arriving in larger numbers in the fourteenth. By the late seventeenth century, nearly three-quarters of the world's Jewry lived in the Polish-Lithuanian Commonwealth. In the eighteenth century, before the partitions, Jews constituted about 10 percent of Poland's population, which made them that country's largest minority. Before World War II, they may have grown to as much as 13 percent. Polish Jews created impressive religious institutions, political movements, a secular literature, and a distinctive way of life. In modern times, Polish Jewry gave rise to Yiddish and Hebrew culture, which crucially influenced Diaspora cultures in Europe and the United States.

All of this meant that throughout much of Poland's history, Jews were a highly visible and socially significant presence — a constituency that had to be reckoned with and one that could even pose challenges to the Poles themselves. In this respect, the nature of the Polish-Jewish relationship is exceptional. In contrast with Western European countries, where Jews were usually a tiny minority (below 2 percent of the population in modern Germany) and where, therefore, they were a mostly imaginary Other, in Poland, the Jewish community comprised a genuine ethnic minority, with its own rights, problems, and powers. We have become skilled nowadays in analyzing the imagery of Otherness, that unconscious stratum of preconceptions, fantasies, and projections we bring to our perceptions of strangers. Such subliminal assumptions and archetypes can and do have a very real impact on how we see and treat each other. But in intergroup relations that were as extended in time and as complex as those between Poles and Jews, the material realities of economic competition and practical loyalties, of policy and political alignments, also played a vital role.

Indeed, it might be possible to see the story of Polish-Jewish coexistence as a long experiment in multiculturalism *avant la lettre*. In the imagination of the West, it has been consistently assumed that Western Europe has been the norm and standard in the light of which Eastern Europe has often been judged as backward, or at least less advanced. And it is true that Eastern Europe has often lagged behind the West in economic development and in sheer political power. But criteria of historical judgment can change sharply as values change in the present. Progress is usually seen as that which precedes us, and from the perspective of today, aspects of Eastern European history are beginning to look presciently relevant, and to foreshadow some of the dilemmas with which advanced contemporary societies are struggling. This is particularly true of the problems of pluralism and ethnic coexistence. Poland especially has interesting precedents to offer in this respect, since during several periods of its history, it was a truly multicultural society. At the height of the Polish-Lithuanian Commonwealth in the sixteenth century, Poland had substantial German, Italian, Scots, Armenian, and other minorities; at some intervals, less than half the population was ethnically Polish.

However, the Jewish minority was usually the largest, and

the most important. Over several centuries, the Polish-Jewish experiment went through different phases of trial and error. In the premodern period, Polish attitudes toward religious minorities were surprisingly liberal, even by our own post-modern standards. While the young Jewish communities in Poland suffered their share of religious and folk prejudice, they were also to a large extent protected by laws and special privileges. There were times, particularly during the Renaissance, when Jews saw Poland as a refuge from other, more hostile places, and when they believed that the word "Poland" was the same as the Hebrew "*polin*," which means "here thou shalt lodge" in exile — that Poland, in other words, was a kind of promised land. This happy state wasn't always sustained. As Poland's economic and political fortunes declined, from the middle of the seventeenth century onward, relations between Poles and Jews deteriorated into suspiciousness and economic competition. In the twentieth century, the period between the two world wars saw both an amazing efflorescence of Jewish political and literary culture and eruptions of ideological, and sometimes virulent, anti-Semitism.

The question of the proper relationship between the two peoples was a matter of ongoing debate throughout Polish history, and the proposed answers varied on both sides of the ethnic divide. There were Polish and Jewish thinkers who felt that the two groups were ineradicably different in spirit and outlook, and that the best they could achieve was respectful separateness. There were assimilationists, again on both sides, who proposed cultural blending, or even conversion, as the only solution to the tensions between the two groups. But there were also Enlightenment thinkers who wanted to combine a degree of Jewish integration into Polish society with spiritual autonomy for everyone. There were Jewish patriots who fought for Poland and Polish romantics who thought that the Jewish legacy was an integral and enriching part of the national identity.

A mixed story, then. The multicultural experiment was rarely completely "correct" or completely successful, but it can hardly be judged a complete failure, especially when we have more recent experience to show us how difficult such experiments remain today. And in light of that experience, it might be possible to understand some of the conflicts that arose between Poles and Jews in terms of majority-minority relations rather than exclusively under the category of anti-Semitism.

✧   ✧   ✧

The shtetl — the word is a diminutive of the Yiddish *shtot*, or town — was where the multicultural experiment was at once most intimate and least tested. The Jewish community in Poland was never homogeneous. There was the equivalent of a class system among Polish Jews, as well as political factions and differences of religious conviction. There were, early on, Jewish merchants, craftsmen, and court advisers. There were, later, Hasidim, Orthodox Jews, and secularists; wealthy industrialists and assimilated professionals, writers in Yiddish and poets who adopted the Polish language. And there were, most of all, big-city Jews and shtetl Jews.

In the postwar Jewish imagination, the shtetl, particularly for those who never knew it, has become the locus and metaphor of loss. It has often been conceived as the site of greatest Jewish authenticity, defined either as spirituality or as suffering. For some, the word "shtetl" summons poignant, warm images of people in quaint black garb, or Chagall-like crooked streets and fiddlers on thatched roofs. For others, it means pogroms and peasant barbarism. Yet while it existed, the shtetl was neither a utopia nor a dystopia but a coherent, curious, and surprisingly resilient social formation. Until the twentieth century, the shtetl, perched among the farming landscapes of Eastern Europe, retained its deeply religious and deeply traditional character. Piety provided the order both of concrete daily rituals in which everyone participated, and of seemingly eternal verities and values by which everyone was guided. Perhaps the main virtue of the shtetl for its inhabitants was the extent to which it was a community — small, closely interwoven, reassuringly familiar. Nobody in these rural enclaves needed to suffer from the modern malaise of uncertainty and nonbelonging. But for the restless and inquisitive spirits, for those who left for the big cities or still farther shores, for the intellectual rebels and outside commentators, the shtetl appeared to be insular, superstitious, and opposed to every progressive trend. Before its unnatural destruction, the shtetl, after centuries of near stasis, was already yielding to the unavoidable forces of modernization and might have gradually given way to something new and unpredictable even in the natural course of events.

It should not be forgotten, however, that "shtetl" refers not only to a specifically Jewish phenomenon, but to places where Jews lived side by side with the local population. Polish shtetls were usually made up of two poor, traditionalist, and fairly incongruous subcultures: Orthodox Jews and premodern peasants. Morally and spiritually, the two societies remained resolutely separate, by choice on both sides. Yet they lived in close physical proximity and, willy-nilly, familiarity. In the shtetl, pluralism was experienced not as ideology but as ordinary life. Jews trading horses in a small market town, speaking in haphazard Polish — that was the shtetl. Poles gradually picking up a few words of Yiddish and bits of Jewish lore — that was also the shtetl. Jewish bands playing at Polish weddings and local aristocrats getting financial advice and loans from their Jewish stewards — all that went into the making of the distinctive, mulchy mix that was shtetl culture. This was where both prejudices and bonds were most palpably enacted — where a Polish peasant might develop a genuine affection for his Jewish neighbor despite negative stereotypes and, conversely, where an act of unfairness or betrayal could be most wounding because it came from a familiar.

As an example of Polish-Jewish relations during World War II, the shtetl offered the most extreme scenario. The villages and small towns were where Jews and Poles were at their most exposed and vulnerable, and where ongoing political conflicts were at their sharpest. This was where Jewish inhabitants experienced acts of the most unmediated cruelty from their neighbors — and also of most immediate generosity. In the dark years of the Holocaust, the shtetl became a study in ordinary morality tested, and sometimes warped, by inhuman circumstances.

ᴔ   ᴔ   ᴔ

Why remember, to what end, and in what way? In the post-Holocaust era, we have taken the obligation to preserve memory as sacred — as indeed, when rightly understood, it is. But if they are merely recited or heeded without active understanding, the injunctions never to forget can become formulaic, an invitation to a ritual rather than to a moral act. How we remember, how much effort and pressure of intelligence and imagination we bring to the process, also matters. On the Polish side, the great pitfalls in relation to the wartime past have been amnesia on the one hand, and the willfully tendentious uses of memory on the other. But this also needs to be admitted: several decades after the Holocaust, there is a danger, for those of us who did not live through it, of a kind of automatism of Jewish memory; of reiterating narratives of tragedy without any longer bothering to think about them; of identifying with martyrdom without having earned the right to it; of remaining fixated on the most awful moment so that we don't have to look back to the more ambiguous past — or forward to the troublingly uncertain future.

At this point, the task is not only to remember but to remember strenuously — to explore, decode, and deepen the terrain of memory. Moreover, what is at stake is not only the past but the present. In Poland, the lacunae in collective consciousness, the blank spots, as Poles themselves call them, have had harmful and disturbing consequences. In the last few years, together with a revival of interest in Jewish history and culture, there has been a resurgence of anti-Semitic rhetoric in Poland, which is particularly insidious in that it is rhetoric without a real object. It is as if, with the lifting of Communist repression, the prewar prejudices have reemerged from their Pandora's box in an unreconstructed — because unprocessed — form. The contents of the Pandora's box, the demons and ghosts haunting the Polish psyche, need urgently to be confronted and examined.

In the United States, where Poles and descendants of Polish Jews come into direct contact, visions of the past have a vital impact on the continuing, still highly charged dialogue between the two groups. In a sense, that dialogue is a particularly painful example of multicultural debate on the whole; and possibly, in its very intensity, it offers a model of both the hazards and the possibilities of cross-ethnic conversations in general.

In its worst-case version, the Polish-Jewish dialogue has taken the form of a moral war and has proceeded in escalating rounds of accusation and counter-accusation, exaggeration and denial. The Polish participants in such exchanges discern in all

Jewish statements an attack on their country and its ideals. The Jewish respondents read the entire past as an agon between oppressors and victims. After a while both positions harden, as each side, in response to rising attacks, pulls up the drawbridge to protect its moral fortress.

Such forms of cross-cultural encounter are unfortunately all too familiar. But the patterns of suspicion and grievance not only prevent us from looking at the actual object of inquiry; they also perpetuate damaging patterns of thinking about multicultural relationships, even if they are relationships between majority and minority groups. The history of Poles and Jews was hardly a tale of pure good intentions on the Polish side, but neither was it a one-sided struggle between brute Polish power and passive Jewish powerlessness. Nor, starting from the other end, was the past a narrative of Polish martyrdom and Jewish selfishness. The various forms of Jewish attachment to Poland and participation in historical events cannot be reduced to disloyalty or a simple lack of patriotism. In any case, such categories as "Poles" and "Jews," as we have learned from looking at other groups and areas of the world, are too large to be anything but fictitious and dangerously misleading. If cross-cultural discussions of difficult histories are to be at all fruitful, they need to start with acknowledgment of complexity rather than insistence on reductiveness.

Ideally, in such encounters, both partners would feel enough equality and strength to supplant accusation with self-examination, and to talk fully and openly about their own histories *to each other*. It is of course necessary in such a conversation for the majority culture to admit its history of dominance or injustice; but the dialogue cannot proceed if the minority group continues to hold the majority moral hostage in perpetuity, or if the history of powerlessness is taken as proof of moral

superiority. And it is unproductive, always, to counter prejudice by denying facts. It does not help to respond to a Jewish
interlocutor who claims that "all Poles are anti-Semitic" with
the equally absurd statement that "there was never any anti-
Semitism in Poland." Conversely, it is unhelpful, because
untrue, to meet the Polish thesis that "Jews were harmful to the
interests of Poland because they wouldn't assimilate" with the
retort that Jewish separateness was entirely a function of Polish
anti-Semitism. It is tempting, and all too commonplace, to
resort to such strategies, if only so as not to give our opponent
the satisfaction of exposing our weaknesses. But if we are to
come to a better understanding of a shared — if embattled —
past, it is necessary to abolish the double standard for "internal" and "external" self-presentation, and to admit even shameful intra-tribal problems, so to speak, into the discussion. It is
the better part of dignity to be able to take such risks, but it is
also the beginning of perceiving one's own history and one's
present more three-dimensionally. For a Polish participant in a
dialogue to admit irrational prejudices; for a Jewish person to
acknowledge that an ethos of separateness has its price; this
may be the beginning of a more probing self-exploration. In
that sense, how we remember is crucial not only for the sake of
those who have perished, but for our own sake as well.

In memories, too, begin responsibilities.

ᔂ   ᔂ   ᔂ

All acts of memory are to some extent imaginative; we can no
longer reconstruct "the full truth" of the Shoah or of a long and
various past. But one thing is sure: the truth and the past were
far more striated, textured, and many-sided than either nostalgia or bitterness would admit. This book is a modest attempt to
reach into the past without assuming too many partisan posi-

tions or stereotypes. It is primarily the story of one Polish shtetl called Brańsk. Situated near the Russian border, Brańsk had about 4,600 inhabitants before the war, over half of whom were Jewish. Today there are no Jews left there. Therefore, this is a book of memory and about memory — or rather, of and about multiple layers of memory. On the more immediate level, this book springs primarily from several quests and encounters. There is the quest of Marian Marzynski, who made the documentary film *Shtetl* from which this book is partly derived. For Mr. Marzynski, who survived the war as a Jewish child in Poland, the attempt to find out what happened in Brańsk was, as he indicates in his film, a way of investigating his own past from a bearable distance. Many members of his large, extended family lived in a shtetl very much like Brańsk. Most of them perished during the war. His film, then, springs from a need to fill in a lacuna in personal knowledge. But the lacuna is public as well as private — what happened during the war in the small, remote towns of Poland is still often obscure and unrecorded. In a sense, Mr. Marzynski's documentary is a race against time, an effort to capture on camera faces and images that still connect us to the life and death of the shtetl before they disappear forever.

Marian Marzynski's journey is, in turn, mediated by two other, very different kinds of quests. One is the project of Zbigniew Romaniuk, a young Brańsk historian who has become fascinated by his town's lost Jewish heritage and has turned into its archaeologist and archivist. I record my meetings with him in the body of the book. The original quest, however, which was the impetus and to some extent the inspiration for the film, was undertaken by someone who died before the book was begun. This was the search of Nathan Kaplan, a Jewish American from Chicago, whose mother came from Brańsk. Like so many people who had been cut off from the continuities of their own history, Mr. Kaplan, rather late in life, became interested in his ancestral origins. But unlike many, Mr. Kaplan — who in the film comes across as the gentlest and most moderate of men — attacked his researches with an obsessiveness that verged on a kind of ferocity. After finding a notice placed in the American Jewish press by Zbigniew Romaniuk, Mr. Kaplan commenced a correspondence with the young Pole that runs to several hundred pages and that led to what was clearly a deep friendship.

From the beginning, they seemed to be made for each other, in that both loved and understood the value of details. Mr. Kaplan wanted to know everything: where the synagogues in Brańsk were situated, whether the river running through town flooded in the spring, how the interior of a Jewish house would have looked in his mother's time, what people ate and wore. Mr. Romaniuk tirelessly and factually explained. It was as if the elderly American wanted the young Pole to convey to him on paper the mysterious and unreachable world in which his mother once lived. In turn, Mr. Romaniuk plied Mr. Kaplan with questions about the Jewish faith, customs and rituals that, for all his interest in things Jewish, he had never seen. Their letters are a living illustration of the great historical rupture: Mr. Kaplan knew almost nothing about the place of his mother's youth, and Mr. Romaniuk, who lived in the place, had never met its former Jewish inhabitants. But the two men's correspondence and their meetings as recorded in the film also exemplify the best possibilities for dialogue that is healing rather than divisive, and for understanding that is genuine and mutual.

In writing this book, I was also engaged in a personal, as well as a historical, enterprise. Before the war, my parents lived in a small town not very far from Brańsk. Although I grew up in

Cracow after the war, in a secular, urban environment during the Communist era, I believe that something of the atmosphere of the shtetl, of its mental habits and moral attitudes, of its human gestures and emotional language, penetrated my psyche through the words and personalities of my parents. And so, as I search for the facts and the inwardness of shtetl life, I search also, to some extent, for my own history and its inwardness.

In order to truly understand the life of the shtetl and the people who inhabited it, I felt it was necessary to reach further into the past, to learn something of the historical context from which the shtetl emerged. In trying to sketch the outlines of the Polish-Jewish story, I have drawn on a growing body of scholarship undertaken in Poland and in the West in the last few decades. I am immensely indebted to the work of the many historians, sleuths, and thinkers who are reviving a long dormant field, and whose work I have used freely, and gratefully. I have indicated the sources of direct citations in the Notes on the Sources. Other works, from which I have gleaned background information, or which are useful in studying the history of Polish Jews, are included in the Bibliography.

And there is, finally, the little town of Brańsk itself, with its physical presence and its tantalizing traces, promising to reveal something to us through its mute stones and its village streets. It is only through the efforts of imagination and memory that the shadows can be made to speak.

1 ♫
The World of Polish Jews: Historical Background

B R A Ń S K : a little town about 180 kilometers east of Warsaw, close to the border of what was, until recently, the Soviet
Union, and what is now, uncertainly enough, Belarus. To get
there, I take a fast train from Warsaw and disembark at the
nearest, tiny station in the town of Szepietowo, where I am met
by Zbigniew Romaniuk, a local historian who will be my guide
to this region. I have come here in the deep of winter, and we
walk toward each other through high, crunchy snow. Zbigniew
is a young, sturdy-looking man with blondish hair and a broad,
open face. As we get into his tinny Polish Fiat, he tells me that
Szepietowo was a gathering point for Jews who were being
transported to the concentration camp of Treblinka. Instantly,
the pleasant station building loses its air of innocence. Instantly,
I flash to the scenes that must have taken place here. But the
rural scene we're entering has, for me, associations with other
layers of the past. Something in the crispness of the air, the
sparkling flatness of the packed snow, reminds me of the Polish
winters of my childhood. And, in its smoothed-over state, the
country we're passing in Zbigniew's box of a car has acquired
the stunning serenity of a Japanese scroll painting: horizontal
surfaces of untouched white, two-dimensional; calligraphic
signs of bare tree trunks, vertical and tensile; broader strokes of

stumpy brown willow trunks with their punk, spiky branches; lithe, white-on-white birches, processions of majestic poplars; the aesthetics of human markings superimposed on the beauty of nature. Farther on — tantalizingly close, but inaccessible in winter — there is the Białowieża *puszcza*, the largest expanse of primeval forest left anywhere in the world, the source of poems and legends, the home of bison, hermits, and conspiracies.

Instantly, the landscape in my mind is diagrammed by two sets of meanings. How to reconcile them, how not to blame the land for what happened on it? Moreover, I am aware that for the young Pole sitting next to me, the countryside is marked by another set of symbols still. Historically, this border area has been the scene of wars, occupations by various foreign powers, and bitter conflicts with Russia, later reincarnated as the Soviet Union. And perhaps precisely because it is a peripheral zone, this eastern region has often stood as a resolute bulwark against the uncertainties of borderliness. Zbigniew tells me that the hamlets and villages we see on our way have been a bastion of patriotic "Polishness," in distinction to towns just a smidgeon farther east, which have a larger Belarusian population and whose loyalties are therefore oriented more toward Russia. Here, Poles and Belarusians have occasionally clashed violently. And here, unbelievably enough, combatants of the non-Communist resistance army continued to hide in the forests and carry out vendettas against the Communists and others well into the 1950s.

But aside, or beyond, politics there is the landscape, and as we drive on, I fancy that none of its inhabitants could stay insensible to its dreamy, lyrical spell, that their moods and temperaments must have been affected by the slants and rhythms of the land, wherever they originally came from. And they came from many places. This was an area of mingling and crisscrossing populations, of Belarusians, Lithuanians, Germans, and, earlier, Armenians. And, of course, Jews. Until the war, this eastern region was dense with Jewish life. In Białystok, the nearest big city, more than 50 percent of the population was Jewish in the interwar period, and the region as a whole was more than 17 percent Jewish — compared to 13.5 percent, at the peak of growth, in all of Poland. There was local pride among these eastern Jews, too. Warsaw Jews or the Galizianers from the surrounds of Cracow may have thought they had cultural superiority, but the Jews of the eastern provinces felt they were the authentic Yiddish heart of Polish Jewry.

But now we are approaching Brańsk. In Zbigniew's description, his town has been characteristic of this uncertain, overcertain region — both a very Polish and a very multiethnic place. It extends in a long, narrow strip alongside the slow, mirrorlike Nurzec River — iced over in winter, blending liquidly into a flat, marshy expanse in summer. These days, Brańsk looks typical in its ordinariness and its uncombed charm, a postcard illustration of a rural Polish town. Overlooking the river on a high embankment is a central square, its character defined by a large Roman Catholic church, rebuilt from near ruin after the war, with a Baroque-style façade in creamy yellow. Nearby, a sprinkling of dismally gray postwar cement buildings, housing a few local institutions and some rudimentary shops. Moving away from the river, these make way for streets of low, long wooden cottages, many of them constructed after the war, but in a peasant style unchanged for centuries. Among them are a few older huts, some of them so tiny and sunken into the ground that I wonder how it is possible for anyone larger than a child to live in them. In one of these almost rural streets there's a Russian Orthodox church, small and blue with a rounded cupola and a single onion-domed steeple. There

are still a few Belarusians in Brańsk who use it. Of the old Jewish neighborhood almost nothing is left. There's the lengthy
Binduga Street, which was the center, the very Broadway, of
Jewish trade and commerce; there's a cottage, toy-sized, in
which the caretaker of the main synagogue lived, before he was
thrown into the burning building with his family by the Germans. No traces remain of this synagogue or the five others that
once existed here, or the shops, or the *cheders* in which young
boys studied. Like so much of Brańsk, all this too was destroyed in the war, during a seemingly unmotivated Luftwaffe
bombing in 1939, which may or may not have been directed at
the Jewish quarter.

ᔓ   ᔓ   ᔓ

It is Zbigniew who is my cicerone to the town's geography and
to its several histories. Zbigniew — or Zbyszek, the diminutive
by which he's known to his friends — is a native of Brańsk and
its self-appointed and largely self-taught chronicler. He is in his
early thirties, and his manner is so plain and forthright as to be
sometimes disconcerting. He's not a person given to sentiment
or the pursuit of mystery. But he seems to be endowed with
something like a sixth sense for the past. From childhood,
Zbyszek looked at the landscape around him and found in it
signs of human history. In the earth itself, he discovered artifacts — a piece of a granite saw, a time-polished arrowhead —
that dated from as far back as 2000 B.C. Later, when he was in
his twenties, he started noticing objects that were much more
recent, but to him just as unfamiliar: the artifacts once belonging to Brańsk's Jewish community. Zbyszek knew almost nothing about this other group, which before the war constituted
more than half the citizenry of his town, but the historian in
him began to be intrigued, particularly by large gravestones

carved with Hebrew inscriptions, which he kept stumbling upon in odd and inappropriate places. He found several in the streets, where they had remained as paving stones since the Nazis ordered them placed there in a gesture of desecration. Once Zbyszek discovered a whole row of stones hidden under newer paving in front of the parish house, which had served as the Nazi command center during the war. The priest who now presides over the parish allowed him to dig up the sidewalk and extract the stones from underneath. Zbyszek also discovered the tombstones in farm buildings, where they had been used to sharpen knives and scythes, by peasants unaware of, or insensitive to, the objects' meaning. On an impulse he is still reluctant to define, Zbyszek, with the help of a friend, started reclaiming the stones from their abused status, and then cleaning and restoring them, so that the inscriptions became visible. Then he and some other young men transported them to a wooded spot right outside Brańsk which had been, before the war, the Jewish cemetery. By then, Zbyszek was intrigued enough by the history contained in the inscriptions that he wanted to be able to decipher the words and letters. To that end, he painstakingly taught himself some Hebrew from textbooks and dictionaries.

These were, needless to say, extraordinary acts. There was no external incentive for Zbyszek to pursue his strange task, no ulterior interest or hope of reward. And yet he disclaims any special sentiment in relation to the Jews whose past he has excavated. He is, he says, simply a historian by temperament and preference. He loves rummaging in archives and unearthing the curious fact, the telling number. He relishes exactness. He likes to investigate the past through the testimony of dry data — statistics, dates, the information in birth and marriage registries. He wants his attitude toward the vanished Jews of Brańsk to remain just as impartial. "Everyone is equal before history," he says when I ask him whether the tragic nature of this particular past plays a part in his dedication to it. If he has more personally tinged motives — a hidden guilt or nostalgia, a desire to make symbolic reparations to those who died, or to achieve perverse grandeur by association with catastrophe — then these are well camouflaged.

Perhaps Zbyszek's attempt at impartiality requires a certain naiveté, given the vexed context surrounding the matters he is unearthing. And gradually I will come to wonder whether a sustained labor of restoration, such as his creation of the memorial cemetery, can be carried out without at least some subliminal urge to restore what has been lost and repair what has been wounded on a more symbolic level. But it may be that his detachment is also natural to someone of his generation. After all, Zbyszek grew up without knowing any Jews or hearing much about them. That he didn't learn about this important part of Polish history in school is, of course, to the discredit of the educational system under which he grew up, but it was not in any way his fault. Still, given this utter blankness of information, I cannot help but think that, whatever his prosaic tone, the discovery of a layer of the past so close to the surface and yet so perplexing must have seemed, for a moment at least, uncanny. The information he was digging up had been a part of the familiar world, and yet it was thoroughly unknown. But in his own account, Zbyszek's relationship to Jewishness seems almost unnervingly rational, unmarred by the exoticizing, idealizing, or obsessive impulses that drive many others who become fascinated by this subject. Zbyszek wants to know — that is, to know the facts. He wants to know about the Jews of Brańsk because they were part of his town's heritage. He has written thoroughly researched, if rather dry, articles about their history in a journal about Brańsk he has founded.

These days, it is often people like Zbyszek who are the custo-
dians of Jewish history in Poland. Cadres of young scholars —
most of them non-Jewish — are learning Hebrew and writing
their dissertations on Jewish subjects. Perhaps some of them are
driven by a dubious nostalgia or unexamined guilt, but there is
surely a large kernel of legitimate curiosity in their pursuit.
With the disappearance of the Jews, Poland has been denuded
of a vital dimension, and for a historian, to learn about them is
to rediscover a fuller kind of "Polishness."

It is through Zbyszek's articles that I first delve into Brańsk's
Polish-Jewish history. The first records of Jewish activity in the
town appear only in the seventeenth century. There remains,
from that time, an obscure allusion to a quarrel between a Jew
and a non-Jew about the ownership of a flour mill; the outcome
of the dispute is unknown. For several decades afterward, even
this minimal kind of information disappears, and the trickle of
facts thickens into something like a written record only in the
eighteenth century.

But this was late in the story. By the time a handful of Jewish
settlers reached Brańsk, Jews had lived in Poland for several
centuries; they were, in some sense, Polish Jews. As I try to
imagine who these first arrivals were, what they were like —
what expectations they might have brought with them, what
hopes, habits, and fears — I know that I must delve further
back and try to reconstruct something of their origins, their trajectory, and the conditions that had formed them.

⟋   ⟋   ⟋

The origins, as is so often the case, are not amenable to precise
vision. But flickeringly, one can imagine. The Jews were Europe's archetypal Other, but they were never completely absent
or unfamiliar. For almost as long as there is a written history of

Europe, there are scattered mentions of Jewish merchants, scholars, wanderers. Most of these notations come from Western European sources. But in Eastern Europe as well there were probably Jewish settlements dating from as far back as the Babylonian dispersion. Very little is known about them, with one exception, which is so peculiar as to seem almost mythical. The exception is the Khazar Empire, which existed from the seventh to the tenth century in the forest-steppe regions of what is now Ukraine and Russia. If one were to write a history of alternative models for organizing nations, one might well look to the Khazars for some ideas. Their idiosyncratic domain, which has given rise to so many speculations and legends, was a multiethnic state in which, as scholars are now ascertaining, much of the ruling elite was Jewish, or had converted to Judaism in order to resist Muslim dominance. An Arabic visitor to the Khazar capital in the first half of the tenth century noted that in the city there were seven judges — two each for the three major religions of Judaism, Christianity, and Islam, and a seventh for the "pagans." It is estimated, from Arabic sources, that more than thirty thousand Jews lived in the Khazar Empire.

Even when they were not forced into wandering, Jews were medieval Europe's quintessential travelers. In that great epoch of trade, Jewish merchants traversed the European continent, carrying goods and coins of various description. Possibly, even before there was such an entity as Poland, traders from the East made their way to the flat country inhabited by the "Polanie," or "field people," bringing glass products or furs or amber. By the time the Polan clans began to consolidate their state in the tenth century, Jewish merchants from Spain and elsewhere were crossing Polish territories frequently in search of new markets.

It seems that by then the Jews already had a shared knowledge of the Continent as a whole. Their conception of Europe was not like any other. Just as they had their own calendar and parsing of time, so they had their own categories of geography. In Jewish nomenclature, Europe was divided into "Ashkenaz," which consisted of what today is Germany and France; "Sephard," which included the Iberian peninsula, Italy, and north Africa; and "Rus," which took in the Slavic-language lands east of the German territories.

Knowledge of geography had practical applications, as traders made their way with their caravans across strange lands, picking up words of different languages along the way. Among themselves, Jews of Germany, Italy, and southern France spoke a language called Laaz at that time, while the Jews of Eastern Europe employed a language called Knaanim, based on Slavic dialects. There was much contact and interchange among the dispersed fragments of Israel. A group of "Radanite" Jews who were based in the Frankish territories (although the Radanites initially emerged in Islamic lands), for example, regularly visited the Khazar domain. At least one Khazar clan apparently converted to the Radanite brand of Judaism as a result of these encounters, and the Radanites may well have brought the word *zhid* to Eastern Europe.

In the middle of the tenth century, the Khazars were supplanted by the Kievan Rus Empire, which also counted about eight thousand Jews among its population. Kiev itself had a "Jewish," or Zhidovskye, gate, perhaps indicating a Jewish quarter. By the twelfth century, there are allusions to Rus Jews studying in Western European centers of Jewish learning.

Gradually, the dim echoes of Jewish presence in Poland begin to gather into more solid evidence. By the mid-eleventh century, accounts written by Western European travelers point to the existence of a Jewish community in Cracow, and of other small communities scattered within Poland. It is just possible that some of the early settlers traced their origins to the pre-Ashkenazic Jews of Eastern Europe, from where they might have migrated to Poland via Hungary, or later, via Prague. For example, a small group of Jews probably came to Cracow from Prague in 1096, after fleeing a pogrom that took place during the First Crusade. A number of others may have made their way to the Slavic territories from the old Jewish communities on the Adriatic coast.

But by far the largest number of early Jewish immigrants in Poland came from German and Saxon lands. Some of them may have been escaping persecutions or harsh prejudice, some may have been seeking economic opportunity. They were Ashkenazic Jews, who brought with them an already developed tradition of Talmudic learning and the Yiddish language, which emerged from German dialects around the tenth or eleventh century. These arrivals must have found their way in the new country rather quickly, because by the middle of the eleventh century, we hear of Jews in Poland being active in monetary trade and running princely and royal mints. Among the more fascinating artifacts extant from that time are a few coins bearing the Polish sovereign's name in Hebrew letters. One surviving document is a deed naming a Jew as the proprietor of a village near Wrocław — indicating that Jews were not barred from owning land.

How were these immigrants seen and greeted? It is possible that the early Polish princes thought that Jews, skilled in the ways of trade and commerce, might bolster the economic fortunes of their realm. In any case, the few fragments of evidence we have from that period suggest that Jews were not only tolerated in medieval Poland, but, at least at some social levels, welcomed. This impression is borne out by the first document that formulates official policy toward the Jews for the Wielkopol-ska, or "Great Poland" region. Known as the Statute of Kalisz, it was signed by Prince Bolesław the Pious in 1264, and it is in many ways a startling piece of legislation. Its text, consisting of numerous clauses and provisions, shows an awareness of the vulnerabilities and the needs felt by a small subject group which is sophisticated even by contemporary standards. In many of its points, the statute was similar to other documents sanctioning "Jewish privileges" common in European countries at the time. It conferred upon the Jews the status of *servi camerae*, or servants of the chamber, which meant that they were subordinated as a community to a prince or king and were to pay communal and individual taxes to these personages. It guaranteed full protection of life and property to the new settlers, as well as of synagogues and cemeteries; it gave them freedom to practice their professions and forbade discrimination against them in court. But in addition to undersigning these basic rights, Bolesław the Pious made far-reaching attempts to address the actual prejudices and inequities from which Jews suffered, and discourage or counter them by force of law. One of the most frequent forms of persecution against Jews in medieval Europe was "blood libel" — the accusation that Jews use the blood of Christian children for ritual purposes. In response to this, Bolesław the Pious stipulated that Jews were not to be slandered with blood libel, "because their law prohibits the use of any blood." Moreover — and this is perhaps the most astonishing clause of the Statute of Kalisz — any Christian falsely accusing a Jew of such a crime was to suffer the same punishment as the Jewish person would have received if the accusation were true. Altogether, the statute tried to assure Jews of equal treatment in Polish courts — specifying, for example, that a Jew's oath was to be made on the Torah. This was in marked distinction to the customs obtaining in countries such as Germany, where a Jew reciting an oath was subjected to various humiliations, such as being made to stand with one leg raised on a three-legged stool or to stand on the skin of a pig. Yet another article of the statute stated that Jews should not be forced to extend hospitality to Christians if they did not wish to, and that a Christian who failed to help a Jew attacked in the night was required to pay a fine.

And so the official experiment in Polish-Jewish coexistence began, in that remote epoch, with a set of laws that could serve as an exemplary statement of minority rights today. The author of the Statute of Kalisz clearly recognized that certain prejudices against Jews were common in his time, but the norms he wished to install were ones of tolerance and civic equality. For whatever reasons — they may have been in part economic — he seemed to want the small group of foreigners in his realm to feel safe and comfortable.

Of course, as we know from our own experience, there is often a discrepancy between the good intentions enshrined in political documents and the ordinary, grassroots realities of people's lives. Yet official legislation does establish a set of standards, a tone, and a social climate that are not themselves without significance. It makes a great difference to people's sense of basic security to know that they have rights to call on in cases of trouble or conflict. It probably makes a difference in the perceptions of others to know that a particular group has the dignity of rights and protections.

The actual texture of Jewish experience in the early Polish kingdom, the degree of alienness Jews felt, or the alienness that was attributed to them — such things are much more difficult, from this distance of time, to reconstruct. But there are enough sharp, revealing details to enable us to draw some connecting lines, and the picture that emerges is noteworthy, as much as anything else, for its ordinariness.

The Jews in medieval Poland seemed to be a rather normal part of the social landscape, and relations between them and Christians included a good deal of unstrained contact and even companionship. Indeed, the degree to which Jewish people were incorporated into daily Polish life came as a surprise to visitors from Western Europe. As far as we can tell, Jews lived in all areas of Polish cities without segregation, although they tended naturally to cluster in particular streets or neighborhoods. They dressed pretty much in the common manner, and the colorfulness or the opulence of their costume depended on the degree of their wealth rather than other distinctions or prohibitions. Although the Catholic Church at times tried to restrict Jews to certain quarters and to impose dress codes on them, such injunctions were rarely followed. (In Western Europe Jews were required to wear a distinguishing item of clothing — often of yellow, a foreshadowing of much later and much more sinister symbolism.)

On the seamier side of cross-cultural contact — the side that is usually recorded and thus remembered — we get glimpses, as late as in the fourteenth and fifteenth centuries, of Jews drinking and gambling in Polish taverns, brawling with Polish neighbors, and joining thieving bands to steal horses. We hear reports of Poles attacking Jews on the highways, but also of Jews attacking Poles. On the better side of trust, there were non-Jews guaranteeing Jewish debts, and vice versa; there were instances of Polish city officials, and even bishops, defending Jews or mediating disputes between various parties. The system of legal representation in Poland seemed to be nondiscriminatory in practice as well as in theory. In internal disputes among themselves, Jews could use their own courts and methods of arbitration. However, if they chose to resort to Polish courts, they could apparently be represented by Jewish lawyers. On the other hand, if Christians sued Jews in court, they had to supply Jewish witnesses to support their suit.

Within itself, the Jewish community in Poland was never entirely homogeneous or perfectly united in its opinions against the outside world. In the early epoch, internecine tensions sometimes seem to have arisen from simple struggles for power. For example, when a group of Jews arrived in Cracow from Bohemia after fleeing yet another pogrom, there soon ensued a battle for control between the "Polish" and "Czech" rabbis and their constituencies — a quarrel ending with victory for the "native" Polish Jews.

Professional hierarchies developed early as well. The new Jewish immigrants pursued a variety of occupations. They were artisans, merchants, traders, moneylenders. Some owned houses and land. A few became wealthy, establishing and expanding family businesses through several generations or becoming traders on an international scale. A number of Jews worked for princely households, running their mints, or managed estates for the small gentry. Perhaps they were hired by the nobles because they had some financial resources the early aristocracy needed, but it may be that Jews were attractive candidates for such positions because they were somewhat better educated than the rest of the population. The Jews who came to Poland carried with them, after all, an already ancient, highly elaborated tradition of learning, which had helped them retain their identity through centuries of dispersion, and which centered on the Book and on reverence for the written word. Even in early medieval times, at least some Jewish households in Poland had Hebrew books, while the Polish populace, with the exception of the aristocracy, was wholly illiterate.

Paradoxically, the seeming ease of Polish-Jewish relations in the nascent Polish society may have been a function not of Poland's advancement but of its relative (as understood in conventional terms) backwardness. Medieval Poland was distant from the centers of imperial and religious power, and therefore, perhaps, from the more centrally controlled codes of morality and behavior. For one thing, Poland did not come under the aegis of the Holy Roman Empire; neither, at this early stage, did it fully conform to the authority of the Roman Church. Polish princes adopted Christianity only in 966, and as late as the twelfth century, pagan cults survived in Polish woods and fields side by side with the new worship. Even the Catholic clergy were sometimes less than rigorous in fulfilling their religious duties. For example, Polish bishops consistently refused to participate in the Crusades. And the Polish Church incurred Rome's displeasure for failing to keep the Jews separate from the rest of the population, or to ensure that they adhered to the required dress regulations.

At the same time, Jewish communities in Poland, living as they were in a peripheral country, remote from the old centers of rabbinical authority, may have become lax in following their own religious laws. To rabbis visiting from Western Europe, Polish Jews seemed a rough lot, lacking in cultivation and piety. Some had fallen into such ignorance that they didn't know Hebrew at all. Others were remiss in observing both the spirit and the letter of the Torah. Young Jewish women were seen dancing on holidays. Jewish butchers did not know the techniques for making meat kosher.

These were undoubtedly troubling matters for the rabbinical dignitaries. But the relaxation of religious rigor may have made it possible for Christians and Jews to live together without the rigid barriers that obtained elsewhere. Perhaps in the still fluid, uncentralized country — a country that did not yet identify itself as a monolithic, Christian state — it was easier to retain a certain fluidity of individual self-definition and therefore to cross borders between group identities.

Poland began to coalesce as a sovereign kingdom under the stewardship of Kazimierz the Great in the mid-fourteenth century. This monarch remains a figure of Jewish folklore and is remembered as "the king who was good to the Jews." During the decades of his reign, Poland again took in large numbers of Jewish refugees. Most of them were fleeing from Western Europe, where the ravages of the Hundred Years' War, the Black Death, and famine resulted in new waves of anti-Jewish atrocities. Poland, which was spared these disasters, readily absorbed not only Jews but other immigrants, particularly from the Netherlands and northern Germany. In relation to the Jews, Kazimierz the Great confirmed the liberties set out in the Statute of Kalisz, extending them to the entire Polish state. He also actively sought Jewish help in his great enterprise of urbanizing Poland. It was said of him that he found Poland made of wood and left it built of stone — and the Jews contributed substantially to this transformation.

It was also said of Kazimierz the Great that his friendliness toward the Jews — considered excessive, or even indecent, by some critics — was motivated by personal sentiment. The king was rumored to have a Jewish mistress, Esterka, to whom he was devoted, and with whom he supposedly had four children: two sons, who were raised as Catholics, and two daughters, who retained their mother's faith. The historical truth of this account seems impossible to establish, but whether it was fact or fiction, the story of Esterka became, in later times, a kind of symbolic Polish legend, used by Jewish and Christian writers alike for various purposes: to praise King Kazimierz or condemn him; to underline the natural affinity, a historical "marriage," between Poles and Jews or to point out the dangerous, seductive powers of the wily aliens, who were capable of penetrating the body politic even unto the king's bedchamber.

Of course, such mixed attitudes were already evident in medieval Poland. Alongside the country's receptiveness to foreigners and the liberalism of its laws, there were in early Poland — as in all of premodern Europe — powerful strains of prejudice against Jews. However, although it may appear precious or unseemly to inquire too closely into the nuances of such an unpleasant phenomenon, it is possible that even within the general category of prejudice we need to distinguish several strands of feeling, preconception, and response. Jews were perceived first of all as strangers, and at least some of the automatic antagonism directed toward them should probably be understood as "anti-Otherness" rather than as anti-Semitism in its specific and strong sense. Why this basic form of prejudice should be so difficult to extricate from the human soul is, in a sense, both mysterious and obvious. The human psyche apparently cannot exist without identifications. We initially define ourselves by our similarities and connections with others, by feeling that we are part of a family, tribe, group, nation. And, in our more primitive psychic processes, such identifications seem to be almost inevitably accomplished, or at least accompanied, by the strategies of rejection and contrast — by distinguishing our tribe, group, nation from everyone outside. In the naive view, to be Like Us is good; to be Not Us is, on the face of it, Not Good. The Not Good can take different colorations. In ancient Greek, the word used for "foreigner" was "barbarian"; the two terms are also synonymous in Japanese and Chinese. At other times, and in other cultures, foreigners have been perceived as sinister or contemptible or comical, depending partly on their social position. In the folk imagination of earlier ages, strangers were seen, without embarrassment or apology, as fair game for insult and laughter. One could compile a thick compendium of popular prejudices from all countries and tongues, and this collection would turn up many common themes. The English, for example, have their historical lexicon of anti-Irish sentiments that sound, at times, very similar to the Polish folklore of anti-Jewishness.

In Poland itself, Jews were to some extent targets of the same kind of colloquial suspicion as other foreigners. Armenians, Scots, and Italians, as well as Jews, were mocked in proverb and ditty for eating smelly foods and speaking in funny ways. They were all accused of excessive shrewdness (who knows what schemes they were cooking up while speaking in those strange tongues!) and of using their underhanded cleverness to exploit poor, guileless Poles. How significant were such routine expressions of prejudice? We have tended to assume that they always correspond to deeper, dangerous currents of feeling, but it is not clear that this is necessarily so. Especially among people who do not have the inhibitions of linguistic correctness, the vocabulary of denigration can coexist with tolerant or even friendly attitudes toward the very objects of such stereotyping; the words can be used to vent tensions or express sharp amusement at the curious ways of exotic strangers.

It cannot be denied, however, that within this spectrum of attitudes, the Jews in medieval Europe presented a special case. They were, after all, not only foreigners; more crucially, they held different religious beliefs, and in a religious world this was difference at its most fundamental and morally charged. It is hard for most of us today to imagine ourselves into the fully believing mind, but to medieval Christians, their faith was an unquestioned absolute, synonymous with the structure and meaning of reality. Religion gave order and significance to their lives, and it was to be defended to the end of life. Within this philosophical framework, no value was placed on tolerance of other beliefs; indeed, such openness would have seemed disloyal and highly suspect. Jews were infidel in Christian eyes, and a condemnation of their religion was morally authorized, and even required.

As Catholicism took deeper hold in Poland and the Church gradually became its own fiefdom, such attitudes gained voice and articulation. As elsewhere in Europe, the clergy was becoming the most ideologically anti-Semitic segment of Polish society, giving vent to its Judeophobia without restraint and producing some truly poisonous texts. Sometimes lay Christians, too, objected to the Jewish way of prayer. Polish medieval verses and histories describe the individual chants, the swaying gestures, and the "shrieking" noises emanating from synagogues on the Sabbath with undisguised disgust. Church sermons accused Jews of profaning the host and insulting Christian religion in numerous ways. And despite express legal prohibitions against such charges, priests were not above insinuating that Jews committed blood libel. In 1407, veiled allusions made from the pulpit, which amounted to inciting the congregation to violence, led to a riot in Cracow, in which a furious crowd burned and robbed the Jewish section of the city and probably killed some of its inhabitants. (It must be noted, however, that such physical attacks were rare, and when they happened, the monarchy responded by severely reprimanding or, when possible, punishing the culprits.)

In folk pageants and Catholic morality plays, the Jew was often pictured as a frightened, cowering figure, speaking broken Polish and willing to undergo any number of humiliations for financial gain. These qualities were not yet seen in psychological ways, as aspects of character, but rather were symbolized through stereotypical or allegorical figures. But psychologically speaking, one can see how the Jewish caricatures in these popular spectacles served the function of absorbing all the undesirable qualities — venality, mendacity, disloyalty, cowardice — that the Poles preferred to suppress or expel from their own notion of themselves. This mechanism worked on both the social and the metaphorical level. In the Polish social configuration, Jews filled the vacuum created by the Polish system of preferences and exclusions: they engaged in the activities the Poles disdained, in commerce, trade, and finance. But in the imaginative, moral realm as well, the figure of the Jew filled the rejected space. The Polish system of values was on the one hand chivalric, and on the other rural. The nobility prided itself on its adherence to the code of honor, its love of liberty, and its uncompromising courage. At the other end of the social spectrum was the honest country bumpkin, attached to nature and the land. The Jew, in contrast, was seen as wily, urban, and unrooted.

The mockery of strangers, the fear of strangeness, the disapproval of difference — these were the hallmarks of a mentality that was not yet self-conscious about intolerance, as they often remain the unacknowledged aspects of many mentalities today, when we are hyperconscious of it. Even in our politically correct era, it takes a considerable capacity for self-examination to overcome our fears of the unfamiliar, or to understand our own mechanisms of projection, through which we all too readily attribute to others the disturbing qualities we cannot bear to recognize in ourselves.

In the age of belief, religious anti-Semitism was part of the prevailing atmosphere throughout Europe — in fact, the regnant world-view. And yet, even while the Catholic Church in Poland began to conform more closely to this ideology, there seemed to be countervailing forces at work in that country which created a climate of relative safety for the Jewish community and enabled it to progress and prosper. As the Middle Ages waned and the Renaissance began, Poland continued to be the place to which Jews went when they were expelled from other countries. Through immigration and natural growth, they were gradually becoming the largest minority in the kingdom, with considerable professional achievements, collective economic power, and an exceptional, though undefined, social status. How do we reconcile this seeming contradiction, if indeed it is a contradiction in the first place?

The discrepancies in Polish attitudes can be understood partly in class — or, less anachronistically, caste — terms. From the beginning of the Polish-Jewish story, certain tensions become discernible within Polish society which were destined to increase during the long subsequent narrative. The main dividing line ran between the elite and the less powerful, or the virtually powerless, groups. It was the upper strata of Polish society that seemed most capable, if not of positive friendliness, then at least of unthreatened openness toward the Jews. Throughout the late Middle Ages and the Renaissance, Polish kings continued to encourage Jewish immigration and participation in the commercial growth of the country. They also continued to employ Jews in the royal court as minters, doctors, scholars, and advisers.

Then there were the grand and lesser nobles, whose role was just as central to the development of Jewish life in Poland. The nobility — or *szlachta*, as they called themselves — were a large and very powerful estate, quite different in character from the aristocracy of Western European countries. Rather than deriving their power from a monarch, the Polish aristocracy emerged from independent clannish groups, and maintained their autonomy resolutely, with far-reaching consequences. The *szlachta* came to include nobility of all stripes, from the major magnates, some of whom commanded small armies and owned vast stretches of land, which they governed as virtually independent principalities; to middle-rank families living in country manors; to the *szlachta* smallfry, who were often no more than farming gentry with a claim to a title or pedigree.

From early on, the nobility entered into an economic alliance with Jewish businessmen, employing them as managers of manorial estates and leaseholders of mills and inns, calling on their services as financiers and, on occasion, forming commercial partnerships with them. The custom of leasing properties to Jews was widespread enough to become a kind of institution, known as the *arenda* system.

The alliance between the two groups was undoubtedly a marriage of convenience rather than of love, and was based on mutual profit and interest. But even this limited, pragmatic relationship would not have been possible without some tolerance of cultural differences on the nobles' part. Perhaps their relative lack of bigotry sprang from their particular and strong code of values, and model of identity. The Polish aristocrats prided themselves on their complete freedom from constraint, their ability to ignore conventions, and their cussed right to follow the dictates of their whim or conscience and be their own law and definition. Wealthy or poor, the *szlachta* prided themselves most of all on their pride. It is possible that this deeply ingrained libertarianism and high-handed confidence gave the nobility the wherewithal to deal with the Jews without fearfulness. They could encounter these Others without feeling their own identity to be under threat, without needing to tame and subdue the Jewish mode of being.

However limited the alliance between the *szlachta* and the

Jews, it caused considerable unease among other strata of society. The resentments were especially strong among Polish burghers, who felt themselves to be in direct economic competition with Jewish merchants. Burghers repeatedly complained about the protected treatment supposedly enjoyed by Jews at high levels. They frequently charged that the nobles practiced an early version of affirmative action — that they treated Jews better than peasants or Polish merchants, and that Jewish favorites were lifted above others in their privileges and station. "In our country, the leaseholder is a Jew, the doctor is a Jew, the merchant is Jewish, and so is the miller, the secretary and the most faithful servant, since they've gained the upper hand in everything," complained one fourteenth-century writer of the burgher class. Altogether, in "middle-class" opinion, the Jews were often perceived as dangerous competitors who looked out exclusively for their own interests and attained their wealth and success at the expense of native Poles — who, in contrast, were pictured as hard-working, sincere, and too honest to achieve much in the world. Over time, burgher scribes created a considerable body of secular anti-Semitic literature in Poland. It needs to be noted, however, that there was much less of this kind of writing in Poland than in other countries, and that on several occasions rabidly anti-Semitic texts were censored or banned from publication.

At the lowest rungs of the Polish social ladder, prejudices against Jews were less rational and more mythical. Among the peasants — unlettered, dirt poor, living in a condition of near serfdom — Jews were perceived less in terms of worldly Otherness than of mysterious alienness, and feelings about them were tinged with superstitious awe and fear. In peasant lore, Jews were believed to have supernatural powers and dark, peculiar customs. According to one folk belief, all Jews were born blind and needed blood to become sighted. (A similar belief was applied to the inhabitants of the Mazowsze region, who were also supposedly born blind and gained sight only after several weeks.) At the same time, Jews were actual figures in peasants' lives, often standing in a complicated relationship with them. Although little is documented about neighborly village relations in the early period, we know that Jewish estate stewards, who acted as collectors of taxes and rents, met with particular resentment, since they were seen by the peasants as their direct exploiters, rather than the intermediaries they really were.

Perhaps, though, when trying to reconcile underlying paradoxes of Polish attitudes toward Jews — or of other cross-ethnic relationships, for that matter — we need to think in terms not only of social hierarchies but of strata, or dimensions, of experience. After all, few of us are completely consistent or monolithic in our views. We may like our neighbor one day and scorn him the next, or like and scorn him simultaneously. We may harbor totally unfounded affection for an entire group of people and secretly dislike another. Under ordinary circumstances, however, we rarely follow to the bitter end the consequences of our collective hates or loves. In each individual psyche there is a layer of moderate, civilized feeling and an undercurrent, an undertow, of drives and emotions that we would rather not admit into the light of day — an aural blur of language that we would rather not hear too clearly. And in each society there is an underbrush of aggression, of irrational groupthink, of hate speech. But these do not always erupt into full rage; the underbrush doesn't always ignite into brushfire. There is much evidence to suggest that in peaceful periods, Jews in Poland did not feel under constant threat of hostility or humiliation. Whatever the ideological currents of anti-Semitism in the larger society, Jews were commonly treated with civil acceptance, or at least benign indifference.

One of the vital and eternally recurring questions in cross-ethnic or cross-cultural relations is why at some periods the free-floating, amorphous prejudices circulating among the populace remain dormant, and why at other times they erupt into unqualified hatred or into violent action. The answers are surely complex and, to a large extent, determined by specific conditions. But perhaps one can hazard some general conjectures. Obviously, the role of real, material circumstances is crucial in intergroup relations. Members of different constituencies are more likely to remain on amicable terms if their interests converge, or at least do not impinge on each other. If such interests become too sharply opposed, the latent tensions are much more likely to crystallize into conflict. The degree of harmony or discord in Polish-Jewish relations varied with the degree of compatibility or divergence in the groups' economic and political concerns.

But aside from the force of immediate self-interest, the climate of collective feeling and opinion can be significantly influenced by the broader political arrangements within which people live and act. Such larger structures can provide a framework for controlling or containing conflicts. The legal protections extended to Jews in Poland constituted one important framework. In terms of actual behavior, a group of angry Polish townsmen, for example, might think twice before launching an attack on the Jewish quarter if they knew they were likely to be punished for it. But on the psychological level as well, the image of Jews might be subtly modified by the realization that they could not be denigrated with impunity. Faced with external restraints, the Polish townsmen might eventually learn that the impulses of anti-Jewish fear or scorn had to be moderated by self-restraint, which is close to a kind of respect.

What of Jewish attitudes toward the Poles? We tend to forget that minority groups are not powerless in their perceptions;

that they, too, exercise judgment and gauge the character of others; and that, much as they may be the targets of prejudice, they are not themselves immune to it. That the Jews had their views of the people among whom they lived we cannot doubt, but their ordinary opinions, ideas, and preconceptions are largely inaccessible to us, since almost no secular Jewish literature is extant from the early period. We do know, however, that Jews had their exclusionary and monopolistic prescriptions, prohibiting rights of residence to outsiders in their quarters, and strictly guarding certain business practices and "secrets" from non-Jews. The use of *hazakah*, which involved control of rents and leases, lasted well into the eighteenth century. We can take it for granted, moreover, that fierce religious disapproval traveled both ways. Just as Jews were infidel in Christian eyes, so Jews were convinced that Christians were wrong, deluded, and blasphemous. And from both sides of the divide, the conviction of the other's wrongness created essential, and increasingly rigid, spiritual barriers. As the Jewish communities in Poland became more settled and began to establish stronger religious institutions, Polish Jews became more rigorously observant. They began to shun intimate contact with Christians, if only on account of the dietary laws.

The Poles, then, were the Jews' radical Other, just as much as the other way around. Of course, there was a crucial asymmetry in the position of Christians and Jews, which gave their perceptions and prejudices a different meaning and weight. The Jews were the minority; they knew they were in their host country as invited guests at best, on sufferance at worst. At a time when there was no citizenship or clear legislation defining the relationship of individuals to the state, the status of the Jews was perennially uncertain. Although there was no threat of expulsion from Poland, the Jewish people had had a long history of expulsions and persecutions — and an accumulated memory of such events, which undoubtedly bred in them a basic sense of existential insecurity.

Insecurity — and flexibility. The fundamental fact of Jewish existence in the Diaspora was the necessity of adjustment and accommodation. In a way, the Jews' opinions of the Poles didn't count outside their own communities; what mattered was their ability to understand these Others to some extent — at least enough to be able to negotiate with them, to incur their favor and avoid their ire.

At the same time, unlike other minority groups, Jews had no wish to assimilate, to take on the coloring of the surrounding culture, to become like the others. This was the stubborn will of the stiff-necked people throughout centuries of wandering and banishment: they wanted, above all, to preserve their identity intact and unaltered, to remain loyal to the teachings of their ancestors and keep the thread of continuity unbroken. For that they needed a certain degree of autonomy and spiritual privacy, and from the beginning this is what the Polish conditions gave them. Quite exceptionally, the Jews in Poland were pressed into neither exile nor assimilation.

The Polish polity continued to develop in a fashion conducive to the possibility of simultaneous coexistence and separateness. Throughout the late medieval and Renaissance periods, Polish society was marked by less pyramidal and more horizontal forms of organization than Western European models. Significantly, the idea of the divine right of kings was never imported into Poland, and Polish monarchs never aspired to, or attained, absolute power. The *szlachta* continued to act as a highly independent estate, whose policies often diverged from the royal court's, and which had the wherewithal — including private armies — to effect its wishes within the country and abroad. This de facto division of powers, and the *szlachta's* insistence on its rights and liberties, resulted in an early establishment of quasi-democratic institutions. Poland had the earliest elected monarchy in Europe and the earliest form of limited democratic representation. At the Treaty of Lublin in 1569, Polish nobles and Lithuanian princes decided to create a united but dual state, in which the Polish kingdom and the Grand Duchy of Lithuania were to be jointly governed by an elected king. The elective body consisted of the entire nobility, which came together to form a Sejm, or Diet. After 1572, the elected monarch had to agree to a covenant guaranteeing broad powers for the nobles.

The *szlachta*, then, were becoming the real ruling elite. At other levels, too, Polish society — in this respect resembling most of Europe — was divided into nearly independent domains, which could perhaps be compared to castes. The burghers and the clergy, as well as the *szlachta*, each formed a separate estate with their own legal statutes. The peasants, of course, had no laws or rights to speak of, but they were expected to keep their fixed place in what seemed to be the natural order of things, and to be satisfied. Members of various estates dealt with each other from within their distinct roles and spheres. A burgher was expected to have different manners, morals, habits of dress, and aspirations from a nobleman. And both were expected to remain firmly circumscribed by their given identities. The boundaries separating social realms were nearly uncrossable, though this did not mean that relationships between them could not be respectful, or even amicable.

In this system, the Jews, who were growing more numerous and visible, could be thought of as another estate, with its own place in the ordained social order. Moreover, the clarity of borders between distinct castes may have meant that differences were felt to be containable, and therefore less threatening.

The nascent democratic tendencies in Polish society and the

szlachta's relish of individuality may have contributed to the climate of tolerance that prevailed in Poland and that was often remarked upon by travelers from other lands. Ethnically, Poland was becoming an unusually heterogeneous — in effect, a multicultural — state. There were fairly settled Armenian communities living there, as well as Italians, Scots, Germans, and others. Even more surprising to foreign visitors was the flourishing religious diversity. During the decades of the Reformation, when Western Europe was racked by religious violence, Poland became a haven for doctrinal dissidents of all kinds. Sects like the Hussite Czech Brethren, Anabaptists, and Mennonites found refuge there, and the Polish Brethren, also known as Arians or Anti-Trinitarians, produced radical theological tracts that, for example, denied the divinity of Christ. None of these sects were persecuted; indeed, in 1573 the principle of religious tolerance was formally enshrined in the Statute of General Toleration. At the height of its Renaissance power, Poland prided itself on being "a land without stakes." The climate of acceptance was becoming an ethos. In later times — to indulge in historical foreshadowing — the ethos turned into a national myth of Polish tolerance that did not always reflect current realities, and could be used to justify an unwarranted sense of moral superiority.

The Jewish presence in the country continued to be, by European standards, markedly visible. The papal nuncio Francesco Giovanni Commendoni, who traveled in Poland between 1563 and 1573, wrote that although Jews there, as elsewhere, engaged in moneylending and usury, there were also many who "farm, trade, and devote themselves to learning, especially astrology and medicine." There were Jewish businessmen, the visitor noted, who attained great wealth, surpassing that of the natives. According to his observations, Jews didn't wear head

Above: Polish coins from the eleventh and twelfth centuries, made by Jewish minters and bearing Hebrew inscriptions. *(Jewish Historical Institute, Warsaw)*

Below: "Persons of Various Stations Lament the Death of Credit" (that is, the dearth of ready money), artist unknown, late sixteenth century. The figure at the top left is a Jew. The others include an Orthodox Christian, a painter, a butcher, a musician, a tailor, a merchant, and so on. *(Polish Academy of the Arts and Sciences, Cracow)*

A wooden synagogue in Zabłudów, in the Białystok region, probably dating from the sixteenth century and destroyed in 1941. Its design shows the influence of Polish folk art. *(From* Synagogues and Jewish Communities in the Białystok Region *by Tomasz Wiśniewski; reprinted by permission of the author)*

The Dance of Death, artist unknown, second half of the seventeenth century. The inscription on this anti-Semitic (or anti-infidel) image, in an approximate translation, reads: "Obscene Turks and ugly Jews, how Death does not recoil from you. To Jewish smells it pays no heed, with savage nations it consorts and leaps." *(Bernardine Church, Cracow)*

Top: The Horse Market by Jan Piotr Norblin de la Gourdaine (1745–1830). Horse-trading was a common Jewish occupation. *(Czartoryski Collections, National Museum, Cracow; photo by Ryszard Kubiczek)*

Bottom: A Scene at the Inn on the Mound by Michał Stachowicz (1762–1825). Inns were traditionally leased and managed by Jews. Here the celebrants are Polish and the innkeeper, in the background, is Jewish. *(National Museum, Warsaw)*

Left: Portrait of Salomon Maimon, artist unknown. Maimon was a late-eighteenth-century thinker of the Haskala (Jewish Enlightenment), a philosopher and the author of an autobiography. *(Jewish Historical Institute, Warsaw)*

Below: The Death of Berek Jose-lewicz in Kocek by Henryk Pillati (1832–1894). Berek Joselewicz was the leader of the Jewish corps formed by Tadeusz Kościuszko in 1794 as part of an insurrection against the Russians. Joselewicz died in 1809, in another battle for Polish independence. *(National Museum, Warsaw; photo by E. Sęczykowska)*

Above: A Jewish Wedding by Wincenty Smokowski (1797–1876). *(National Museum, Warsaw)*

Left: Jankiel's Concert, by Maurycy Trębacz (1861–1940), illustrates a famous scene in the Polish romantic epic *Pan Tadeusz* by Adam Mickiewicz. Jankiel, a Jew and one of the poem's central characters, plays the dulcimer, recounting Polish history through music. *(Jewish Historical Institute, Warsaw)*

Above: The Funeral of the Five Martyrs in Warsaw in 1861 by Aleksander
Lesser (1814–1884). At this funeral of victims killed in an uprising against the
Russians, two chief rabbis of Warsaw officiated together with Polish religious
leaders. *(National Museum, Cracow)*

Below: Simchat Torah, by Tadeusz Popiel (1862–1913), depicts the joyous
holiday celebrating the completion of the yearly reading of the Torah. *(Jewish
Historical Institute, Warsaw)*

Above: A rabbinical court in Vilno, 1875. This engraving, by an unknown artist, first appeared in the Jewish publication *Kłosy.* *(Jewish Historical Institute, Warsaw)*

Left: A Jew Praying at Night (1887) by W. Leszczyński. *(Jewish Historical Institute, Warsaw)*

Above: Interior of the Great Synagogue in Orla, near Brańsk, showing the *bimah,* a place of honor from which prayers are chanted. Construction of the synagogue probably began in the first half of the seventeenth century, and the ornate decorations suggest the prosperity of the Orla community.

Left: The *bimah* of the Great Synagogue in Tykocin, near Brańsk. This beautiful synagogue, built in Renaissance style, was finished in 1642. After falling into disuse, it was restored and now serves as a museum.

(From Synagogues and Jewish Communities in the Białystok Region *by Tomasz Wiśniewski; reprinted by permission of the author)*

coverings to distinguish themselves from others, and some even carried swords.

The Jewish population was becoming more differentiated, certainly in terms of wealth, but also in social status. The categories of rank were different from those obtaining in Polish society and less expressly defined, and yet they were clearly recognizable. Among the Jews living in villages, a portion were employed as leaseholders of inns, mills, or even whole villages. But most Polish Jews lived in towns and cities, and acted as traders and merchants, or as middlemen between Polish and foreign merchants and Polish producers and buyers. These trading intermediaries sometimes bought goods abroad and sold them in Poland, or vice versa; in this they were undoubtedly helped by having what amounted to an international language and a far-flung network of contacts. In the eastern territories of Poland, where they were more populous, Jews were becoming involved in the new fur and lumber industries. Some formed trade companies, and were becoming quite wealthy.

The fledgling Jewish "middle class" continued to fill the gaps created by Polish predispositions. As another traveler, a Venetian envoy to Poland, Pietro Duodo, wrote perceptively, if rather cynically, in 1592: "There are many Calvinists and Lutherans [in Poland], but most numerous are the Jews; because the nobility is ashamed of trade, the peasants are too backward and oppressed, and the burghers too lazy, the entire Polish trade is in Jewish hands. The aristocrats treat them with respect, because they have profits from them, the government treats them so, because when in need, it can extract great sums from them."

Aside from this early Jewish bourgeoisie, there were, of course, poor Jews: cobblers, carpenters, and blacksmiths who plied their humble crafts, and modest merchants who acted as go-betweens. At the other end of the scale were people who worked for the aristocracy and who by that association had a higher social standing. There were, first of all, the managers and accountants who ran the manorial estates. At the highest rung were Jews who worked directly for the monarch or who had the official title of crown servitors. The court itself often employed Jewish doctors and secretaries. Other servitors did not necessarily come in direct contact with the court, but were formally freed from all taxes and border restrictions, and could use their title as a kind of passport guaranteeing royal protection when traveling abroad. One famous servitor, a man known as Becal, paid a large sum to the king in return for a license to collect royal tolls in Ruthenia and Volhynia — in defiance of a law prohibiting Jews to lease royal customs. Over time, some of the more successful Jews began to identify with the *szlachta*, adopting its dress, comportment, and sometimes its arrogance.

The Jews, then, seemed to have some freedom to maneuver in Poland, and were able to find ways of using the resources available there to further their fortunes. And whatever the uncertainties of their situation, there is considerable evidence that Polish Jews themselves thought they were living in a relatively hospitable environment. One commentator, Itzhak of Troki, writing in Hebrew at the end of the sixteenth century, declared that the horrible mutual persecutions of Catholics and Protestants during the Reformation in England, Spain, and France were a punishment for the "spilling of Israelite blood" and the earlier persecutions and expulsions of Jews. In contrast, Itzhak of Troki wrote (undoubtedly with some exaggeration), "Such actions never took place in Poland. . . . Indeed, here they hold those who do ill [to Jews] responsible, and punish them severely; here, they even support Jews with favorable privileges, so they can live happily and peacefully. The kings of this land

and their dignitaries . . . are lovers of magnanimity and justice . . . and that's why God gave this land mightiness and peace, so much so, that those differing in their religion don't feel hatred and don't persecute each other."

ᴣ ᴣ ᴣ

The sixteenth century was a high point in Polish history, when the Commonwealth was a prominent and peaceful European country and the Jewish inhabitants were a prominent domain within it. In manners and morals, they were becoming a securely distinctive group. Although dress codes were not imposed on them, Polish Jews had developed their own style of clothing, derived from that of the Polish nobility: black caftans tied at the waist and fur-trimmed hats for the men, black dresses for women, with strings of pearls and other jewelry for the wealthier ones. In matters of collective character and mentality as well, the Jews were conscious of themselves as an entity, with qualities and differences they proudly embraced. It may be that the prosperity and expansiveness in the Polish Commonwealth in that period helped to create a capaciousness of attitude and the benign, or at least permissive, assumption that Jews could exist side by side with Poles without intruding on each other's freedom or interests. In any case, Polish rulers continued to act on the premise that, within their own territory, so to speak, Jews had the right not only to observe their own customs and spiritual principles, but also to create their own political institutions and laws. In this climate, Polish Jewry began to develop communal and religious structures that became a model for Ashkenazic Jews everywhere and lasted for several centuries.

The most important of these structures was a form of self-government adopted by Jewish communities throughout Poland. Each community chose a body of male elders, a *kahal*, to oversee and guide all of its affairs. The chief personage among this gathering of wise men was the rabbi; the others were appointed on the basis of their religious learning. Wealth and useful contacts with the Poles were also important criteria, but the primary system of ranking and prestige in Jewish communities was based on Talmudic erudition — and the kind of sagacity and good sense that were supposed to proceed from it. Once appointed, the elders exercised enormous power. In the Jewish world-view of the time, there was no separation or contradiction between religious and secular authority, and the elders were invested with both. They collected taxes, deployed the community's finances, and adjudicated legal and doctrinal disputes. They were in effect a court, which could charge people with crimes and administer punishment. They could also grant or withhold divorces, give people spiritual imprimatur for their actions, and place the awful curse of anathema on those who committed religious transgressions. The *kahal*'s decisions were arrived at by an informal system of discussion and religious disputation, and its rulings were often delivered in the form of Talmudic aphorisms and pronouncements. In a sense, the government of elders was a very old form of tribal autocracy, harking back to a world in which religious and secular understanding of the world was not yet riven.

The extent of control that these local governments exercised over people's private and public lives left room for considerable demagogy, and sometimes this led to conflicts with the communities themselves or occasionally open rebellion. But there is no doubt that the *kahal* system proved of great importance in sustaining a strong collective Jewish identity. It enabled the communities to govern themselves and gave the Jewish population throughout Poland a uniform pattern of organization and, at times, a basis for united, nationwide action.

The system of Talmudic learning elaborated in Poland also set the standard for Ashkenazic Jewry everywhere. Jewish education was almost entirely religious, and was intended only for boys. Girls' instruction was limited to some private tutoring in Hebrew and Yiddish. Boys, on the other hand, were taken through a series of very precise, if very narrow, steps. Between the ages of four and eight, they attended *cheder*, an elementary school of sorts, where they memorized parts of the Bible, learned Hebrew and Yiddish as well as some basic arithmetic and principles of good conduct. Between the ages of eight and thirteen, pupils went on to study the Talmud, a corpus of commentary on the Bible that had accumulated from the Babylonian exile onward. Boys who were considered conscientious or gifted scholars went on to attend academies, or yeshivas, for more advanced Talmudic study. By the sixteenth century, the yeshivas of Poland — in Cracow, Poznań, Lvov, and Lublin — were renowned among European Jews, and their master scholars attracted students from all over the world.

In some fundamental ways, then, Polish Jewry was becoming highly coherent and self-sufficient, enough to think of itself as a nation. The spirit of autonomy culminated in the creation of an institution unique in the history of the Diaspora — a kind of Jewish parliament known as the Vaad Arba Aratzot, or the Council of Four Lands. It is not widely known that a legitimately elected Jewish assembly existed in Europe for about two hundred years, long before the formation of Israel. Even today, in our intentionally multicultural societies, it is hard to envision an arrangement whereby a minority group might form a legislative body of its own. The council arose from the conditions of political life in Renaissance Poland, and to some extent echoed and paralleled them.

The council began to coalesce in the 1550s, when Polish kings recognized the Jews' right to select their own leaders. From then on, the Jewish communities started to convene local and regional meetings of their *kahal* representatives. However, it gradually became evident that certain problems and issues could be better dealt with on a national level, and the Council of Four Lands, representing four regions of Poland (with a separate delegation for Lithuania), was formed.

The Vaad was similar in many ways to the Polish Sejm, and it is possible that the conception for this Jewish institution was an instance of fruitful, if not entirely conscious, cultural borrowing. It would surely be surprising if, after several centuries of close proximity, the two cultures did not cross-fertilize to some extent. The delegates of the Sejm, like those of the Vaad, were elected at regional Sejmiks (little parliaments) that met all over Poland, and there were similar disputes in the two bodies about the order of seating and other procedural matters. The organization of the Vaad may have seemed natural to its founders because a precedent for it already existed. In turn, the *szlachta* may have found it easier to give their imprimatur to the Vaad because it resembled their own legislative body. More fancifully, one may speculate that the tenor of Jewish political life as we know it even today, with its tendency to animated discussion and fiery disputatiousness, was to some extent incubated in the Polish political climate. Certainly, the Sejmiks and Sejms were rowdy, often chaotic gatherings, with barrels of beer a regular part of the scene. The very principle of disagreement and disarray was encouraged by the rule of liberum veto, which allowed any one person to block the action of the entire assembly. The *szlachta*'s approval and relish of argument, and even anarchy, was indicated by a slogan that declared, "Poland stands on its nongovernment" (or, on its "disorder").

Unfortunately, most of the Vaad's records, or *pinkas* books, have been lost, but enough documents remain to give us considerable insight into the workings of that institution. At the peak of its effectiveness, the Vaad met twice a year and arbitrated a variety of matters. Its main role was the collection of taxes for the crown. This actually enhanced Jewish autonomy, because it meant that all taxes were collected and paid by this central body, and no Polish officials were directly involved in gathering money from the Jewish communities. But the Vaad exercised other forms of governance as well. In a way, it was *kahal* government writ large. The Vaad was a rabbinical body, and it acted as a religious and moral overseer of the Jewish population as a whole — making sure that the various communities under its jurisdiction followed the laws of the Torah, and punishing infractions, sometimes to the extent of pronouncing *herem*, or anathema, on offending members. In addition, there was an element of foreign policy in the Vaad's deliberations. It regularly apportioned part of its funds for charity to Jews in the Holy Land, and there were instances when German Jews turned to the assembly to settle their disputes with Polish Jews.

It is hard to define the Vaad's precise status vis-à-vis Poland itself. Perhaps the closest comparison would be to a government of a protectorate or a federated province — a political body answerable to a central governing power, but nevertheless having some genuine internal independence. Or perhaps the Vaad expressed something for which there are still few analogies: the status of the Jews as a fully autonomous minority culture. In any case, Polish rulers recognized the Vaad's authority to represent the Jewish community, and apparently they considered it in their interest that this authority should remain effective. This is indicated by the fact that on the rare occasions when the Vaad's dictates were flouted, Polish magnates stepped in to enforce them. In turn, one of the Vaad's most important and delicate tasks was maintaining and managing relations with the Polish governing powers. Informally, the Vaad tried to influence Polish policy toward the Jews by sending diplomats or liaison officers, called *shtadlanim*, to the regional Sejmiks and the national Sejm. The *shtadlanim*, who were chosen at both the local and national levels, played a crucial role in carrying messages from the Jewish communities to the government and in keeping those communities informed about Polish political moods and policies that might have a bearing on Jewish life. The chief *shtadlan*, who represented the Vaad at the main Polish parliament, was chosen with great care and received a salary and traveling expenses. Not surprisingly, there were many contenders for such influential positions, and there were express warnings against unauthorized competitors intervening in the corridors and cloakrooms of the Sejm. In trying to exercise their influence, both local and national *shtadlanim* often resorted to the one strategy by which anything was accomplished in the unruly Polish democracy — giving money "on the side" in exchange for favorable rulings. Bribery was an open secret, and was practiced not only by Jews but by other interest groups wanting to sway the Sejm to their interests. In the Vaad's proceedings, money for such purposes was allocated as a regular part of the budget.

The Vaad's sessions were probably never as chaotic as the Sejm's — for one thing, no beer flowed at them to loosen tongues — but needless to say, during the two hundred years of its existence, the Jewish parliament was hardly a perfectly united body. The most frequent subjects of dispute were money and the distribution of tax burdens among the towns and villages. At the end of the seventeenth century, the disagreements between Polish and Lithuanian representatives of the Vaad about their respective contributions to the general budget reached such a pitch that the two communities decided to act separately, even in dire cases of emergency or expulsion.

The Vaad, created at a zenith of Polish confidence and prosperity, was also a high point in Polish-Jewish relations. But the centuries of the Vaad's activity coincided with a succession of disasters for Poland, which led to that country's rapid decline and impinged directly on the Jews. The worst of these catastrophes were the Chmielnicki invasions of the mid-seventeenth century, events that acquired the hues of a dark legend in both Polish and Jewish imaginations. Bogdan Chmielnicki was a Cossack chieftain who, in 1648, rallied the disaffected masses of Ukrainian peasants, as well as the warrior caste of Cossack and Tartar horsemen, to rise up against their Polish overlords. This did not happen without provocation, as the Poles had exploited and abused the peasants very thoroughly. In the annals of Ukrainian history, Chmielnicki is remembered as the first leader to rebel against the oppression of the Polish state. In Polish memory, he is demon incarnate. Certainly, the invasions conducted under his leadership were ruthless in the extreme. For nine years his seemingly unstoppable armies rampaged through southeastern Poland, burning and pillaging every village and town in their trajectory, and raping, torturing, and murdering their inhabitants with wild and cruel savagery. Large swaths of Poland were devastated; hundreds of thousands of people were killed. The Ukrainians and the Cossacks, who were Russian Orthodox, attacked two groups with particular relish and impunity: the nobility and the Jews. The Catholic clergy, although not the main target of the invasions, also came in for its share of persecution.

How did Jews and Poles get along in what was, to some extent, a shared crisis? In many ways, their positions during the massacres prefigured the complexities of their relations during

World War II — and from this distance, it may be easier to discern in the earlier event the unhappy pattern of the predicament in which everyone was caught. Both Poles and Jews were horribly and fundamentally threatened, but they were in curiously unequal positions even in the equalizing face of death. It was for the Polish nobility that the Cossacks reserved their most elaborate tortures; the Jews were usually "merely" burned alive, often inside their synagogues. But the Poles were in a far better position to defend themselves, to fight back and be treated as a serious adversary. The Jews were, on the whole, unarmed and helpless. Both Poles and Jews suffered enormous losses of life in the course of the invasions, but Jewish people were butchered on a mass scale. It is estimated that as much as 20 to 25 percent of the Jewish population, or between 70,000 and 80,000 people, were killed in the massacres.

However, Jews were not entirely without the power or capacity to resist. In several towns they joined the Poles in military self-defense, and in some instances they took up arms themselves, fighting for their towns after everyone else had given up. Where the Jews were without the means of self-defense, the *szlachta* sometimes came to their aid; in some instances, Jewish chroniclers write, Polish nobles conducted campaigns to avenge the Jews. But there were also times when the Poles abandoned their more vulnerable neighbors as they looked to their own survival. Moreover, the invaders often set Poles and Jews against each other, so that solidarity was difficult to maintain.

The testimony of a Jewish chronicler, written in 1650, about the defense of the town of Tulczyn, shows all the wrenching conflicts created by the invaders' brutality. The account begins with a description of Jews in military action, joining the Poles in common cause. "About 600 courageous men, the nobles, barricaded themselves in the fortress," Meir of Szczebrzeszyn writes. "Approximately 2,000 of the scattered sheep [the Jews], accurate marksmen, joined them. The noblemen received them and they joined together, making an honest covenant between them; each would help the other. The noblemen were deployed inside the fortress; the Jews stood around on the battlements, on guard with bow and arrow. When the smouldering butts [Cossacks and Tartars] attacked, they shot at them with arrows and flames. The Greeks [the attackers] recoiled in fear and trembling and the noblemen and Jews chased them, smiting a mighty blow against the rebels."

But the compact between the nobles and the Jews was short-lived. It was broken by the attackers, who first demanded that the nobles give them all Jewish property in exchange for their lives. The Jews deliberated and reluctantly consented, knowing that the alternative was sure death for everyone. The enemy demands then escalated: they now wanted the Jews themselves, or they vowed to burn down the fortress. The nobles went along with this ultimatum as well, and delivered up their comrades-in-arms, who were promptly massacred. The Poles' reprieve, did not last long, however. Within days, their fortress was penetrated, and they, too, were murdered to the last man.

One can see the moral horror of it all too clearly: with life itself at stake, tribal loyalties reassert themselves in the most naked form, and in either-or scenarios, betrayal of others is turned into a seemingly necessary choice. Despite the self-preserving allegiances, however, some Jewish people felt a sense of identification and shared suffering with the Poles. Natan Hannower, writing some time after the massacres, chronicled the awful tortures to which Jews were subjected, but noted that the Cossacks "acted no differently with the Poles, especially with the clergy." To another Jewish historian, Shabbetai HaKohen, the attacking hordes were "a contemptible nation . . . vile, base, unreliable and vacuous. . . . Peasants and farmers gathered from near and far and raised their hand against the king, his noblemen and retainers, a great and powerful nation, like the giants."

For Poland, the disasters were hardly over. The decade of Chmielnicki's atrocities was followed by a long and economically devastating Swedish invasion, which left many Polish towns and villages razed to the ground yet again. This, in turn, was succeeded by a Turkish war and by Russian incursions into parts of Polish and Lithuanian territory. In the midst of the manmade destruction, the country was racked by famine, fires, and epidemics.

The position of the Jews worsened substantially during this period of decline. Jewish communities suffered more than their share of calamity with every eruption of violence, and the financial levy exacted from them, partly to pay the costs of war, grew ever larger and harder to meet. After the Chmielnicki massacres, the Vaad became additionally burdened by enormous expenses designated for the aid of Jewish victims. Although Polish nobles habitually borrowed money from the Jews, now Jews increasingly got into debt by borrowing from the nobles and even the clergy.

As Poland's position and status deteriorated, its climate became less hospitable to differences of all kinds. During the period of the Counter-Reformation, the Catholic Church began to reassert its strength by stepping up the rhetoric of religious antagonism. For the first time (and much later than other countries), Poland witnessed persecutions of Protestants and other "heretics." In the last decades of the seventeenth century and the beginning of the eighteenth, several hundred Jews were accused of blood libel and executed. During the same years, more than a thousand women were accused of witchcraft and burned at the stake.

Secular attitudes toward Jews also became more hostile. The harshness of economic life played its part in these tensions. The hard-pressed burghers routinely and unjustly accused Jewish merchants of ruining Polish towns and undermining Polish townsmen by unfair competition. Others pointed the finger at Jewish innkeepers, charging them with destroying the peasantry by drink. The Sejmiks and the Sejm passed acrimoniously worded resolutions barring Jews from residence in major cities — although these were rarely effective, and individual princelings still recognized the value of Jewish contributions by inviting Jewish merchants to restore towns emptied by war.

The Council of Four Lands was dissolved in 1764 as part of a general fiscal reform in Poland, undertaken as the country's economy slid into disintegration. With the Vaad's dismantling, the Golden Age of Polish Jewry was over. Not all that surprisingly, the closure coincided with the end of Poland's Golden Age, and preceded by only eight years the first of the partitions, during which Poland was systematically swallowed up by three neighboring empires. The fate of the Jews was, inevitably, contingent on the fate of the host country.

During its existence, the Vaad embodied the possibility of reconciling resolute separateness and a tenable coexistence. But this equilibrium, so rarely achieved in majority-minority relations, was never easy to sustain. For one thing, Jewish autonomy depended very much on Polish goodwill, and from the Jewish point of view, the solution symbolized by the Vaad carried the germ of its own conflicts and contradictions. Undoubtedly, their self-containment helped Polish Jews reach a level of cultural coherence that is a form of strength. The ability to follow their customs undisturbed enabled them to develop and nurture traditions of civic life and learning that made them a central force of world Jewry.

However, separateness was not without its price. It precluded deeper familiarity between Jews and Poles, and it is only superficial familiarity that breeds the superficial reaction of contempt. At the higher rungs of the social ladder, where more intimate, or at least ongoing, contacts between Poles and Jews were most frequent, relations between the two groups were relatively open and friendly. The *kahal* elders could conduct negotiations between their own communities and the outside world with relative ease, but they discouraged "ordinary people" from fraternizing with the Poles. Dietary prohibitions meant that Jews could not eat in Christian homes, and neither Catholics nor Jews would think of entering the other's house of worship.

The hazard of insularity is not only that it leads to social isolation, but that it creates a certain solipsism — or, to put it in more worldly terms, parochialism — of perception. In some Jewish texts, events in the larger world were understood entirely in light of Jewish concerns. For example, some commentators interpreted the partitions of Poland as a punishment for the dissolution of the Vaad. In an extreme example of ethnocentrism, Rabbi Levi Itzhak preached to his flock that "all of the nations were created for the sake of Israel, for the good of Israel; for sometimes, for some reason, good comes to Israel from the nations. . . . Were it not that there is some good, they would not have been created at all."

The distance between Poles and Jews was desired by both parties, although for different reasons. Both nations had their syndromes of superiority, although with unequal powers of acting upon them. The impact of Polish prejudices was perforce far more injurious to the Jews than vice versa. The Poles were hardly ready to admit Jews into full Polishness, or full humanity. But Jewish separatism was also an active choice, and it also had its consequences. It meant that Jewish individuals and communities cultivated their own alienness, and that although they were willing to engage in contractual relations with the Poles, they did not wish to enter into a shared world with them.

The Polish view implicit in granting broad autonomy to Jews was that they were foreigners of sorts who should be allowed to follow their own laws and customs, however arcane or irrational these may have seemed. But the Jews were not yet seen as a "foreign body" within a united body politic. This may have been because the polity was not yet sufficiently unified, its notion of itself not so homogeneous as to give rise to such conceptions. In a sense, Jews were accepted insofar as they were foreign, insofar as they were a separate caste, and did not have to be embraced as "Polish." But as Poland began to move toward the modern idea of nationhood, and as its geopolitical condition simultaneously deteriorated, the discussion of the Polish-Jewish relationship took more complicated turns.

Indeed, in the second half of the eighteenth century, the "Jewish question" became firmly installed as one of the central topics on the national agenda. By then, it was widely recognized that Jews were a permanent and prominent element of Polish life. Numbers are not always reliable for this period, but it is estimated that the Jews numbered around 900,000, or about 10 percent of the total population. In addition, since the seventeenth century the Jewish population had been growing much faster than the Polish one. This was due in part to the continuous influx of immigrants, driven to Poland by expulsions and persecutions to the east and west. Numerical expansion was also aided by the institution of early marriage (Jewish girls were often betrothed by the time they were twelve) and by a lower infant mortality rate than that obtaining among the rest of the population. Jewish laws regulating diet and hygiene may also have contributed to demographic growth.

As Poland tried to cope with its internal problems and to define its political identity in the changed climate of the eighteenth century, the issue of a large minority's position in the social structure gained new importance in public discourse. Ideas on the subject covered the whole political spectrum. In the Sejm, the discussion was dominated by conservative voices, but the tone of intellectual argument was set by a group of progressive thinkers influenced by the secular, universalist ideas of the Enlightenment. These social philosophers wanted to change the very definition of a person and the nation. In their writings, they tried to lay down the principles governing the individual's relationship to the state, to articulate the rights, privileges, responsibilities, and commitments that members of a society owed to one another. They espoused the principles of religious tolerance, judicial equality, economic freedom, and broadly based education for everyone. And at least some of them were radical enough to advocate extending these principles fully to Polish Jews.

What of the Jewish attitudes toward these larger trends? As the discussion of reform and of the Jewish position in the potential new state gathered force, Jewish opinion on such matters remained divided. This can be seen in a revealing debate among three writers at the time, aptly enough, of the French Revolution. The first exchange of views took place in 1789 between Mateusz Butrymowicz, a Polish exponent of Enlightenment ideas, and Herszel Józefowicz, the rabbi of Chełm. In an essay entitled "A method for forming Polish Jews into useful citizens of the nation," Butrymowicz, who was a delegate to the

Sejm, started with the good Enlightenment premise that "man is born neither bad nor good, neither intelligent nor stupid," and that everyone is shaped by education and circumstances. Therefore, the project of shaping Jews into Polish citizens was an achievable goal, and Butrymowicz proposed several measures to attain it. He acknowledged that religion was a matter of private conscience, but thought that Jews should adjust their holidays to the Christian calendar. As it was, he calculated that Jews spent one quarter of the year "in strictest idleness," thus depriving the country of valuable labor. He also recommended that they be required to use the Polish language, in writing if not in speech, and that they dress in the same manner as others, so as not to incur the mockery of the populace. At the same time, he considered it a grave defect of the Polish constitution that Jews did not have a clearly defined social position, and suggested that this should be rectified by endowing them with the status of burghers. In this capacity, Jews would come under the jurisdiction of Polish courts. "To give Jews an estate, and from eternal wanderers to make them into citizens of this country, in which until now they were guests, should be the very first aim."

The rabbi of Chełm responded in a tone of respectful humility, but he protested energetically against being improved, educated, or regulated by the Poles. He objected to Butrymowicz's charges of Jewish idleness (aside from the Sabbath, by his count, there were only twelve nonworking holidays in the Jewish calendar), and he bridled at a phrase Butrymowicz apparently used, describing Jewish innkeepers as "leeches sucking people's blood." One must wonder, Herszel Józefowicz said, who installs these leeches in the first place, and who derives the highest sums of money from them. As to the suggestion that Jews should come under the jurisdiction of Polish courts, he argued that this would necessitate violations of the many religious injunctions Jews had to follow. "We know very well that we are subject to the country's government," he wrote, "to which we are always obedient," but he pleaded that his community be left to its own devices, in its full differentness and separateness.

The rabbi of Chełm was probably speaking for the majority of Polish Jews. But the Jewish community in Poland was becoming fractured, even in its religious beliefs. Segments of that community were also affected by the wider European intellectual currents and by the environment in which Jews had lived for several centuries. There were students and travelers among Polish Jews who considered themselves to be part of the modern European culture. There was even a Jewish Enlightenment movement, known as the Haskala. Indeed, the divisions among Jews mirrored one of the basic oppositions of the age — between religious and social traditionalists of all persuasions and the secular, humanist reformers from all countries and backgrounds. In discussions of the Jewish role in Poland, the adherents of the Haskala — known as *maskilim* — allied themselves with the representatives of the Polish Enlightenment, and against Orthodox, rabbinical Jews.

One exponent of Haskalic ideas who entered the Polish-Jewish dialogue was Salomon of Vilno, the court doctor of King Stanislaus August. Writing three years after Butrymowicz, Salomon of Vilno implicitly agreed with almost all of the proposals set forth by the Polish reformer. In his essay "A project in regard to the reform of the Jews," Salomon also argued that the Jewish community should come under the aegis of Polish law and thus become a more integral part of the society. He too wanted Jews to receive burgher status, although he advocated that Jews who did not have a skilled trade or other source of income should be encouraged to farm. He thought that Jews should learn Polish and reform their dress customs. Salomon of Vilno was more sensitive than Butrymowicz to symptoms of Polish prejudice; he urged that the word "unbeliever," routinely appended to the word "Jew," should cease being used, and that other pejorative terms should be actively discouraged. On the whole, however, he adopted a patriotic tone, and framed his project for Jewish reform within a context of concern for the general improvement of Poland.

The debate on the "Jewish question" reached its political climax during the so-called Four Year Sejm of 1788–1792. This prolonged parliamentary session had as its task nothing less than the reconstruction of the Polish state and the systematizing of rules governing the country's institutions and social relations. The burning national issue was the creation of a Poland strong and orderly enough to defend itself against foreign powers, especially the Russians, whose aggressive intentions were becoming ominously unmistakable. As far as the Jews were concerned, the chief problem was the regulation of their rights to reside in cities and to practice all trades and professions. The actual status of Jews in these matters was still governed by an eclectic patchwork of prescriptions and provisions that had accumulated since medieval times — although in practice these were rarely followed to the letter. In addition, the laws governing Polish institutions were just as capricious. There were, for example, different tenets for lands owned by the crown and for so-called private cities; there were villages owned by the nobility and towns with their own charters. At the time of the Sejm, a much larger proportion of Jews lived in towns than in the country. Legally, though, their rights of residence were limited, and they were barred from a number of professions, and from owning land.

During the Four Year Sejm, representatives of various Jewish communities — mostly Haskalic Jews themselves — submitted, together with a group of liberal deputies, a number of petitions asking for the admission of Jews to full residential and civic rights and for the lifting of various professional restrictions. The reformers, however, were routinely outflanked in the Sejm by the much larger conservative faction. In the society at large, the fiercest opposition to full Jewish enfranchisement came from the burghers and townsmen, whose own rights remained uncertain. The townsmen, like the Jews, did not have full privileges of municipal citizenship; and the burghers, who were a small and relatively undeveloped estate, felt directly threatened by Jewish competition. The acute rivalry among these groups erupted in anti-Jewish riots in Warsaw in 1790.

Perhaps in response to the general climate of opinion, the Sejm did not significantly alter the status of the Jews or, for that matter, of the other, relatively disenfranchised groups. It is worth noting, however, that the rhetoric of opposition to Jewish rights was at that point economic rather than racial or religious. Among certain segments of society, Jews were feared, even reviled, but the danger they supposedly represented was perceived as emanating from their economic prowess, not their "strangeness" or their faith.

The conservative mood predominating in the Sejm might yet have swung in another direction had the partitions not rendered all Polish resolutions moot soon thereafter. In 1792, near the end of the Four Year Sejm, the progressives, working secretly with the weak but liberally disposed king, resorted to a strategic ploy in order to pass a document known as the Constitution of May Third. This was the first written constitution in Europe, and it was hailed throughout the Continent as a revolutionary piece of legislation. In fact, the constitution was not all that radical, but the liberals intended it as a blueprint for further changes, which they hoped to introduce later. Among other matters awaiting reconsideration was the question of Jewish status. Indeed, discussions were already resuming between Jewish representatives and the king's counselor when external events once again harshly intervened.

As it was, the partitions were about to eliminate Poland as a political entity, and to initiate a 125-year period of Polish colonization and diaspora. But even on the eve of that painful event, there were instances of solidarity between Poles and Jews that were perhaps inspired by the ideas of the Enlightenment. One such occasion came in 1794, when Tadeusz Kościuszko (who was also a hero of the American Revolution) mounted an insurrection against Russian armies that were in effect already occupying Poland. In a rare gesture of fraternity, Kościuszko called on Jews to serve as troops, under the leadership of one Berek Joselewicz. Some five hundred volunteers responded to his call. In his proclamation announcing the formation of a Jewish regiment, Kościuszko drew parallels between Jewish and Polish traditions, between ancient Israel and beleaguered Poland. Alluding to King David and other Old Testament figures, he declared, "Out of such valiant men a nation was constituted. Albeit meager in itself, it terrified its invaders. With a small handful it dispersed the numerous armies of great Eastern powers. The rebuilding of Jerusalem offers a most splendid display of the character of this nation. While holding a cutlass in one hand and a trowel in the other, the people restored their native walls and fought for their native land."

In turn, Berek Joselewicz, calling upon fellow Jews to join his light cavalry regiment, spoke in tones rarely encountered in Jewish rhetoric before the military speeches of Israeli generals: "Beloved brothers, I expect of the Eternal Almighty, nor do I doubt, that the propitious time has come for us to humble our enemy. . . . We need only be honorable and have a valiant and heroic heart. . . . Awaken, help us to retrieve a hitherto down-trodden and oppressed Poland. Faithful brothers! Let us fight for our country to the last drop of our blood. Even if we do not live to see it, our children will live freely and safely, and they will not roam about like wild beasts. Beloved brothers! Awaken as lions and leopards."

There was soon even more reason for mutual identifica-tion between the two peoples, as Poles were about to go into their own period of wandering and internal exile. For all their united spirit, the Polish and Jewish forces were hopelessly out-numbered in their insurrection, and the great Warsaw battle of November 4, 1794, was lost. Empress Catherine of Russia, who had been the effective ruler of Poland for some years, negoti-ated the final agreement with Austria and Prussia whereby the three empires carved up the country. In what was one of the great political scandals of the time, Poland had been ruthlessly swallowed up by the great powers of the day.

Berek Joselewicz left Poland, but returned twelve years later, to the Duchy of Warsaw, where, under the short-lived Consti-tution of 1807, all inhabitants, including Jews, were guaranteed equality under the law. In 1809, he organized his legion once again, and died in another battle for Poland.

It is hard to know how the Polish-Jewish relationship might have evolved if the existence of Poland had continued un-broken. Before the partitions, the contradictions of that rela-tionship were reaching the point of high tension. Maintaining simultaneous separateness and friendliness between groups is, as we know from today's multicultural societies, a tricky bal-ancing act — and the balance was no longer holding. If relations between Poles and Jews were not to become permanently hos-tile, the terms by which the Jewish minority lived in Poland needed to be renegotiated in the direction of greater enfranchisement and integration. But both ideas met with resistance. Conservative Poles felt that as long as the Jewish community remained separate, it did not deserve equal rights. At the same time, they feared that if the Jews received those rights, they would soon come to dominate the indigenous Poles. Religious Jews, for their part, felt that Poland had not given them sufficient reason to merit their full loyalty. Moreover, they feared that integration would lead to a loss of integrity and identity.

It was only the liberal theorists who felt that equal rights were a first principle, and that all members of society were entitled to them. Polish progressives argued that it was against Poland's interests to have a large minority that remained unincorporated into national life; the most radical thinkers suggested that Jews had to be granted full enfranchisement in good faith, before loyalty or commitment could be demanded from them. In their version of these ideas, Haskalic Jews felt that Polish Jewry needed to accommodate itself to modern conditions and to assume active membership in the society in which they had been living for several centuries. None of these thinkers wanted to eliminate religious distinctions or convictions, but they believed it was possible to combine public loyalty to country and state with a private cultural and spiritual self.

What did Poles owe to the Jews, and Jews to the Poles? What were their mutual responsibilities, and how were they to reconcile their differences with social cohesion? Disagreements about such basic questions often became incendiary, and at times led to mutual alienation of the two groups. But the questions were not, on either side, a function of pure pride or pure prejudice. They were legitimate problems, arising from the changing relations among all parts of society and the changing nature of the social contract itself. For various reasons, the frictions between the two groups were becoming, on the eve of the partitions, unsustainable. Since expulsion of the Jews was not on anyone's mind, it seems probable that new accommodations would have had to be reached eventually. But with the partitions, Poles and Jews became subject to the laws of three different powers, and the relationship between them entered an even more complex and unhappy phase.

It is at this point that the history of Brańsk's Jews really begins.

2

Shtetl: The Beginnings

FOR NO LESS than five hundred years, the Brańsk market has convened every Monday, come rain or snow, war, partition, or Communism. In earlier days it must have been a colorful, bustling place — a meeting point for Poles and Jews, of course, but also for Belarusians, Armenians, and Germans, bringing produce from the neighboring villages and exchanging it for items made in the town, shouting, laughing, shaking hands on a bargain. It is from markets like these that a Jewish saying, which I sometimes heard in my childhood — "Sell the head of a fish, buy the tail" — derives. But these days the market presents a more mundane spectacle. I have come here with Zbigniew Romaniuk on a wintry day, and the large, fenced-off area contains only a few trucks, a row of parked cars, some makeshift stands with items of clothing blowing in the wind. A few Ukrainians from over the border have set out their truly pitiable collections of goods directly on the ground: an old shirt here, a few chipped plates there, nails, used stockings, cartons of cigarettes. Commerce as hopelessness. The Soviet Empire, after all those decades, redux.

At the other end of the market, trading looks less dismal, if not exactly brisk. A few young, dirty calves have been brought out of their long, covered trucks to be exhibited and examined.

Ruddy-faced farmers in sheepskin coats and high leather boots
stand next to them, stomping their feet in the snow for warmth.
I observe them with a double vision. They are rough-and-
ready-looking men, huddling in small groups, exchanging idle
remarks. That is all. But in post-Holocaust ethnography, they
have come to be seen as allegories of anti-Semitism. In their
faces, if you look at them a certain way, nothing but this essential hatred can be discerned — the way, undoubtedly, that to
some of them a Jew was a pure type, of greed, cleverness, and
manipulativeness. I know that there may be some truth to the
Polish stereotype: that in some of their hearts anti-Semitism
sprouts. But I know also that on both sides these are reductions,
pure, simple, and sometimes very dangerous.

Reductions that, in their purity, are undoubtedly more possible from a distance. When the market was a weekly meeting
place for Poles and Jews; when a Polish farmer haggled with a
Jewish merchant and they arrived at a price; when the same Polish farmer later went to relax at an inn run by a Jewish leaseholder; then archetype might have been modified by actual contact, by a few sentences of conversation, a moment of shared
jollity. Side by side with preconceptions — "Jews are shrewd
and greedy"; "Poles are foolish and primitive" — some consciousness of real persons, of men and women who were more
or less amiable, witty, attractive, wise, honest, or strong, would
have played its part as well. But now, as far as Poles and Jews
are concerned, we are in an era of almost wholly abstract typol-
ogies, and we have to reconstruct past perceptions from fragments, scraps of recollection, condensed phrases, a few flashes
of memory.

Zbyszek leaves me to do my reportorial researches, and I
approach a group of men, who greet me politely. When I tell
them I'm writing about Brańsk, they instantly assume I'm inter-

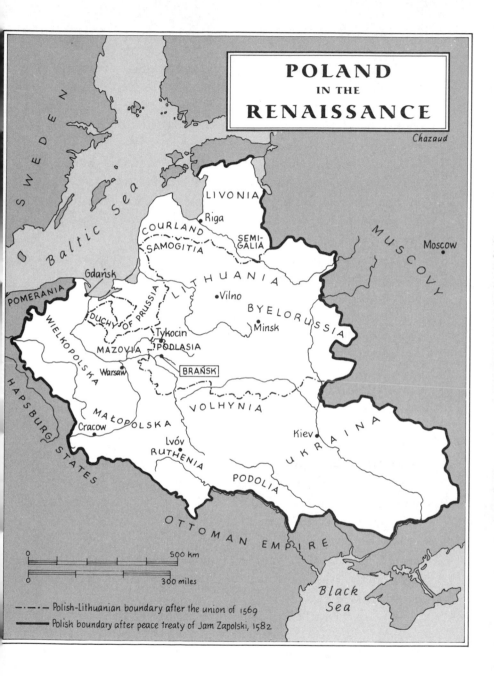

POLAND
IN THE
RENAISSANCE

Chazaud

SWEDEN

Baltic Sea

LIVONIA

Riga

COURLAND

SAMOGITIA

SEMI-GALIA

POMERANIA

Gdańsk

DUCHY OF PRUSSIA

WIELKOPOLSKA

LITHUANIA

•Vilno

BYELORUSSIA

Minsk•

MUSCOVY

Moscow•

Tykocin

MAZOVIA

PODLASIA

Warsaw

BRAŃSK

MAŁOPOLSKA

Cracow

Lvóv

RUTHENIA

VOLHYNIA

Kiev•

UKRAINA

HAPSBURG STATES

PODOLIA

OTTOMAN EMPIRE

500 km

300 miles

Black
Sea

—·—·— Polish-Lithuanian boundary after the union of 1569

——— Polish boundary after peace treaty of Jam Zapolski, 1582 ested in the new politics and instantly try to satisfy my putative curiosity, speaking with a quick eagerness.

"So you see, they are coming back again, but we won't let them! The West isn't helping, but we won't give in! We won't let them!"

"They," in this little riff, refers to the Communists, who in a different guise have returned to govern Poland again. Yet another Them, satisfying perhaps some perennial human need for an enemy, or at least an Other, through whom we can become We.

I tell the men — expecting a shift into unease — that actually I am interested in the history of Brańsk's Jews. But there is no unease.

"There were various kinds," a tall farmer leaps in. "Good ones and bad, just like in every nation."

The youngest one among them interrupts, speaking earnestly, even passionately. "They lived well together," he says, bending intently toward me. "My dad told me. There were all kinds of people, sure, some were good and some weren't. Some were friends, sure. My dad traded with them, he told me."

An older farmer, short and dark, addresses me with the formal "Pani," used in its old-fashioned, class-tinged way, which suggests the respect owed by a peasant to someone of a higher station. "Pani," he says, speaking very fast, "I'm stupid, but what stupid person invented that about the Poles — that they're anti-Semites? They helped, they helped a lot, would Jews have helped like that? I'm stupid and more stupid, but what are they saying about Auschwitz, that we must get out of there? How is that?"

Defensiveness: the first note struck before I have even asked any questions. This conversation, in his mind, has already had many twists and loops, and by now he's responding not to his own memories but to an implicit accusation: all Poles are anti-Semitic. And in this kind of conversation, accusation is answered with accusation, and the past and present are all intermixed in his mind. The Auschwitz incident he is referring to concerns a convent built in 1984 right outside the concentration camp, whose presence has been angrily protested by American Jewish groups. I confess I can see his point of view in this quarrel. Although the numbers are not comparable, Auschwitz was the site of Polish suffering as well as Jewish martyrdom. To his mind, a convent is a sign of respect. Why should it be seen by others as an offense?

"We got along, sure," another one chimes in, bringing the conversation back to safer matters. "My father did business with them all the time, he had a friend who came over every week, sold my dad some things."

"I took food to people in the ghetto," the old farmer informs me offhandedly, as a sort of afterthought.

"Really?" I ask, my curiosity rising.

"Sure. I went up on my bicycle. My father told me to take some bread and other things."

"And what happened?" I ask.

"What should happen? I just handed some food to people over the fence and rode away on my bike. I was only eleven, nobody noticed me. Well, goodbye," he wraps up, and walks away briskly. And there it is, a moment remembered and arrested in time. I can see it: a young boy, almost a child, not afraid of what he was doing because he probably did not grasp the danger he was courting, the fraught meaning, at that time, of his ordinary gesture.

"They only ate the forequarters of the calf, not the hindquarters," another farmer informs me. "So we bought the hindquarters from them."

The remarks go on. But what do they correspond to? Former realities? Memories received from the older generation? Or some sense of what I want to hear?

But no, these men do not strike me as self-conscious enough to present a calculated image of themselves. My impression is soon confirmed by another meeting, on the way out of the market. Another peasant, in high leather boots, tall and beefy, his healthy face belying his seventy-five years. He must at least guess that I am Jewish, and yet, speaking to me in a confidential though respectful tone, he unfolds before me a farrago of classically anti-Semitic notions.

He says exactly what men like that, in the folklore of anti-Semitism, are supposed to say. He speaks like an archetype. He gives me a long account of how Jews manipulated and cheated everyone. They lorded it over the peasants. At least Piłsudski — the Polish leader before the war — knew how to handle them, but Wałęsa didn't, he let the Jews get out of hand. But even with Piłsudski, they tried to slip him a Jewess . . .

Really? I ask, wanting to test his reality-testing. The conjecture about Piłsudski is so far-fetched that I haven't heard it before, even as a rumor.

Oh yes! he assures me. And then, in a collusive tone, he avers that if they — this time the word stands for the Jews, not the Communists — came back and took over in Poland again, the way they did before, it would be bad. Oh yes, a few of them tried to come back after the war, but one got killed and the rest got scared off.

These are the most chilling words I have ever heard spoken by a Pole. But there he stands, talking to me jovially — though by now he surely knows that I am Jewish — and taking me into his confidence. Clearly, he doesn't feel that he has anything to be ashamed of; he is simply expressing ideas that seem to him entirely natural.

My voice is temporarily throttled by fury and disbelief, but I want to know more. How, I ask, did the Jews cheat and manipulate the peasants?

Oh, you know, he says, they always lowered prices before Christmas, or when they had too much produce ... Always knew when to lower the prices and then raise them again.

So that's it. The famous Jewish shrewdness, the practically demonic cleverness — it came down to this! But I shouldn't be too surprised, for this rather naive man is exhibiting the naive mechanisms of prejudice. His belief that Jews were wicked exploiters comes first, and all evidence is absorbed into this deep-seated preconception, as drops of water are absorbed into the soil.

And now? I ask. What goes on at the market now, without the Jews?

He thinks for a moment. "Oh, now it's even worse!" For a moment he looks surprised. "Yes," he laughs, "ours are just the same. Everyone always walks all over the peasants."

But the peasants manage somehow, I suggest.

Oh yes, he readily admits, sure they manage. And he goes on to tell me with relish about the pieces of land and the cattle he's bought since he's inherited his farm.

"After the war we worried that without the Jews, nobody would know how to trade. But ours know how to do it too."

Zbyszek has stood by during the conversation, looking a bit uneasy but letting me take the lead. Now he confirms that many people in Brańsk worried about this after the war: without the Jews, no one would know how to trade. Of course, they learned. Trade does not involve higher mysteries, although for a long time it had been associated with the Jews, and mystified by this association. Buying and selling for profit was supposed to take devilish cleverness; it was supposed to be inherently dishonest.

"Oh yes, ours know all the tricks — they'll take your money as well as anybody," the ruddy man adds, as if he's stumbled on a terrific bit of insight. Is that all it takes, then, to talk him out of his prejudices? A simple argument? No, undoubtedly he will return to them before he has had his supper. They go far back, his notions, although by now it is impossible to disentangle their roots or remember where they came from, impossible to account for one man's friendliness, another's indifference, and yet another's hatred.

ॐ   ॐ   ॐ

The shtetl, in the absence of living actualities, has become a trope, a metaphor frozen in time. In our minds, it tends to be unchanging, filled always with the same Sabbaths, the dybbuks, the fear of Cossacks, the family warmth. But although it is true that the shtetl changed reluctantly and slowly, it was not exempt from the forces of accident, conflict, and development — in other words, from history.

In Brańsk, as in so many shtetls, history began with the market, or at least with the marketplace. And in Brańsk, the Polish-Jewish story began slow and late. Until the mid-sixteenth century, there is very little written information about Jews in the town, although this does not mean they were not present in the area. Until 1569, parts of the Podlasie region were under the jurisdiction of Lithuanian princes. In 1495, Lithuania's Prince Alexander had banished Jews from his country, but several years later they were allowed to return and reclaim their property in exchange for a handsome collective ransom. Some of them may well have settled in the Brańsk area.

Later, the Jewish population was increased by arrivals from central and western Poland. Many of these migrants would have been part of the drive to settle the eastern territories, which were Poland's early frontier, thinly populated and potentially fertile. The Jewish settlers came in search of better opportunities. Some of them may have been encouraged to relocate by a wealthy nobleman or a town's owner who hoped they would liven up the local economy. In private towns, the fledgling Jewish communities were protected by the local magnates. But most of the wanderers would have come with more tenuous dreams. They would have been among the humblest people, traveling in covered wagons, in their black garb, carrying a few books of the Talmud, stopping at Jewish inns along the way. By the mid-sixteenth century, there were at least two communities with their own *kahals* in the region — in the town of Tykocin and in Bielsk, only a few kilometers from Brańsk. In Tykocin, a beautiful Renaissance synagogue still stands, from a somewhat later time, its high-style architecture and grand dimensions testifying to the wealth and self-confidence of the local Jewish community.

But the royal towns of the region had a privilege called *de non tolerandis Judaeis*, which gave them the right to bar Jews from full-time residence. Brańsk was one of those towns. It was, in the sixteenth century, no more than a large farming community, administered by a royally appointed elder and inhabited by small gentry and by peasants classified variously as villeins, rent farmers, and toilers.

Despite the formal restrictions imposed on them, Jews probably weren't entirely absent from the town's precincts. The first real fact we get on this subject dates from 1560, and tells us that seventeen of Brańsk's flour mills were operated under lease by Jews. Then, a long silence — until 1613, when there is a mention of an innkeeper named Moshe and his wife, Ciba. Moshe died in 1620, and his place at the inn was taken by Abraham. Another named inhabitant was one Hreczko, who ran a mill.

These are bare bits of data, and yet on them hangs an economic tale. The local gentry hired Jews not from any ethnic preference, but in the hopes of increasing their yields and profits. Experience had apparently shown that enterprises run by Jewish managers were more productive, and in Brańsk the flour mills were the most successful part of the local economy.

From the gentry's point of view, then, Jews were welcome in their domains because they were useful for business. From the peasants' perspective, things might have looked different. The lower orders of peasants were kept in a state of near serfdom; in the Brańsk area, there were repeated reports of their disaffection, their protests against extortionary taxes, and their violent rebellions. One can get a glimpse of their condition from descriptions of soldiers swooping down on villages and summarily wresting farm animals from their owners. We know from various documents that some elders worked the local peasantry ruthlessly, and punished them with beatings or imprisonment.

To these hard-pressed toilers, the Jews who occasionally appeared in Brańsk may have seemed an unreasonably favored caste. Managing mills and inns paid relatively well and was not as physically demanding as farming. The Jewish leaseholders, on the other hand, must have experienced the essential insecurity of their position; they knew that their very right to live and work in Brańsk depended on the goodwill of their employers. And so the seeds of petty resentment were probably sown early, as they always are when two kinds of underprivilege are brought together.

Still, there are reports of neither great enmities nor minor incidents between peasants and Jews. Indeed, after the mention of mill managers in the mid-sixteenth century, there is, as far as information about Brańsk's Jews is concerned, another long, almost two-century pause. The silence on this subject may have to do with the noisy turbulence on other fronts, for while in the

Jewish narrative of Brańsk this was still a prehistoric period, in the Polish tale history was already marching at a brisk pace. In the next two hundred years, Brańsk found itself almost constantly in the path of violence and catastrophe.

Although Chmielnicki's horsemen didn't reach that far north, shortly after the invasions an epidemic of Black Death swept through the area, undoubtedly affecting Jewish families among others. No descriptions of that episode survive from the Podlasie region, but Jewish texts from other parts of the country describe dire scenes of death, of bodies piling up without proper burial, of families fleeing their homes in a desperate attempt to escape the pursuing plague.

In the relentless progression of disasters, the next one came in 1655 from the direction of Sweden. In Brańsk, the situation during this period was particularly tangled. The town's elder, a Lithuanian magnate named Bogusław Radziwiłł, changed sides and entered into an alliance with the Swedes. As a result, army divisions faithful to the Polish king decided to punish the traitorous noble by destroying his properties. Whole estates, villages, and peasant farms were torched and leveled to the ground in this revenge action.

We do not know what the provincial Jewish villagers would have made of these internecine quarrels, but they may well have found themselves in the kind of dilemma that Jews had to face all too often in their history. If they remained loyal to the Lithuanian magnate on whom their immediate fate depended, they would have incurred the wrath of Polish soldiers; if they declared their allegiance to the Poles, they might have lost their protection and their businesses. What we do know is that during the Swedish Wars, most of the flour mills in Brańsk were burned down, eliminating an important source of livelihood for the local Jews.

To compound the destruction, Brańsk was soon visited by another epidemic and subjected to further military attacks. In a statistic not untypical of the region, the town's population fell by a stunning 64 percent as a result of the combined events. Throughout the eighteenth century, soldiers of Swedish, Russian, Polish, and other armies continued to clash and pillage on Brańsk's border territory. The lot of peasants grew harder as more taxes and obligations were imposed on them. It was only in the second half of the century that the economy of the region took a turn for the better, and the township began to develop again.

It is during this more peaceful period that history proper of Brańsk Jews begins. Toward the end of the eighteenth century, perhaps attracted by the growing need for labor, Jewish people of assorted trades and professions started coming to Brańsk in larger numbers. At that time, they were still not allowed to reside within the town's borders, so they lived in nearby villages and traveled to Brańsk to work. Among the first groups to be mentioned and counted were the traditional leaseholders of inns and mills, and also medics, leather tanners, and caretakers of municipal property.

Culturally, these Jewish villagers cum townsmen were a hybrid species. They were rural people, tending their horses and farmyards, cultivating a bit of orchard or garden. But they were also carriers of an internal legacy that originated long ago in another part of the world. This was a tradition whose visible signs Jews reestablished wherever they went. As soon as their numbers were sufficient, they built synagogues and appointed *kahals* even in the tiniest, most peripheral hamlets.

They lived on two levels, then. In the external world, they plied their crafts, traded, and exchanged practical information with the people around them. As a result of such daily dealings, their everyday language, Yiddish, was absorbing a sprinkling of Polish words and expressions. But among their fellow Jews, they entered another universe, in which their most important task was to maintain the continuum of their laws and beliefs, to uphold the faith that made them who they were, that constituted their very selves.

At the same time, the scattered Jews of the Podlasie area may have been aware that their faith was beginning to fracture and splinter. The latter part of the eighteenth century was a time of great spiritual turbulence for Polish Jewry, and reverberations of the storms were felt even in the remote Brańsk region. In 1760, for example, a woman in one of the neighboring villages converted to Catholicism and received the surname Nowicka (from "new"). Perhaps hers was an individual decision, but it is more likely that the convert was acting under the influence of a strange movement known as Frankism, which briefly arose among Polish Jews around midcentury. The movement — not the first of its kind — was led by a fascinating figure named Jakub Frank, who in the 1750s declared himself the Messiah. Frank accompanied his own deification with some highly peculiar notions, which nevertheless have an oddly familiar ring. In his personality and beliefs, Frank prefigured any number of today's swamis and gurus, suggesting that the messianic mentality follows certain patterns, independent of the tradition from which it emerges. Frank styled himself as a worldly figure — half Turkish pasha, half Polish nobleman — and surrounded himself with a paramilitary entourage. For a while, he had a notion of carving out a separate Jewish kingdom within Poland, over which he would naturally preside. But short of this, he declared that Poland was the Promised Land and consoled himself with fantasies of becoming the country's king. In religious matters, he had a tendency to tailor his beliefs to his own preferences. He believed, for example, that one could destroy evil by indulging in it — that, to quote Joseph Conrad, one should "in the destructive element immerse." In Frank's case, the element seemed to be mostly sexual, and he proceeded to plunge into it with enormous appetite, conducting ritual orgies. He repudiated Talmudic teaching, but not the Old Testament, and asserted that Jews could profess any religion as long as they felt themselves to be Jewish.

In 1759, acting on these ideas, Frank converted — with the Polish king himself acting as the godfather at his baptism — and many of his acolytes followed suit. Despite the heretical and seemingly un-Christian elements of his teachings, Frank and his followers were welcomed by the Catholic Church, and most of them were immediately rewarded with noble titles. Apparently these new converts were accepted into the aristocratic ranks without much objection. The perennial rumors about the Jewish ancestry of Polish aristocrats which circulate in Poland to this day can probably be traced back to the Frankist conversions.

It is impossible to know whether a village convert like Nowicka received a noble title; more likely, she would have been admitted into the farming gentry. She may have been welcomed by the local Catholic church and pointed at by peasants as a living example of Christ's power. But her Jewish neighbors would have viewed her defection with shock and anger. The rabbi might well have pronounced anathema on her, and preached against her in the synagogue.

But it may be that theological disputes were not the first thing on Jewish minds in Brańsk, that more immediate, practical shifts in their world occupied them. The major political change in the area came as a result of the partitions. In the division resulting from the partition of 1795, Brańsk came under Prussian rule as part of a territory renamed New Eastern Prussia.

This event had a direct bearing on the Jewish inhabitants of the province, since the Prussian administration encouraged a resettlement of Jews from villages to towns, largely to facilitate and centralize tax collection. For the same reason, the new government required Jews to accept surnames and to designate a definite address and source of income. Until then, the Jewish custom was to use a patronymic — to call someone, say, "Sarah, daughter of Moshe." The many Germanic surnames that Jews bear to this day were given to Polish Jews during the Prussian and Austrian occupations.

The Prussians' policy toward their multiethnic subjects was more energetically assimilationist than the Polish stance. The new governors abolished *de non tolerandis Judaeis*, and as a result, Jews started settling in Brańsk permanently. In a census taken in 1799–1800, there were 80 Jewish inhabitants in the town, out of a total population of 1,145. This small group included two prosperous merchants, who exported goods to the port city of Gdańsk, as well as housepainters, medics, butchers, bakers, confectioners, and lumbermen.

However, the Prussian rulers discouraged the formation of independent *kahals* and communal tax collection. They extended their assimilationist policy to the Poles as well, requiring all of Brańsk's children to attend Prussian schools, where lessons were conducted in German as well as Polish. Polish courts came under the supervision of Prussian legal commissions, and a Prussian squadron, made up of Bosnian soldiers, was stationed in the town.

It is hard to know whether the recipients of these policies approved of them or not. On the whole, Prussian rule seemed like a fairly benign form of domination, but it did not last long enough to leave a real mark on Brańsk's character. After eleven years there was another round of power plays, and in 1807 Brańsk came under Russian control. According to a Russian census of that year, the number of Jewish inhabitants had grown to 156, or 12 percent of the population. This was a large enough group to support an independent synagogue, and it is possible that one of the community's buildings was designated as a prayer house.

But if so, it would have been destroyed in 1812, when Brańsk was burned to the ground yet again. This time the fires were set by Napoleon's armies retreating from Russia. For the Poles of Brańsk, Napoleon's defeat would have spelled disaster and great sadness, since the Polish nobility had put its faith in the conqueror, seeing him as a potential liberator of Poland. But the Jewish neighborhoods might have been thrown into terror by the French soldiers. In addition to the usual fear of armies, there was a superstition circulating among Jews (the origins of this are unclear) that the French were cannibals, and in particular, child-eaters. In the town of Brody, not too far from Brańsk, Jewish men came out and faced the bedraggled soldiers with homemade weapons, to avert the threat of child snatching, and worse.

It was only a few years later that a period of stability allowed Brańsk's Jews to establish themselves more securely and to start laying the groundwork for a permanent community. Brańsk was becoming a regular shtetl, among so many dotting the landscape of the eastern Polish borderlands.

It is about this time, too, that the written history of Jewish Brańsk begins. It starts in a rather dry way, in 1816, with a *pinkas*, or chronicle, that recorded the notable facts and events in the community's life. The first entries in this register mark the building of a synagogue and the formation of a burial association — the basic blocks in the structure of a shtetl society.

In the story of Brańsk, the acquisition of a burial ground was an important event, because it signaled the young community's growing self-sufficiency. Until then, Brańsk's Jews were included in other *kahals*, and their dependent state had begun to rankle. Sometimes they bridled at the Tykocin *kahal*, which siphoned off an unfairly large share of taxes from Brańsk's inhabitants. The burial arrangements weren't satisfactory at all. The Bociek community had consented to bury the bodies of Brańsk Jews — but at the price, sometimes, of living souls. When the Russian army began to take a quota of Jewish conscripts from each *kahal*, the Bociek elders decided to demand one young Brańsk male to be counted as one of their recruits, in exchange for ten buried bodies. After a while, such bargains got aggravating enough for the Brańsk Jews to suspect — given a sufficient clash of interests, enmity is easy to generate — that the Bociek *kahal* was out to destroy them.

In 1820 the Jews of Brańsk decided to go independent. This could only happen with the agreement of the Russian authorities, which required the formation of a council to represent the community to the Russian administration. Within its own precincts, however, the *kahal* was organized along traditional "Polish" lines. Soon Brańsk had all the institutions necessary to a Jewish community's spiritual and material functioning: a *cheder*, a synagogue, a cemetery, a *mikvah* (ritual bath), and a hospice. Legend has it that when the first body was buried in the Brańsk cemetery, someone had to sleep near it every night until the second funeral took place. In Jewish law, the dead cannot be left alone.

Aside from the *pinkas*, the written history of Brańsk has one other great source: the Brańsk Yizkor Book, or the Book of Memory. This text was written in 1947, along with several dozen such volumes compiled shortly after World War II, in a great act of collective commemoration. The importance of written witness was apparently felt immediately after the destruction, and dozens of informal scribes from dozens of communities began to set down, often in awkward and untutored style, everything they and their fellow survivors could remember of their communities' past. The Word preserves; the Word honors; the Word, perhaps, solaces those who use its powers, and eases their burden of obligation to, and their sorrow for, the dead.

The two authors named on the cover of the Brańsk Yizkor Book are Alter Trus and Julius Kohen, although it is said that Alter Trus did most of the actual writing. But the manuscript, like all the Yizkor Books, was in any case the fruit of a wider collaborative effort, and contains information garnered from other survivors as well as from the authors' own recollections. It is, in its Polish translation from Yiddish, a rough-hewn text, utterly plain in style, clumsy in formulation, sometimes ungrammatical. It was written in a state of still fresh loss, and this tinges even ordinary episodes with a premonitory gravity. And some former Brańskers will whisper confidentially that the book is tendentious in other ways — that Alter Trus, a former member of both the Brańsk town council and the *kahal*, had socialist leanings, and that this affected his reading of events. Memory, even when it is so close to experience — or perhaps especially when it is that close — is multiple and contentious. The past depends on the angle from which it is seen, and from which it has been lived. And yet the book's elementary narrative, its naive sentiments and homey, homely details, add up to a vivid diagram of the shtetl — its institutions, its concerns, even something of its mentality.

The picture that emerges from these details is of a social microcosm organized with an almost iconic precision. The structures of collective and personal life in Polish shtetls were so exactly defined as to be infinitely replicable — as the structure of a honeycomb is replicable throughout a beehive. Each shtetl was a self-contained world, and each was utterly recognizable as an instance of its kind. This consistency, the patterned predictability of life, was undoubtedly part of the shtetl's strength. But it also meant that the shtetl was a deeply conservative organism, resistant to innovation, individuality, or rebellion. It is hard to think of any analogues to the early shtetl society, for its character was part untouchable and part Brahmin, simultaneously ancient and pioneering, both pragmatically materialistic and sternly religious. It was a peculiar, idiosyncratic form of a rural, populist theocracy.

Like the *pinkas*, the Yizkor Book begins with a listing of synagogues and rabbis, although it expands the bare facts into something like a story. In 1821, the first synagogue, known as the Alter Beth Midrash (the Old Synagogue), a simple brick building, was inaugurated. Ten years later, the wealthiest Jews in Brańsk donated money for the creation of a second synagogue, known as the Neue Beth Midrash, which became the prayer house of the town's elite. Later, other synagogues were added, including one for tailors and other poor people, and, in the twentieth century, a small prayer house for the Hasidim.

In 1822, one Meir Nechis, described as a "highly educated man, worthy of being the spiritual leader of a generation," was appointed the first rabbi of the Brańsk *kahal*. On the subject of rabbis, the Yizkor Book is sometimes unintentionally sad and sometimes just as unintentionally comic. Meir Nechis apparently wasn't happy with the conditions of his work. His apartment, in the Alter Beth Midrash, is described as dark and dank, resembling a prison more than a home. His pay was very low, and the catalogue of bonuses he received on holidays — tea, sugar, a bottle of wine — provides a further glimpse of the extremely modest material circumstances in which the Brańsk community began.

Rabbi Nechis initiated a long period of rabbinical bad luck in Brańsk. The second rabbi died young, as had Nechis, perhaps from the dampness of his rooms. The third, probably bearing the example of his unfortunate predecessors in mind, took a more energetic approach and protested the conditions of his living quarters. When no better alternative was offered by the leaders of the *kahal*, he decided to resign and accept another post. On his departure, his cart was forcibly stopped by a number of his faithful followers, some of whom threw themselves on the ground in front of the vehicle, crying, "Rabbi, don't abandon us." In none too tactful tones, he is supposed to have replied, "My place isn't with you. You have insulted me and nothing good will come of our cooperation, but I forgive you everything, and God help you."

One might think that the narrators of the Yizkor Book would be a bit miffed at the rabbi's impertinent treatment of his humble flock. But it turns out that the authors place the blame squarely on the shoulders of the *kahal*'s elders. In the Yizkor Book rendition of the story, these stubborn and shortsighted men not only mistreated the third rabbi; they went on to underestimate the fine qualities of the fourth, who was highly popular with the ordinary people of Brańsk. Once again, the rabbi was saddled with that unpropitious apartment, as well as other unsatisfactory arrangements. Sure enough, he became very ill. But even then, his congregants were unable to move the hard-hearted community leaders to action. The fourth rabbi died when he was only forty-three.

Is this Alter Trus's socialism showing? Possibly. But conflicts between ordinary, poor Jews and wealthier, more influential elders were hardly unknown either in the shtetl or in the bigger cities. References to such quarrels can be found in *pinkas* records of all periods, although they became more frequent in the second half of the eighteenth century. Often these tensions had to do with unfair allocation of taxes or desirable offices; sometimes fights arose about purely symbolic matters of prestige, such as one's place in formal processions in the synagogue. Occasionally frictions spilled over into violent riots or revolts. In the town of Leszno in 1763, the Jewish populace, angered at rising taxes and arbitrary imprisonments, dragged the offending *kahal* officials off to a synagogue and forced them to swear an oath that they would resign immediately. Interestingly, the Polish town owner intervened on behalf of the Jewish elders and ordered three of the rebels punished, albeit quite lightly.

In Brańsk, nothing so dramatic occurred, and luck turned for the community with the arrival of the fifth rabbi. This may have been because — finally! — the *kahal* came up with different, much better living quarters.

Synagogues and rabbis were the foundation stones and pillars of the shtetl. In the Yizkor Book, the next place of importance is given to various associations. To a modern reader, it comes as a surprise to discover how tightly organized the shtetl was almost from its first days. The Jews of Brańsk from the beginning established a network of professional "brotherhoods," voluntary societies, and study groups, which addressed all of the community's fundamental, as well as higher, needs. The burial society and the gravediggers' society, concerned as they were with ultimate matters, were the oldest and the most important, but the Yizkor Book also lists, among others, a society of tailors, a Torah study group, and charitable organizations. Some of these associations were supported by communal taxes, and grew wealthy enough to draw the resentment of ordinary folk. The burial society was known for holding opulent feasts, at which, it is noted approvingly in the Yizkor Book, "there was no lack of 90 proof liquor."

The dense web of communal associations embraced just about everyone. No one was left out — and no one, for that matter, was allowed to escape it. Even the poorest and most improvident members of the community were included in the communal net. Charity was an important value in the shtetl's ethos, and there were ritualized ways of administering it. The authors of the Yizkor Book devote some space to a category called "Women Leaders" and, in a word hard to translate, "Announcers." These were women whose main function was to help the needy and also to announce the order of prayers in the women's section of the synagogue. Among the charitable women, several are remembered by name. There was Frumele, who went from house to house each Friday, collecting challah and rolls from the housewives and distributing them among the poor, so that no household went hungry on the Sabbath. There was Chaja Esther, who belonged "to the same type of woman as Frumele. Wherever someone was sick, hungry or barefoot, she knew about it." The work undertaken by such women was considered praiseworthy, for they ensured that no Jewish person would ever fall out of the communal fellowship into destitution or abandonment.

These institutions gave the shtetl a kind of horizontal coherence, but the social map was also diagrammed vertically, by professional status and other forms of hierarchy. The Yizkor Book details at some length the sources of livelihood available to the Jewish inhabitants of Brańsk, and these suggest a considerable degree of diversity. At the high end of the social scale were the managers of the large estates. In the Yizkor Book these middle-management figures are viewed with some disapproval, as lackeys who had to please their capricious masters and who would compromise their integrity in return for favors. This may not have been the view of the ordinary folk, to whom the well-positioned and sometimes handsomely rewarded managers might have seemed quite enviable. But the majority of Brańsk's Jews were small merchants and craftsmen who probably remained poor all their lives — innkeepers, housepainters, cloth merchants, shoemakers, and peddlers who each week wended their way through the surrounding villages, selling everything from needles to shoes, coats, and cartwheels. With time, the number of small shops in Brańsk grew, and several of these developed into successful workshops or factories. One of them manufactured leather belts that were sold in Russia. (In the Yizkor Book there is mention of an unnamed rich personage, before whom even non-Jews "took off their hats.")

The early, aspiring businessmen of Brańsk would undoubtedly have been interested in the stories of Jewish merchants beyond the town who had attained great wealth. Tales of such legendary figures were spread throughout Poland by travelers from the cities, but the success stories might also have reached Brańsk via the printed word. Until the end of the eighteenth century, the only kinds of books published in Hebrew in Poland were theological tomes or histories. With the rise of Jewish secularism, there arose a new sense of human individuality, and with the emergence of individual personalities came a genre hitherto unknown among Jewish scribes: autobiography. An assiduous reader in Brańsk might have come upon a memoir written at the end of the eighteenth century by a prominent businessman named Ber of Bolechów, whose career reveals much about Polish-Jewish relations in better-educated circles. Ber was the son of Judah, a wine merchant who was already worldly enough to give his son both a Jewish and a Polish tutor.

Judah was apparently a charming man, with a gift for story-telling and equally fluent in Yiddish, Polish, and Hungarian. "My father was welcomed everywhere," Ber writes. "People were glad to see him again, Jews and Gentiles (Christians) alike." Judah acted as an interpreter at high diplomatic levels, and was sent by Polish noblemen on missions to buy fine wines in Hungary.

Ber himself, in addition to his biblical and Talmudic studies, acquired considerable knowledge of French and German litera-ture. He had an impressive library of valuable books, most of them by classical writers. At the same time, he plied his success-ful business, developing a kind of limited partnership. At times, noblemen and clerics became Ber's silent partners, an arrange-ment that could be found in other trading companies.

Figures like Ber of Bolechów would have been unequivocally admired among the people of Brańsk. Until the later stirrings of socialism, prosperity was unabashedly respected in the shtetl, and the nuances of neighbors' wealth were closely watched and widely known. For a traditional Jewish man, the injunction to make a living and provide for his family was as compelling as the duty to pray. Historically, money was one of the only solid forms of security for Diaspora Jews, who were after all deprived of political power and an assured place in any society. There had been enough instances when Jews won their entry into a country or the good graces of elites and rulers with large monetary offerings for the knowledge to seep into the Jewish psyche that money was a crucial currency of influence, and sometimes of survival.

Divisions between the rich and the poor were clearly per-ceived and important, and yet they were to some extent sub-sumed under another system of values — religion. A religiously learned man was prized above the wealthy, simple man; piety was the greatest adornment and merit. In the Yizkor Book, the primacy of belief is taken for granted as something that does not need to be discussed explicitly. Yet religion permeates the entire text, as it permeated the fabric of shtetl life; it was the woof and warp from which the material of existence was made. The communal organizations gave a kind of horizontal coherence to shtetl society; religious observance provided the internal, three-dimensional coherence — a coherence in depth. This is an aspect of the Jewish tradition that has become familiar from a vast literature and informal testimony. But it was the central aspect, without which the character, the atmosphere, and the particular emotionalism of shtetl culture cannot be grasped. The day, the week, and the year were shaped and parsed by ritual signposts: the day by morning and evening prayers, the week by the climax of the Sabbath, the year by the sequence of holidays. Each part of life, from food to sex to marriage and personal hygiene, was governed by a highly elaborate and precise body of religious principles and rules.

The initiation into this highly structured symbolic universe began, for boys at least, at age four, when they started their studies, either under the guidance of a private tutor or, more commonly, at a Jewish elementary school, the *cheder*. Moreover, in Brańsk "there were also people who simply could not afford even a grosh [penny] to pay for a teacher." Since it was unthinkable that Jewish children should not "know how to pray," a public school, or Talmud Torah, was instituted in Brańsk sometime in the nineteenth century. The authors of the Yizkor Book sketch an unflattering picture of this little center of learning. The school was located in a room of the Old Synagogue, and the teacher — the *melamed* — who also lived there, was a disaffected man who "spit bile" and beat his students mercilessly, knowing that nobody would intervene on their behalf. His pupils were orphans or children whose parents were so burdened by the hardships of making a living that — this is rare enough to be notable — "they weren't interested in the upbringing of their children."

This was a poor children's school, but judging from many other accounts, the typical *cheder* was not all that different — indeed, often it was worse. Here is a description of a *cheder*, in a town not far from Brańsk, by the great Yiddish writer Sholem Aleichem:

> Cheder. A small cottage on chicken legs, covered with straw. Most often slightly leaning towards one side. Sometimes without a roof. As without a cap. Only one window. And if more, at most two. Without window-panes. Instead of a window-pane, they'd stick a piece of paper on the window-frame. Floor made of clay. On Saturdays and holidays, they'd sprinkle it with yellow sand. A large part of the cheder was taken up by a stove, with a sleeping place on top, and a cot. On the cot sleeps the rebbe. On the stove sleep his children. Near the wall stands a bed. On the bed sleeps the rebbe's wife. . . . On this bed, on a white sheet, from time to time there appears a cutting board for the cutting of noodles or dough for cracknel. . . . Sometimes, if it's very sick, they put a child in the bed. Under the stove, there's an opening [where] they raise poultry for sale. . . . In the middle of the room, a long table, with two long benches.
>
> This room is the cheder. Here the school takes place, here the rebbe conducts his lessons. Everyone is shouting all the time. The rebbe shouts and his pupils shout. You can also hear the shouting of the rebbe's wife, who is scolding her children. She's scolding them to make them stop shouting. The aviary under the stove is cackling from fear. . . . The devil take it!

Clearly, the spiritual purpose of this institution was often at odds with its actual incarnation. But what did the students learn in the course of their education? The curriculum, aside from some rudimentary arithmetic, was entirely religious and followed the patterns set several centuries earlier. At the "secondary" level, study was often practically uninterrupted. Boys bent over their books all day long and sometimes through the night. They fell asleep at their benches and woke up to the great tomes before them. These pedagogic methods were accepted without protest. The authority of the *melamed* — poor figure though he might cut otherwise — was unquestioned. Or rather, perhaps, it was the authority of the thing he represented: the Book, the Word, the Tradition.

At the higher, yeshiva level, young men — certified as such by the initiatory ritual of the bar mitzvah — entered into a deeper engagement with the Talmud. The object of their study merits description. In its printed version, the Talmud consists of a wide central column in Aramaic, surrounded by several columns in Hebrew, set in smaller type. The central column is the Mishnah, the first written compilation of Jewish laws and rules of conduct, written during the Babylonian exile, approximately between 580 B.C.E. and the sixth century C.E. The Hebrew columns are the rabbinical responses and commentaries on this basic codex, accumulated in the Diaspora over the span of centuries. On the page, the commentaries adhere to the main Aramaic text like layers of bark to a tree trunk, in a graphic representation of slowly accreting knowledge and of a philosophical conversation carried on in defiance of geography and time.

In the yeshivas, the young scholars sat in pairs, concentrating on a discrete passage of the Talmud each day and questioning one another about its meaning and message — or, its meanings and messages. The method of exegesis they employed, developed in Poland and disseminated throughout the Ashkenazic world, was evocatively called *pilpul*, or pepper. It involved a painstaking search for contradictions and paradoxes between the Bible and the commentaries, for multiple significances of words, and for hidden puns. In other words, the students were looking for those grains of pepper that disturbed the harmony of the text and that might therefore be a clue, an opening, to further truths. When this methodology was carried to excess, it was called *hilluk*, which means something like hair-splitting.

It is no wonder, perhaps, that later so many Jewish students turned to the study of law, which depends on a similar kind of argumentation, or that scholars who emerged from the Talmudic tradition went on to become masters of modern literary textual exegesis. Talmudic education nurtured certain modes of thinking that have proved very durable. Above all, it stimulated the powers of memory. Even a middling yeshiva student could quote some passages of the Talmud by heart. The great scholars, such as the renowned Gaon of Vilno in the mid-eighteenth century, performed prodigious feats of memorization, which was considered a form of devotion. In committing all of the Mishnah, or the Gemarah (the first set of commentaries), to memory, in learning them "by heart," the rabbis made themselves into the literal carriers of the Jewish tradition. The history of their people and their faith was inscribed on their psyches and contained within their persons.

For all its virtues, by the end of the eighteenth century, Talmudic education started coming in for criticism from progressive Jewish thinkers, who pointed out the extreme narrowness of traditional Jewish scholarship, its formulaic nature, and its increasing irrelevance to the needs and demands of contemporary life. These intellectuals, many of whom were educated in

the yeshivas themselves, worried that Talmudic thinking promoted the insulation of Jewish communities by cutting them
off from scientific knowledge and from all forms of modernity.

In provincial shtetls like Brańsk, dissidence from Orthodoxy
was extremely rare. The Yizkor Book, in an undated story,
gives us a chilling glimpse of the fate awaiting those who dared
step outside its bounds. A man named Chlawne could not find
the means of supporting his family in Brańsk, so he left for the
bigger town of Kamień Podolski to look for employment.
Once there, he met with a group of local Haskala intellectuals
and became infected with the germ of secular learning. He
proved to be intellectually gifted, and eventually he was
accepted by the medical faculty at the University of St. Petersburg. None of this implied, for him, a disavowal of Jewishness,
or even of religion, but when he went back to Brańsk to rejoin
his family, he was greeted by a hail of stones and booted out of
town. His wife demanded a divorce, and his children were hidden from him. Brokenhearted, Chlawne left again for the
depths of Russia, where he apparently decided to make a virtue
of necessity, and to convert in earnest.

For girls in the shtetl, the progress of life was quite different.
Their education consisted of some private lessons in Hebrew
and Yiddish, and stopped at marriage, which usually came in
early adolescence. The Yizkor Book is silent on questions of
courtship and matrimony, but we can imagine something of the
marriage customs that prevailed in Brańsk from descriptions
of other shtetls. One of the best sources is a wonderful autobiography written at the end of the eighteenth century by
Solomon Maimon.

Maimon was a fascinating figure with a career worthy of a
picaresque novel. He came from a shtetl not far from Brańsk,
but after breaking away from it made his way to Germany,

where he studied science and an early version of psychology. In Berlin he met important intellectuals of his day, enjoyed a rakish love life and the patronage, not always reliable, of several aristocrats. Maimon's memories of his Polish childhood are both pastoral and disturbing. His grandfather was a prosperous leaseholder of several villages on a princely estate, but he lost his property through the schemes of envious Gentiles, and the family fell on hard times. Maimon himself was a lively and precocious child who refused to attend the local *cheder*, run by a man of truly sadistic temperament. This pedagogue routinely thrashed his pupils to unconsciousness, and sometimes pulled off parts of their ears, or put out an eye. His way of dealing with protesting parents was to beat them off with a stick and shouted imprecations. Solomon was fortunate to find a rabbi who attended to his education in a more benign manner, and he excelled at his studies.

By the time Solomon was eleven, his fame as a brilliant scholar had spread, and he found himself in great demand as a prospective husband. His intellectual gifts made him particularly desirable, but such extremely early contractual marriages were the norm. Courtship rituals were conducted on the premise that it was the boy who was the coveted prize — he was, in effect, bought by the bride's parents. Solomon's father tried to make the most of his son's marketability, taking bids from several parties and in the process acquiring gifts from all of them. After a series of misunderstandings, Solomon was married, at eleven, to a bride three years older than he. He was so unhappy and confused by the event that he refused to attend his own wedding feast. The wedding night was not a success. However, by the time he was fourteen, Solomon had fathered a child — as he was fully expected and encouraged to do by the anxiously watchful adults.

Maimon found the institution of enforced early matrimony appalling, but it would be the custom, in Brańsk as elsewhere, until well into the nineteenth century. By their early teens, most of the children in the community were paired off, and prodded by impatient relatives to produce offspring. The young husbands were expected to live with the bride's family and devote themselves to further study. For the girls, their period of childhood freedom was over, and they had to adjust as best they could to their appointed roles as wives and mothers. Open rebellion was out of the question for them, though disaffection may have expressed itself by more subterranean means. With psychological hindsight, we can perhaps discern in I. B. Singer's stories of dybbuk-obsessed young girls, or in Sholem Aleichem's portraits of perennially ailing women, some hints of a deeper malady.

Although women's status in the shtetl was constrained, it would be a mistake to envision it, as we are sometimes wont to, from our liberated distance, as hopelessly passive. One of the contradictions of traditional societies is that they often afford women considerable authority within their limited domains. In the shtetl, the possibilities of learning and high spiritual attainment belonged to the men, but in the practical sphere, women had some room to maneuver. In the domestic fiefdom they ruled undisturbed. More surprisingly, the daily management of business affairs was often left in women's hands — a situation depicted in numerous fictional scenes in which a harassed but confident wife bustles about in the front store while the absent-minded husband sits in his study in back, absorbed in the misty realms of theological speculation. The Yizkor Book mentions a few such women in passing — rabbis' wives mostly, who ran small businesses of their own, buying and selling candles or sugar or embroidered cloth.

Altogether, while life in these small towns was confined within strictly prescribed bounds and people's energies were forced into narrow channels, the shtetl was not a place of pure suppression and repression. On the contrary, the atmosphere conveyed in fictional accounts and actual memories is one of bustling, animated life. There was the constant traffic of visits, gossip, matchmaking; there were people's personalities and eccentricities to observe at close quarters; most of all, there was the unending stream of vivid talk — speech that mixed Talmudic quotations with profane proverbs, Polish imprecations with Jewish curses. The famous Yiddish humor — skeptical, self-deprecating, salty — was basically shtetl humor. The curses were so colorful and varied that Sholem Aleichem, for one, chose to record whole lists of them. He took them, as it happened, from his harridan stepmother, who seemed to have an inexhaustible vein of invention in this genre, and who answered just about every word with a curse — in rhyme! "Eat — may the worms eat you!" she would say. Or: "Sew — may they sew a shroud for you!" Or: "Sit — may you sit on infected wounds!"

Religion, for all its rigors of doctrine, was also a vehicle for expressiveness. In the shtetl world, people were distinguished not by their tastes, literary preferences, or style of dress, but by the character of their observance. One of the chapters in the Yizkor Book is devoted to "Those Who Pray Before the Public" — that is, men knowledgeable enough to lead the congregation in prayers on the High Holy Days. There was one, a housepainter, whose chanting was "sincerely sweet, with such a plea in it. His prayers must have been accepted, one could refuse such a Jew . . . nothing." There was another, a big man, with great emotional power: "During his prayers, the public simply melted in tears. The crying began in the women's section, from where it spread to the men and grew into a big plea, with deep sighs."

In trying to understand shtetl life, this is probably the most difficult leap of imagination required of the modern secular reader: to comprehend, to enter into, the mood suggested by even such minimal descriptions of prayers in Brańsk. A small synagogue in a village street, swept up in shouts and murmurs, weeping and pleas rising in gusts and currents ... pleas to be inscribed in the Book of Life, to be forgiven one's weaknesses and failings. Sighs for daily hardships transmuted into a plaint for the hardships of fate and the Jewish condition. Tears of repentance mingled with self-pity. Prayer was a form of catharsis and of reflection on the human lot.

Although religious learning was a matter of hierarchy, belief and piety were the common medium, the glue holding everyone together. At moments of heightened worship, or on the Sabbath, the shtetl really became a unified organism — each household progressing through the same prayers, gestures, food, and intuiting, perhaps, something of the acceptance and gratitude with which the Sabbath was supposed to be celebrated. Each person was subsumed in the ritual and in an encompassing, time-deep sense of Jewishness, which was unquestioned and unquestioningly inclusive.

The shtetl had all the virtues of its limitations. It gave its inhabitants the advantages of psychological security, a tight web of relationships, the pleasures of a small world intimately known. That was within the community's enclosures, among one's familiars, one's own. But what about the others — or Others — the Polish world next door? In the pages of the Yizkor Book, the Polish Brańsk is rarely in evidence. Until the period of World War II, there are only scarce allusions to actual Polish persons or to relationships between Poles and Jews: there is a mention of the rich man respected by the Poles, a landowner whom his Jewish employees had to mollify; the fifth rabbi was apparently so beloved and wise that he had the regard even of the Christian inhabitants of Brańsk. And that is about all.

One has to take into account the kind of text the Yizkor Book sets out to be: a commemoration of a lost Jewish community. And yet the almost complete absence of Poles from its account of the shtetl's life probably represents a kind of reality as well: the reality of spiritual, if not practical, isolation. The two halves of the town lived side by side, but in a state of considerable ignorance of one another. At the market, in the inn, in the shops, there was mingling, and there must have been acquaintanceships, casual friendships. But in many ways that mattered, the two communities were mutually impenetrable. They did not go into each other's houses or places of worship; they knew little about each other's thinking or concerns.

Still, they saw each other every day. How, one wonders, did they appear to each other at this daily distance? The Poles, of course, had their own hierarchy of status and wealth. At the top was the local *szlachta*, who hired Jewish managers and stewards on their estates, and whose personalities Jews would have known very well. The estate owners were sometimes friendly and protective; others were capricious and disdainful. They might ask their Jewish manager to bail them out of financial trouble, in which case the manager would have to come up with a bundle of money from his own pocket or extract more taxes and rents from the peasants.

On the next rung of the Polish social ladder was a small cluster of educated professionals — a doctor, a teacher, several bureaucrats, a priest. There were a few prosperous peasants, who might know how to read. But most of the Polish population in Brańsk was poor, barefoot, and illiterate.

In many ways, the system of values and of actualities governing the Poles' lives was in great contrast to the Jewish ethos. The gentry still valued patriotism, courage, dash. They drank alcohol in great quantities, hunted, and discussed the question that for them had the most burning import: how to regain independence for Poland. The peasants were bound to the land as firmly as the Jews were tied to religion, and their day, week, and year were marked by the demands of working their farms and tending their animals, as the Jewish calendar was marked by religious signposts.

For the peasants, the Jews may have been an object of economic envy, but this coexisted with an undercurrent of lore and superstition that had nothing to do with social realities. Jews played an inordinately important role in the peasants' mythological universe, as is testified by countless Polish proverbs, verses, legends, and folktales. Some of the lore would have been acquired in church, but peasant piety gave a particular coloring to Catholicism, infusing it with pagan, non-Christian elements. The belief that Jews needed Christian blood for making Passover matzo might have been insinuated by the local priest, and on some subterranean level widely believed, even if no direct accusations of ritual murder were made. It was also assumed that the Jews were a cursed people because they killed Christ — although in some versions of this story, Jews themselves were very sorry they had done this, and accepted their hard fate as a deserved punishment. Some of the folk explanations of Jewish customs were elaborately fanciful. One tale had it that Jews didn't eat pork because they believed that pigs came from human beings and thought that the pig was their "aunt." This was supported by a long story of how Jews tried to play a joke on Jesus Christ, and how he repaid them by this deception. Jews were associated with demonic powers — but also with good luck. If a thief robbed you, a Jew could put a curse on him, so that he would be caught and punished; the peasants thought this was done in the synagogue, during the recitation of the Psalms of David. If a Jew borrowed something from you, that brought good luck in business for the day. Jews were supposed to be excellent healers who did not take advantage of their patients. In the Herod plays, frequently staged in villages, the Jew was often lame and hunchbacked and a target of jokes, but he was also a wise man who could interpret dreams, or who brought first greetings to a newly wedded pair. The Yizkor Book tells us that the saintly fifth rabbi was often asked to advise peasants on various matters and to resolve disputes between Jews and Christians. This, too, was a recurring motif in accounts of shtetl life.

In other words, Jews supposedly possessed magical and esoteric wisdom, which was to be both feared and respected — and this deep belief affected the peasants' real perceptions of the people in their midst. As he crossed the streets of Brańsk, a peasant might glimpse, through the low windows of a wooden house, a bearded man in a black caftan, bent over a large black book covered with strange lettering — and might see not so much a real person as an image of mysterious knowledge. A farming woman might look into the interior of a synagogue on one of the holidays and feel curious and perplexed by the sight of men carrying a long, rounded object. The peasants often discerned in the shape of the Torah scrolls a golden lamb or calf — an especially ironic bit of distortion given the Jewish prohibition against worshiping idols.

To the Jews of Brańsk, their Polish neighbors would have been more transparent, or at least less frighteningly mystifying. Jewish people were long used to other languages, other customs; they understood Christianity as a younger, misguided offspring of Judaism. Shtetl Jews had their own superstitions. The fear of the "evil eye" was widespread among them, and many people wore amulets against its powers containing magical verbal formulas. But the Jewish superstitious transactions were with the dark realms of heaven and earth, with their own spirits of the dead and the sinful, rather than with the Gentiles around them. Jews living in villages might shake their heads at the paganism and naiveté of some of the peasant rituals — such as going out to fields and stables to talk to the animals on Christmas Eve, in the belief that for just one night beasts acquired souls. But such customs would not have awed Talmudically educated Jews. They had learned to be wary of the real power of Christians, but they did not invest Christianity with magic powers. Indeed, in the Jewish attitudes toward Christian religion, there was a definite element of condescension. Solomon Maimon remembers an incident from his childhood when a Polish princess with a hunting party stopped at his grandfather's house. Solomon was dazzled by the glamour of the gathered personages, but his grandfather quickly set him straight: "Little fool," he whispered in Solomon's ear, "in the future life the princess will kindle the stove for us."

The two parts of Brańsk, then, were simultaneously very familiar and quite unknown to each other. The peasants had their magical beliefs about Jews; the Jews had their skepticism about Poles. But the two groups existed — and perhaps this is most important — below the level of meaningfulness to each other. They did not admit each other into the sphere of true, moral life; they did not share a world. This remained true for a long time. Of course the world kept impinging on both communities, and change, however slow, did take place.

3
Shtetl:
Among Foreign Powers

Only in Poland are Jews the most backward, most obstinate Talmudists ... only in Poland have they captured the highest rung of the
country's industry. . . . Only in Poland are they so numerous and each
day multiply that their present population is one-eighth of the country's; and of the population able to compete with their natural opportunities, shrewdness and restraint of needs, they make up more than
half. In Poland only are they today most harmful, or rather, only here
are they harmful. . . . When the peasantry will pull itself out of their
hands and become enlightened ... when Jews themselves will approach us in their customs and will clearly prove that they can be reconciled with the people, the moment will be safer to grant them liberal
advantages.

— From a statement of the State Council of the Polish Kingdom, 1817

The Israelites have been settled in this country for six centuries, they
have become accustomed to this land and they comprise a useful part
of the national whole. They own many properties in the country, both
in the form of houses and even more factories, a considerable part of
the commercial and industrial branch is in their hands and the taxes
raised by them fill a not insignificant rubric in the budgets of the Treasury and the towns of the Kingdom. . . .

If until now not all Jewish inhabitants and not in everything have
entered into a relationship with the general population in regard to

customs and social life, the cause of this — in the opinion of the Synagogue Council — lies entirely in discriminating between them and the generality at every opportunity, and setting for them separate rules and regulations.

— A statement of the Warsaw District Synagogue Council, 1856

Our theological leader Remu, on whose statements the whole House of Israel relies in its tenets regarding nations of different faiths, declares that we should love the native inhabitants of Poland more than the inhabitants of all other countries. Because they are truly our brothers, the sons of our patriarchs and ancestors, the sons of Esau; and he [Remu] wrote that even a dry piece of bread tastes good with peace in Poland, where they do not hate us and allow us to keep to the laws of our holy Torah. . . . Therefore I declare that it is our duty to love the sons of the Polish nation.

— From a New Year's sermon preached by Rabbi Ber Meisels
during the Polish Uprising against the Russians, Warsaw, 1861

THE CHIEF FACT of Polish history from the end of the eighteenth century until the end of World War I was the partitions. Poland had ceased to exist, but Polish nationalism grew all the more fervent for being ruthlessly suppressed. From the Polish point of view, the Russians were the most oppressive and dangerous occupiers, and the nineteenth century was punctuated by a series of conspiracies, uprisings, insurrections, and mutinies against tsarist rule — each of them defeated, and each followed by waves of repression and punishment. A large portion of the Polish elite lived in exile during much of the nineteenth century. It was during this period that Poles developed a sense of their nation's martyrdom to rival the Jewish sense of being singled out for special suffering. The symbol of Poland as the Christ of nations competed with the allegory of eternal Jewish wandering. Occasionally, parallelisms of fate led to identification and bonding between Poles and Jews. More often, politics of the partitions, as well as each group's conviction of the primacy of its plight, created acute conflicts between them. There were episodes, in times of active rebellion, when Poles and Jews acted in concert, leading to surges of fraternal feeling. But common victimization does not necessarily make good bedfellows. Between moments of comity, Poles accused Jews of insufficient loyalty to their cause, to which they were so fervently devoted. Jews, on the other hand, pointed out that they were not given sufficient reasons for abiding patriotism. In the meantime, economic competition between the two groups grew sharper over the course of the century, as the division of roles and kinds of labor became more distinct.

From the perspective of the Jewish communities, the question of the age was how to position themselves within the new sets of laws and conditions — where to place their loyalties, how to protect their interests, how much to assimilate, and into which culture. Were they, by then, sufficiently Polish to ally themselves with the Polish cause, whatever its vicissitudes? Or did they still perceive themselves essentially as guests who had to accommodate to whoever was in charge? The effects of the partitions on Jewish life varied with the colonizing powers, and so did the answers to such questions. In the western regions of Poland under Prussian rule, the proportion of Jewish inhabitants was the lowest, and while the poorest Jews were expelled from the state, the wealthy ones were actively encouraged to assimilate. Partly because of linguistic similarities between Yiddish and German, they did so readily — incidentally provoking Polish reproaches at Jewish unwillingness to accept Polish culture with similar ease. In the Hapsburg Empire, which included the province of Galicia, Joseph II granted Jews full citizenship

500 km
300 miles

SWEDEN

Baltic Sea

Riga

Smolensk

RUSSIA

Gdańsk

EAST PRUSSIA

Vilno

PALE OF

Minsk

Berlin

Annexed by Prussia)

Tykocin
Białystok

Bielsk

BRAŃSK

JEWISH

PRUSSIA

Warsaw

CONGRESS

Łódź

POLAND

SETTLEMENT

(Annexed by Russia)

Kiev

Cracow

GALICIA

Lvov

(Annexed by Austria)

AUSTRIA

Black
Sea

**PARTITIONED
POLAND
1815–1918**

Chazaud

in 1789 and, at the same time, limited *kahals'* jurisdiction to religious matters. In Galicia, the administration of Polish affairs was in effect in the hands of the Polish gentry, and the *kahals* were left pretty much to their own devices, as they had been before. The small piece of putatively independent Poland around Warsaw, established at the Congress of Vienna and known as the Congress Kingdom of Poland, or Kongresówka, was de facto ruled by Russian overseers.

The Russian sphere was the most extensive — Russia gained 60 percent of Poland's territory and 45 percent of its population — and the tsarist policies usually the most repressive. However, in the large Russian-occupied territories there were enormous differences between the central region, where strategies were formed and actions initiated, and the remote eastern provinces, in which Brańsk was situated, where the tempo of change was slower and the pitch of events less intense. The policies varied from tsar to tsar, but in relation to the Jews, they were historically more conservative than Polish attitudes. One precedent was set by Catherine the Great, who in 1791 instituted the Pale of Settlement in Russia, which severely restricted Jewish rights of residence and movement.

The Pale was not extended to the occupied territories of eastern Poland, but there is no doubt that the onset of tsarist rule had powerful repercussions in these peripheral regions. In 1824, for example, Alexander II issued an edict forbidding Jews to wear their traditional clothes; however, this law was largely ignored. For the Jewish community of Brańsk, and for all the shtetls of eastern Poland, the most hated tsarist law was the Cantonist edict of 1827, issued by Nicholas I, which required a quota of young Jewish boys to be conscripted each year into the tsarist army. According to the Yizkor Book, the first response among Brańsk's Jews to this fiat of fate was religious: on receiving the news of the edict, they declared a fast, hoping that this would cause the law to be withdrawn. When the Russian authorities, failing to take note of this method of propitiation, went on to require the registration of all Jewish names and to demand the first three recruits from the Brańsk catchment area, the *kahal* turned to more worldly tactics. After the initial panic, some families fled to other towns, where it was ostensibly more advantageous to register. Others, knowing that married men would not be required to serve, rushed their sons into marriage before they were weaned from their toys. Birth dates were altered and bribes offered.

The brunt of the edict's burden, as is so often the case, fell on orphans and children of poor families. The *kahal*, which was responsible for collecting and delivering the recruits, made up a secret list of the poorest boys, mostly sons of tailors. Some of these children were simply snatched from *cheders* or from the street by Jewish "catchers." At the time of the Yizkor Book's writing, these events were still within intergenerational memory, and people from Brańsk remembered stories of "Lejb Tate," a man known for his sadistic temperament, who came to Brańsk from the town of Orla to catch boys, who were then delivered as part of Orla's quota. In times of threat, loyalties quickly narrow, sometimes to the borders of one's town.

Later, in a nasty twist, Lejb Tate was hired by the Brańsk *kahal* to seize children for them. The boys thus ensnared were kept imprisoned in a room of the synagogue with barred windows. The Yizkor Book's writers recount with some indignation how a delegation of tailors went to the synagogue to protest the unfairness of such tactics to the community elders. "Your children are at home, and you take away our bread-winners from us poor parents," the tailors said. The chief elder ordered the head of the tailors' delegation to be thrown out of the synagogue — a command duly obeyed, and accompanied by a beating for good measure. Protesting mothers were apparently also beaten by Lejb Tate.

The Yizkor Book contains a story, told to the authors by one Reuben Kacew, that suggests why conscriptions were felt to be so catastrophic. Reuben recalled a night, long ago, when Lejb Tate and his cohorts burst into his and his brother's bedroom. Reuben was eight years old, his brother thirteen. The boys tried to escape, but the older brother was caught and carried off to the army. Such children often disappeared into the depths of Russia for decades without a trace. At first, Reuben's family was very sad, but with time they forgot about the missing boy. Forty years passed; Reuben's mother had died. The catcher Lejb Tate had died. Then one day Reuben's brother reappeared in Brańsk, in the uniform of a Russian major. "But my brother was no longer a Jew," Reuben said. "He was converted in the Russian army."

After the brother's repeated pleas, his family agreed to show this stranger-kin his mother's grave. The whole town followed him to the cemetery, and his lamentations broke everyone's heart. "Mother, why did they take me away from you?" he wailed over the grave. "Why did they tear me away from my religion?" Then the Russian major spat and stomped on the grave of Lejb Tate, who had condemned him to his exile all those years ago.

The story does not have a forgiving, prodigal son ending. After the emotional cemetery visit, the brother left Brańsk. He occasionally wrote to people back home, but nobody answered him. This time, he was definitively banished from communal memory. Such personal tragedies were repeated in countless shtetl families. The Cantonist recruits were often mistreated in the Russian army and forced to convert. When they tried to return to their hometowns, they were usually met with rigid rejection.

According to the Yizkor Book, the Cantonist edict caused not only the grief of families but the premature death of Brańsk's first rabbi, Meir Nechis. Apparently, the mothers of the recruits followed their children to the prison room of the synagogue, which was next to the rabbi's apartment. There the mothers lamented, crying and beating their heads against the walls. The rabbi, the story concludes, was unable to bear these sounds of grief, and "for this reason, died at a young age."

This is one of the occasions when the Yizkor Book poetizes ordinary events and turns them into a revealing little parable. Maternal worry, in this brief tale, is turned into epic grief — grief that seems to condense a long memory of persecutions and an almost mythic sense of Jewish suffering.

In fact, Jewish attitudes toward tsarist rule were mixed. In contrast with the Poles, Jewish communities basically accepted the legitimacy of the Russian government, even though they may have bridled against its particular policies. Many Jewish leaders at first thought that their people had a better chance of full emancipation as part of the large, multinational Russian Empire than in a potentially reborn Poland — although their hopes were repeatedly disappointed.

On the local level at least, the Russian authorities — even more so than the Polish ones of the past — were a force to be evaded or outwitted. Under previous Polish rule, the *kahals* were left to govern their people, interacting with the Polish administration only at certain prescribed junctures; under Russian rule, the demands for civic subordination were greater. As a result, the shtetl began to distinguish between its public and its private face. In 1835, the Russian government embarked on a new phase of "Jewish reforms," limiting Jewish rights and the role of the *kahals*. The new laws called for the appointment of so-called synagogue councils, to be made up of an official rabbi, a treasurer, an elder, and a "learned man." Since the post of the administrative rabbi could be filled only by someone with a full secular education, the *kahals* began to appoint two rabbis — one for the tsar and one, so to speak, for God. The official rabbi was the intermediary between the Jewish community and the government; he issued marriage and divorce certificates and kept records of births and deaths. The function of the religious rabbi was now supposedly limited to the clarification of doctrinal doubts and disputes; in fact, it was he who remained the true moral guide and spiritual leader of the community.

The regressive "Jewish reforms" came several years after the first of the big Polish rebellions — the November Uprising of 1830–31 — and were probably part of a wider attempt to gain control over the Jewish population and to break its ties to Poland. Indeed, in regard to Poles and Jews, the Russians practiced deliberately divisive politics. They kept promising full privileges to the Jews in return for loyalty to the tsar, and they tried to turn up the level of Polish wariness by such tactics as using disproportionate numbers of Jews in their intelligence services. But in reality, the Russians kept reneging on their pledges, exploiting Jews financially when convenient and including them in their repressive policies at other times. In 1844, another Russian statute abolished independent *kahals* altogether. Legally, the management of Jewish affairs was taken over by town administrations; unofficially, however, Jewish life continued to be regulated by communal and family structures.

The divide-and-conquer strategy only deepened the rifts that already existed between the Polish and Jewish inhabitants in the Russian-controlled territories. In the Congress Kingdom of Poland, where Poles had some ostensible power, and where seeds of later Polish problems were sown, the mood between the two groups was often tense and rancorous, as it swung from suspicion to resentment to counter-suspicion. The cycle of recriminations began under the earlier Prussian rule, when Poles accused Jews of loyalty to the Germans. Subsequently, the laws governing the Jewish population became more discriminatory, causing great grievances in the Jewish community, which in turn began to think that it was not in the interest of Jews to offer their allegiance to the Poles. In 1809, for example, the government of the Duchy of Warsaw introduced a new edict according to which Jews were not permitted to settle on particular streets in the city. By 1817 the political climate had changed, and the Polish temporary government set up a Commission for the Jewish People and Peasants in an attempt to undertake reforms. This project, however, was rejected by Tsar Alexander II.

Still, by the 1830s the Jewish population in Congress Poland had grown to 20 percent of the general population, and despite political instabilities, the period saw the growth of substantial Jewish wealth. Some of it dated from the Napoleonic Wars, when Jewish merchants became the main suppliers to the Polish Napoleonic legions. Several of these businessmen went on to establish powerful financial dynasties — a phenomenon that caused envy and resentment among the Poles, who saw the fortunes as founded on their misfortunes, forgetting the Jewish contributions to their army.

In the brief subsequent intervals when Polish elites exercised some real power, they failed to grant Jewish inhabitants of their reduced country legal emancipation, or they made full rights conditional on partial assimilation. This in turn encouraged some of the Jewish leaders and bankers to ally themselves with the Russian overseers who seemed to offer more.

In 1830 came the first of the insurrections against the Russians, known as the November Uprising. In the Congress Kingdom, where the uprising began, Jewish allegiances and opinions were split, but a large contingent of the community was disenchanted enough with the Russians to feel it was a better part of wisdom to cast its fate with the Polish rebels. Interestingly, several well-known Frankists played prominent roles in planning the rebellion as part of the inner circle of insurgents. The Polish general at the head of the National Guard, formed to patrol the streets of Warsaw to prevent disorders, initially objected to admitting Jews to the ranks, but under political pressure he reversed his decision. Jews, including many Orthodox men, volunteered in enthusiastic numbers. This détente, however, foundered on petty matters of appearance, as some of the guard's Polish members objected to the Jewish volunteers' beards. In response, the general created a somewhat lesser, "preparatory" Civil Guard, to which Jews of all hirsute styles were admitted. In the meantime, three or four hundred Jews decided to shave off their beards after all and join the National Guard proper, in which some of them were appointed as officers. Among the Jewish soldiers of the November Uprising were Józef Berkowicz, the son of Berek Joselewicz, the hero of Kościuszko's Jewish legion, and Józef's son, Leon Berkowicz. In the end, the uprising — about which Polish opinion was also divided — was quashed, and followed by severe reprisals, thus ending yet another brief episode of Polish-Jewish solidarity in struggle.

The frictions generated by the uprising affected the Podlasie area, albeit in diffuse ways. In Brańsk, Russian vigilance increased, and so did the Poles' suspicions of their Jewish neighbors. The Yizkor Book notes a Brańsk "legend" from that time, according to which an itinerant *chazan* — a man who went from village to village to chant Sabbath prayers — was stopped on the road by local insurrectionists and accused of being a spy. He could not explain the nature of his work to the Poles, so to simplify matters he professed to being a tailor. When put to a test, the poor man couldn't so much as thread a needle. The insurrectionists concluded that he was lying and must therefore be hiding his true errand. In consequence, the *chazan* was hanged.

ᴄᴈ   ᴄᴈ   ᴄᴈ

Between outbursts of political passion, life in the shtetl remained relatively stable. Jews married and multiplied, new synagogues were built, young men went to yeshivas to study. Thirty years passed before the next quake of the political landscape: the January Rising of 1863. This was the century's most important Polish action against the Russians, and in preparation for it, Poles and Jews of Warsaw once again joined forces, this time with the mutual awareness that their fates were linked. The Poles understood that they needed the political and economic support of the Jews for the success of their enterprise; progressive Jews had convinced themselves that they could not expect any great boons from the tsarist powers. In the turbulent period preceding the January Rising, there were stirring declarations of patriotism and fraternal feeling.

After a massacre of Polish patriots in 1861, the two chief rabbis of Warsaw walked side by side with Polish leaders in the funeral commemorations. In the same year, Rabbi Ber Meisels was arrested by the Russians for his gesture of closing synagogues as a protest against the Russian profanation of Warsaw's Catholic churches. He was expelled from the country before the uprising began.

Patriotic fervor had its price, but also its sweet satisfactions.

In 1862, Ozias Lubliner, a Jewish journalist writing from Brussels, addressed the "Poles-Israelites in Poland" in tones full of hope. "The bloody incidents that took place in Warsaw in the year 1861 accomplished a great miracle," he declared. "Whereas until now none of the national insurrections in Poland have brought any political changes for the Jews, whereas the organs of the Polish press even in 1859 held that Jews, although settled in Poland for eight centuries, are always newcomers and foreigners — your active participation in the national events of 1861, your share in exposing your breasts to the Muscovite swords and bullets on Warsaw's pavements . . . all these events, completely unexpected, almost miraculous, have tied Christian Poles with Israelite Poles together with an unbreakable knot. Through the participation on the pavements of Warsaw . . . the Jews have not only gained, but they have won, the right to the title of Polish citizens. This title the Christian Poles have granted them wholeheartedly."

In Brańsk, cells of conspirators began to form in 1861; eventually, a large fighting unit was assembled from the ranks of the peasants and the gentry. The Russian military presence was increased. One can imagine that, amid such tensions, the Jewish community in the town felt caught between Scylla and Charybdis. In the eastern provinces, the Jews were still predisposed to link themselves with the tsar. With the accession of the liberal Alexander II to the throne, the Jews of Russia and the Russian territories gained new hopes that his reforms would extend to them as well. Their hopes were not fulfilled, but under Alexander's rule, Jews did gain more rights, and the hated Cantonist edict was abolished.

Moreover, from a purely pragmatic point of view, the sheer proximity to Russia might made Jewish identification with the Poles much less tenable. The Orthodox Jewish communities in the shtetls knew that to join the Poles in open defiance would leave them more vulnerable than they already were.

It is now possible to follow the events in Brańsk during the uprising years in some detail, on the basis of information made available in newly opened Russian archives, discovered by Zbigniew Romaniuk. In terms of Polish-Jewish relations, the story that emerges from the documents is hardly comfortable for anyone. The drama began with the announcement of the retrograde Russian peasant reform in 1861, which reversed some of the effects of emancipation. The reform led to increased rents and taxes in the annexed provinces and to great unrest among farmers in the Brańsk area. As a result, two Russian army companies were brought to town to prevent rebellion. One of the court trials at the time concerned a band of armed peasants who marauded in the local forests and who, among their other crimes, attacked a saloon run by a Jewish woman, threatening a pogrom. They were judged to be mere bandits and sentenced accordingly, but their activities might have had an anti-tsarist as well as an anti-Semitic tinge.

As political agitation in Brańsk simmered, the Russians, in a typical tactic, brought in a Jewish man from the town of Grodno to act as a spy. The Catholic church was then one of the main forums for Polish conspiratorial activity, and the Grodno man apparently told the authorities about provocative sermons, whose content he learned from fellow Jews. Discomfiting though such information may be, it is interesting that the Russians apparently did not trust a Brańsk Jew to inform on his own townsmen, and it is revealing of some closeness between Polish and Jewish communities that Jews would have known what had been preached in church during Mass.

In the confusing subsequent events, the stance of the Jews seems unclear. In one incident, Jews gave information to the

Russians — perhaps under duress — which led to the discovery
of a hiding place where scythes and other peasant weapons were
collected. In another episode, a Russian official known for his
hatred of the Polish freedom fighters stopped at an inn owned
by a Jewish woman. He was hanged by the rebels during the
night, and the innkeeper was detained under suspicion that she
was in league with the rebels. She energetically denied knowing
them and was released. However, from the testimony of another
Jewish woman, it appears that the innkeeper's husband may
have been involved in the execution of the Russian. A few
months later, another Jewish arrival from a different region was
accused of spying in a nearby village and executed by the Poles,
despite the intervention of a prominent Jewish personage. The
body was brought to the Brańsk cemetery, but the man who
guarded his grave was killed as well, in what appears to have
been an act of gratuitous vengefulness. By that time, tensions
were so high that Jews found it unsafe to travel on country
roads. A number of Jewish families moved from nearby villages
to Brańsk, where conditions were better.

Polish resistance persisted for an unusually long time in
Brańsk, conducted mostly from the thick and concealing forests
— the area was developing a reputation for partisan activity,
and for cussedness. But each Polish defeat was followed by ret-
ributions. After one of the major battles in Brańsk, the Russians
forbade the Poles to wear signs of mourning for the slain soldiers — although this ruling was promptly defied by women
who donned symbolic jewelry, in the shapes of broken crosses,
chains, and the crown of thorns. Several insurrectionists were
sentenced to exile in Siberia or other Russian provinces; some
gentry estates were confiscated and the properties distributed
among Russians. As part of an overall Russification campaign
following the uprising, use of the Polish language was prohibited in public offices.

One ambiguous memento of the uprising has lasted in Brańsk to this day. After the rebellion, every town in the Russian area was ordered to erect a memorial to the Russian hero Alexander Nevsky. In Brańsk, the burden of this fell on the Jewish community. The resulting monument — a graceful enough stone rotunda with columns surrounding a statue of Nevsky — is one of the few structures to escape destruction in the two world wars, and it now stands as an innocent street ornament, shorn of its previous associations.

What is one to make of these muddled events? "Generally, one can say that Jews didn't mix in and weren't interested in politics," the authors of the Yizkor Book tells us. "But miseries from politics they had enough of in all times."

Among the Polish and Jewish intelligentsia of Warsaw, the uprising stood as a high point in interethnic relations. "Good God, where did we not meet with the Jews in 1863," the leading Polish writer Bolesław Prus wrote a few decades later. "In conference halls and conspiratorial rooms, in churches and in prisons, on the battlefields and on journeys to Siberia, and under the gallows as well." After the defeat of the uprising, Jews as much as Poles were punished with imprisonment and Siberian exile. But in the shtetl, there was no such moment of unity to hark back to. The Jewish inhabitants of Brańsk were clearly aware by then of broader Polish politics, and tried to position themselves within its complexities as best they could. But ordinary folk had a strong sense that politics was something that happened to them, and from which they suffered, rather than as something in which they had an interest and a stake. The events in the Gentile world were not really their affair. In Brańsk, one tangible consequence of the uprising was a special punitive tax imposed by the Russians. The Yizkor Book notes that the Poles wanted to raise part of the money from the *kahal*. From the authors' point of view, this was unfair, because Jews did not participate in the rebellion. From the Polish point of view, however, the morality of this position would have been precisely reversed, and Jewish unwillingness to share the tax burden would have been perceived as insult added to the injury of nonparticipation. According to the Yizkor Book, an influential member of the Jewish community got the authorities to agree to a lesser tax. Neighborly relations may have cooled for a while as a result of such developments; at the very least, the events would have been a reaffirmation of moral separateness.

The Jews of the shtetls may have tried hard to remain neutral in the conflicts between the more involved actors, but at times of increased fervor and bloodshed, it was difficult to retain political innocence — or rather, innocence and neutrality also exacted their price. Possibly, though, among the better-educated Jews of Brańsk, a more complex political and social consciousness was beginning to germinate. A broader understanding would have developed not only through experience itself, but also through the influence of the written word. The Yizkor Book mentions that a large portion of Brańsk's Jews remained illiterate — amazingly enough — until the end of the nineteenth century, but their community also included some avid readers. In the mid-nineteenth century, the literate Brańskers would have had at least occasional access to the Yiddish, Polish, and Hebrew books and journals from various Polish and Russian territories. By that time, several Jewish presses operated in Warsaw, publishing in Hebrew and Yiddish. Journals in both languages covered a range of issues and took an active part in Polish-Jewish polemics. The progressive weekly *The Israelite*, founded in 1866, was the most prominent of the publications.

On the Polish side as well, the debate about the "Jewish question" was by then largely conducted in journals and newspapers rather than in the disempowered political forums. In

1859, for example, Warsaw witnessed a so-called "Jewish war" in the press, which began with attacks in a Polish newspaper on the Jewish bourgeoisie and on assimilated Jews; these groups were becoming targets of hostility as capitalist "infiltrators" of supposedly noncommercial Polish society. To everyone's astonishment, the Jewish community responded by suing the newspaper for defamation. Although the suit was lost, the paper — with the encouragement of a prominent Jewish banker — changed its position entirely and began publishing pro-Jewish articles in the years leading to the January Rising. In addition, one Polish newspaper, funded by a Jewish financier but edited by a well-known Polish writer, specialized in topics of Polish-Jewish coexistence.

At least some copies of these publications would have reached Brańsk, stimulating discussion in the streets and synagogues. Or Brańsk readers might have preferred to get their news from the Lithuanian city of Vilno, which was also a lively Jewish intellectual center. The debates in the periodicals reflected a growing political consciousness in the modern sense: the perception of Polish Jewry as a collectivity that had to find a coherent stance toward Poland and Polishness. This awareness, in turn, was a response to the Polish sense of national identity, which was becoming more definite and more defensive. From the Polish point of view, the question was how to awaken and strengthen unified national consciousness among the still separate "castes," including the often noncommitted peasants. And because their identity was so embattled, Polish patriots were prone to feel that "whoever is not with us is against us."

From the Jewish vantage point, the great question was whether or not to assimilate, and to whom. The shades of opinion on this matter bespoke a considerable level of political and social sophistication, and prefigure today's debates, not only among Jews but among other minority groups. A handful of Jews favored full conversion, but they were a tiny minority. A majority of the well-off Jewish bourgeoisie wanted to live within Polish society as potential Polish citizens, but without losing or denying their historical and religious Jewishness. The nuances of nomenclature became quite important and illustrate fine distinctions. Some assimilationists began to call themselves "Poles of Mosaic denomination," or even "Jewish Poles." The degree of loyalty to their Orthodox brethren was a tricky point for many assimilationists, but mostly they wanted to lift these less enlightened brethren out of the mire of traditionalism and backwardness — in other words, if not to Polonize, then at least to modernize them. One can also discern, among some of these educated *maskilim*, a kind of "Jewish guilt" about distancing themselves from their tribe, or a sentimental attachment to the traditional ways they overthrew, but in which many of them grew up. Certainly, disavowal of one's Jewishness — in other words, "passing" — was viewed with great distaste and opprobrium. "If a son of Israel does not live according to the demands of his tradition, if he openly rises up against this tradition and declares that it is not obligatory — he gives the proof of his free-thinking, or indifference to religion," wrote Samuel Zvi Peltyn, the editor of *The Israelite*, in the 1870s. "If he openly converts to another religion, he demonstrates a change of religious conviction. . . . In none of these cases is there anything to shame Israel! But if a Jew hides his faith and wants to pass for something he is not . . . then, besides the ridicule he must incur from those among whom he is trying to steal himself, he also brands his own people with the most ignominious stigma."

In the pages of *The Israelite*, one can also find discussions about whether Jews could still legitimately consider themselves a separate nation whose identity depended on the dream of return to an ancient homeland, or whether they had, in the course of their long history in Diaspora, become de facto Europeans, and should therefore strive toward full membership in the countries in which they were living. Such questions, of course, gained new urgency with the rise of Zionism.

If there were any closet *maskilim* in Brańsk, longing for life in the secular world, they would have kept a low profile. But they might have had their dreams — stimulated not only by the heated discussions of current issues but by fictional and poetic images. Jewish readers in Brańsk would probably have known of a novel that in the 1860s swept its way from Germany to Eastern Europe and Russia, reworked by different authors in several languages and adaptations. The main version of this polemical work, written in Hebrew by Peretz Smolenskin and entitled *The Reward, or The Jews in Warsaw During the Last Rebellion*, contains extended arguments between Jewish protagonists of various ideological persuasions. Among its central characters are *maskilim* of two generations who represent pro-Polish and pro-tsarist positions; there are also assimilationist Jews with self-hating tendencies and Poles representing varying degrees of tolerance and open-mindedness. The readership for this novel was substantial, but we do not know precisely whom it consisted of. Was fiction considered "women's reading" among Jews, as it was in many circles — sentimental pablum unfit for manly consumption? Perhaps not serious fiction with social or political themes, of which the period produced great quantities.

It is doubtful whether Jewish readers in nineteenth-century Brańsk would have turned to Polish literature, but if they had, they would have found works of surprising interest. The partitions and revolts produced a large body of fiction and poetry on Jewish themes or with Jewish motifs. Romantic poets especially were often fascinated by Polish Jews, usually portraying them in a favorable, if melancholy, light as picturesque, enigmatic figures or as emblems of age-old woe. Judging by certain modern criteria, one could say that these poets were engaged in a process of exoticizing, which is a form of unconscious prejudice. But then, perception itself is prejudice. It may be a purist illusion to think that we can understand members of other cultures with perfect impartiality or perfect empathy. We can, however, bring to our understanding more or less curiosity, respect, sympathy, and imagination. For the Polish Romantic poets, Jewish characters were still Other, still seen across imaginative barriers, but in the symbolic universe their figures were endowed with positive, and sometimes deeply felt, meanings.

The positive image of Jewishness reached its early apotheosis in the works of Poland's greatest Romantic poet, Adam Mickiewicz, who almost certainly came from a Frankist background. In his most important work, *Pan Tadeusz* — a matchless epic of rural manorial life written in rhyming couplets — one of the central figures is Jankiel, a Jewish tavern keeper, depicted as the soul of honesty, wisdom, and patriotism. *Pan Tadeusz* is set in Lithuania during Napoleonic times, and Jankiel acts as an intermediary between units of the French army and Polish conspirators who placed such great hopes in Napoleon. It is Jankiel who advises noblemen on military strategy, who soothes enmities in the village — who, in a sense, is the heart of manorial society. In a culminating scene, Jankiel plays a dulcimer at a feast, interweaving Polish and Jewish motifs, and creating a sort of narrative of Polish history in sounds — a musical drama that moves the gathered company to tears.

In his later years, Mickiewicz developed quasi-mystical ideas about the fateful interdependence of Poles and Jews. He saw the metaphorical "Israel" as Poland's "older brother," and he felt that his country's destiny as a second "chosen nation" could be fulfilled only if the Jewish spirit was allowed to permeate the Polish soul. As part of his vision, shortly before his death, Mickiewicz tried to create a Jewish legion in Turkey, which was to help Poland regain its independence by strengthening the Ottoman Empire against Russia.

In Poland, poets were the acknowledged legislators of the world, the keepers of national identity when that identity was under threat, and Mickiewicz's ideas about the spiritual importance of "Israel" would have been taken seriously by his readers. Of course, Polish renditions of Jewishness were not always so idealistic. There were strains of anti-Semitism even in the high literature of the period — for example, in the poetry of Count Zygmunt Krasinski, another major Romantic poet, whose later work is marred by paranoia about converted Jews. But there were also writers who made it part of their program to depict Jewish life realistically in all its social and intellectual variety. Novelists like Ignacy Kraszewski, who specialized in Jewish subjects, explicitly criticized stereotypical fictional portrayals of Jews and tried to make the picture of Jewish life more three-dimensional. Other writers used Jewish history — for example, the oppression of Israelites by the Romans — as an allegory for Poland's own situation.

The shtetl, when it was mentioned in Polish literature, was rarely seen in flattering terms. Travelers passing through the little towns, especially in the eastern provinces, looked out of their carriages and saw dirt, puddles, poverty, backwardness, barefoot peasants amid filthy pigsties, and Jews in black caftans emerging from unkempt shops. Interestingly, in the perceptions of many writers, the dismal character of these small towns was defined not by their Jewishness, but by their specific Polish mix of peasants and Jews. Indeed, sometimes the shtetl was perceived as Polish precisely because it was Jewish. "And do you know what makes every town Polish?" Ignacy Kraszewski asked. "The Jews. When there are no more Jews, we enter an alien country and feel, accustomed as we are to their good sense and services, as if something were not quite right."

These glimpses from the outside undoubtedly missed something vital about the shtetl: the liveliness and the human textures that made the inhabitants of a muddy town feel that it was also a rich, familiar world. But the travelers' comments were not entirely inaccurate. The eastern shtetls *were* poor, backward, and dirty. The Yizkor Book tells us that the Jews of Brańsk lived crowded together, with whole extended families and their numerous broods packed into small houses. There was no indoor plumbing, and waste was thrown into the same Nurzec River that supplied the drinking water. Houses habitually got a thorough cleaning only once a year, before Passover. In the Yizkor Book, these conditions are connected to the diphtheria epidemics that erupted in Brańsk in 1844, 1852, and 1892. "The town was emptied . . . , and the cemetery filled with the dead," the authors write about the first epidemic. Most of the victims were children. During this outbreak, the *kahal* declared a fast and prescribed special prayers; more practically, objects thought to carry disease were burned, and people were encouraged to keep themselves and their houses clean. During the 1892 epidemic, a hospital was built, although according to the Yizkor Book's skeptical account, nobody emerged from it alive.

In addition to epidemics, fires swept through the wooden town every few years. In 1868, a January fire spread far and wide, because water could not be drawn from the frozen river.

The town government came to the aid of people whose houses were burned down, making it possible for them to rebuild quickly. Five years later, fires were deliberately set in several houses, probably by Jewish arsonists avenging themselves for the forced recruitment of their brothers into the army. In an example of legal cooperation, the *kahal* gathered signatures requesting the punishment of the young men, and the Russian administration complied by sending them to Siberia.

The largest fire erupted in 1876, devastating about half of Brańsk. According to the Yizkor Book, people from neighboring villages — we do not know whether they were Jewish or not — brought clothing, bread, and potatoes to Brańsk in their carts and helped the victims rebuild their houses. However, cooperation was not long sustained in the fire's aftermath: since the boundary lines of the new houses weren't precisely indicated, violent quarrels broke out between owners over land. "People came close to killing each other over a scrap of ground," the Yizkor Book informs us.

Despite the ceaseless sequence of natural disasters, the Jewish population of Brańsk was growing apace. In 1857, it constituted 39 percent of Brańsk's 1,845 people. And given generally modest conditions, the second half of the nineteenth century saw considerable economic growth in the Jewish community. Although the exact start-up dates of businesses cannot be ascertained, this was probably the period during which some of the larger Jewish enterprises, such as the cloth-weaving workshop and a small factory producing leather belts, were founded. One of the consequences of development was that the gap between rich and poor was increasing. This trend was highlighted by such events as the construction of the third synagogue, known as the Dritter Beth Midrash, or the Noble Synagogue, by and for the wealthy Jews of Brańsk. Another important sign of eco-

nomic growth was the establishment, in 1863, of a lending society, which made small loans to Jewish borrowers, who used
pieces of jewelry or other valuables as collateral, and retrieved
them on repayment.

At the same time, after the defeat of the 1863 January Rising,
economic improvement became the main focus of Polish
activism. Since it was clear to the Polish elites that the dream of
an independent Poland was not going to be realized easily, they
turned instead to less revolutionary programs of reform in the
occupied country. The leading slogan of the reform movement
was "organic work," which stressed the Tolstoyan values of
self-help, the cultivation of disciplined habits in daily hygiene
and labor, and the creation of farming cooperatives and other
kinds of self-managed institutions. The reformers hoped that
such pragmatic, earthbound strategies would lead to gradual
but real improvements in living standards and productivity, and
that by starting small, at the grassroots level, they could educate
the Polish masses in modern modes of behavior. In its early
days, the leaders of the "organic work" movement saw the participation of the Jews as vital to its success, and invited Jewish
financiers and intellectuals into new societies, charitable organizations, and other associations. But as competition between
Poles and Jews grew sharper, and as the economic roles of the
two groups became more distinct, these links once again loos-
ened and broke.

While peasant lending and savings cooperatives were spring-
ing up in the Polish territories, in Brańsk there was no such
institution until the beginning of the twentieth century. Indeed,
to many Polish peasants, the idea of using currency at all still
seemed mysterious and vaguely suspect. It may be that Brańsk
Poles looked upon a Jewish lending society as further proof of
the wicked cleverness and insularity of the Jews.

And yet there are no indications of hostilities or even great tensions between Jewish and Polish parts of Brańsk in the latter part of the nineteenth century. As the political situation reverted to a kind of equilibrium — after 1863 there were no more attempts at overthrowing Russian rule for several decades — interethnic relations were also restored to stability. After all, the Jews by that time had lived in Brańsk for more than a century; they must have seemed a permanent part of the social landscape, one element of the accepted natural order of things. This was the period when Polish craftsmen — who were usually farmers as well — yielded their places to Jewish artisans. But this did not induce any tremor perceptible at this remove of time. Perhaps the change was gradual enough, and the division of labor sufficiently satisfactory, to go unquestioned. And so the Jews plied their trades while the farmers worked their land. The Jewish peddlers took their horse-drawn carts through the villages; the peasants came to the market to buy and sell, and later to have a drink at a Jewish inn. At the market, women wearing several layers of skirts and flowered scarves mingled with women in wigs and men in black caftans and long beards. A peasant or a Polish gentleman might have a "good" coat made by a Jewish tailor; sometimes a Pole consulted a Jewish medic about some stubborn complaint. Or a Jew might go to a peasant healer for an herbal remedy. To most people of Brańsk, the Jews must have been simply . . . the Jews, "different" people whose existence does not impinge on one's own, and toward whom one feels, among other things, the affection, or at least the recognition, that comes from long proximity. They were, in peasant parlance, "Żydki" (the diminutive of "Jews"), which carried a mixture of condescension and intimacy. Sometimes they were "our Jews," which meant Jews whom one particularly knew, with whom one could come to an understanding.

They were hardly aliens any longer; rather, they had become the familiar, complementary Other — the counterpart by which the rural Poles to some extent recognized themselves.

To the Jews, the Poles had also become the familiar given, the necessary condition of life, viewed with a mixture of friendliness and, yes, condescension. They were simply the goyim, the routine term, still used today, for all Gentiles short of aristocratic status. Sometimes they were — in an inversion of "our Jews" — "our goyim." And although Poles and Jews retained their spiritual separateness, their daily culture — habits, language, cooking, ordinary aesthetics — inevitably intermingled and influenced each other. They lived in similarly constructed wooden houses. Some of the gorgeous wooden synagogues of Polish towns and villages were decorated with Polish folk motifs. Yiddish was permeated by Polish vocabulary: *shmata* for rag, *czajnik* for kettle, *paskudny* for odious, among many others. The peasants picked up Yiddish words, and Jewish themes appeared in their proverbs. Even today, people in Brańsk say, "It's as noisy as a *cheder*", or "She's dressed as for a Jewish wedding" — meaning, dressed ostentatiously. We no longer know whether the origins of chicken soup were Jewish or Polish.

And then there was the music. Each village had its Jewish musicians, to whom everyone was willing to listen. People from Brańsk still remember the Jewish fiddlers and klezmer bands that played at Polish weddings. Their melodies combined Jewish and Gypsy and Polish and Russian influences — that vivid, energetic, melancholy mix that is the Eastern European equivalent of the blues. And surely if they played like that, moving their audiences to dancing and to tears, then their souls must have caught something of the genius loci — the tune, the temper, the spirit of the place.

But toward the end of the nineteenth century, the balance began once again ineluctably to shift. In the Yizkor Book, several revealing details suggest new winds, new currents. Perhaps the most important changes were caused by sudden migrations, both inward and outward. The influx of new immigrants began after the assassination of the liberal Tsar Alexander II in 1881, an event followed by a wave of pogroms and other anti-Semitic persecutions within the Russian Pale. In the aftermath, tens of thousands of Jews, known as Litvaks — so named because most of them came from Lithuania or from parts of Belarus commonly called Lithuania in those days — fled to the Polish territories to seek refuge. These refugees were Russian speaking, for the most part very poor, and very Orthodox. Economically, they were oriented toward Russia, buying and selling products in the mother country, thus raising Polish fears that they would become instrumental in the process of Russification. Such fears turned out to be unfounded, but it was true that the better-educated Litvaks tended to be influenced by Russian political ideas, and later accounted for a large proportion of Jewish leftist parties.

In Brańsk, as in other shtetls, the Litvaks' advent was greeted with ambivalence by Jews as well as Poles. For one thing, the new arrivals dressed differently, and they spoke a different dialect of Yiddish from the locals. Also, the addition of sheer numbers exacerbated the already severe problems of overcrowding. An average one-story house in a Jewish neighborhood had nine inhabitants, and the density created constant health problems. The presence of an impoverished new contingent of people must have created new social demands and frictions. Possibly some of the charitable institutions established during that period — the Society for the Aid of Poor Fiancés, the Society for Good Deeds and Visits to the Sick, and the Society for Fraternal Aid — were a response to the problem and an attempt to incorporate the poorest of the refugees into the communal matrix.

The Litvaks kept coming to Brańsk well into the twentieth century, but the pressure of increasing numbers in turn pushed others out, to seek their fortunes on other shores. The gates of America stood open. As the economic prospects for young Jews in Brańsk worsened through the 1880s, the first trickle of emigrants started leaving for the land of promise. Until then, emigration from Brańsk was extremely rare, although not unheard of. A few young men had managed to elude Cantonist recruitment by escaping, via the Russian-Austrian border, to far-flung places. The Yizkor Book notes that occasionally people had to leave town to avoid disgrace and scorn over a wrong they had committed. The authors tell a rather obscure story of a young woman who had become pregnant out of wedlock and was sent by her parents to Palestine in 1861. The inhabitants of Brańsk only learned about this in 1937, when the woman's legal representative suddenly showed up in town looking for her rightful descendants. She had apparently died lonely but wealthy, leaving her money to such relatives in Brańsk as might still exist. By that time, however, she had been erased from the town's memory. No one was willing to claim kinship, and the representative from Palestine departed without finding takers for his money. But the story gives us an insight into the absolute taboo that surrounded sexual transgressions in an Orthodox community, and also into the human fact that such transgressions occur even in the most constrained circumstances.

In the 1880s emigration became a widespread phenomenon, a new trope of Jewish life. We know its markers and stages mostly from the American side: the immigrants arriving after a long and miserable ship passage, the hopeful faces at Ellis Island, the hard striving in the new country, the eventual triumphs. From the other side — from the vantage point of those left behind — emigration meant the loss of family members, waiting for letters, reading them eagerly around family tables, or asking someone else, embarrassedly, to read them to you. It often took several years before the first word from the emigrants arrived — the years of greatest hardship, uncertainty, and perhaps shame at the lack of instant success. When letters did come, they often exaggerated all that was good and fabulous in the New World, and so different from Brańsk. But even without exaggeration, the reports from the *goldeneh medina*, the golden land, must have seemed, from the perspective of Brańsk's low huts and muddy streets, nearly mythical. In the meantime, to the emigrants themselves, their new lives might well have seemed harsher in some ways than what they left behind. They were mostly young single men, many of them tailors who went to work in Lower East Side sweatshops, laboring long hours in stifling conditions, under close and peremptory supervision. This was a far cry from working in a small room of a family dwelling — albeit a crowded and a noisy one — stopping when you needed to, having meals brought to you by the women of the house.

And yet emigration continued uninterrupted for as long as the borders were open and the ship passage affordable. By 1894 there were already not one but two Brańsk associations in New York, and their membership grew through the rest of the century. Of course, one reason for the stream of departures was the magnetism of America, the lure of possibility, the dream of altering one's life in an unimaginably grand way. But there was also something about life in the Polish shtetl that had ceased to offer enough hope or safety or spiritual sustenance to everybody. Economic conditions were one element; but perhaps, too, the framework of belief had begun to loosen, causing uncertainty in some souls and making the prospects of leaving attractive, if frightening. Even among those who stayed behind, one could sense simmerings of as yet unarticulated energies and unaccustomed doubts about the old unquestioned order of things.

Indeed, the order itself was slowly shifting, as the material conditions that had supported it changed. The Yizkor Book notes a kind of watershed event: the purchase of a machine by the owner of a shop that produced suede jackets. This was such a wonder that "all of Brańsk ran to look into the window" as the automatized worker went through its revolutions. Gradually the owner imported more machinery, bought up an entire building for his enterprise, and employed thirty to forty young women — enough to acquire the honorific name of "manufacturer."

Sometime around then, Brańsk acquired another, colorful new enterprise: a photography shop. It must have been popular, because the authors of the Yizkor Book write that whenever one saw a couple dressed as if for a holiday, walking down the street with prayer books in their hands, one knew they were going to have their photograph taken. And of course we know those photographs: formal, sepia-colored, dignified. A young couple or a family, decorously groomed and dressed, staring straight at the camera — those are our glimpses of Jewish life, arrested in the midst of that walk to the photography shop, in the midst of the moving stream of life.

In general, the divisions between rich and poor were becoming starker and undoubtedly more disturbing. At one end of the spectrum, fairly substantial enterprises were emerging and growing. Most of the applications for building permits of business premises in Brańsk in the last decades of the nineteenth century came from the Jewish side of the population. There is mention in the Yizkor Book of a Jewish tile factory, which for some reason employed mostly "Catholics," to use the text's category. Other people accumulated enough capital to engage in a kind of futures market with the local "Pany" — the lesser *szlachta* and gentry, who had large agricultural properties. These investors bought the prospective products of a field or orchard sometime in the winter, on speculation; they collected the crop in the summer. Apparently, the local aristocrats also came to Jews for loans. The writers of the Yizkor Book complain that some of the "poor but highly respected" Pany sometimes were less than punctual in repaying, forcing the lender to collect his due in wheat or other produce. In a time-honored tradition, Jews were also the main horse traders in Brańsk. The horses were sold mostly to peasants, often on the strength of promissory notes. "The merchant then prayed to God that the farmer would have good crops," the Yizkor Book says, "or that the horse wouldn't die" before the notes were redeemed.

In addition to such ventures, almost every Jewish household in Brańsk had a little booth or stall, offering for sale everything from pins to doughnuts. The most famous one was the Pesach stall, which belonged to a man thus festively named. This shop was a mere four feet square in size, but apparently you could find there just about anything you wanted — most of it for just one grosh! You could even buy one-quarter of a pencil, carefully divided and sharpened by Pesach. Many of these variety shops were operated practically like garage sales, without a permit. When a neighborhood was warned of a government inspector's arrival, there was great hustle and bustle as people hid their jumbles of goods under a neighbor's bed. The authorities must, above all, be outwitted.

Legal or not, these basic businesses could not have produced much income, and most of the Jews in Brańsk remained extremely poor. Town poor rather than country poor: living in crowded spaces, waiting for customers rather than crops, subsisting sometimes on the edge of cold and hunger.

Both the growing wealth and the growing poverty reflected broader trends within the Polish territories. With the belated coming of industrialization to Eastern Europe, the structure of Polish society was changing in fundamental ways. New classes began to form around new conditions and activities. The pertinent distinctions were no longer between castes — the nobility, the burghers, the clergy, Jews, and peasants — but between industrialists and workers, or, as they were more tendentiously called, the bourgeoisie and the proletariat. In this new configuration, Jews once again occupied a highly charged place. Because of their traditions of trade and commerce, they were alert to the possibilities of industrial production and quick to explore and exploit them; therefore, they comprised a disproportionate percentage of the commercial middle class. The Poles, because of their traditions, were late to take up the new occupations. To them, commerce was still a dirty, or at least a dubious, word, and the *szlachta* — the class from which educated industrialists might have come — had its version of aristocratic disdain for ambitious striving. By the time Poles started to engage in industry and commerce, they found sharp and challenging competition in those economic spaces from Jewish entrepreneurs.

This caused — not very fairly and not very surprisingly — new waves of envy and resentment. In anti-Semitic conceptions, the Jew was becoming closely and insistently identified with the Capitalist, the money man who had no deep roots, no attachment to the land, no national loyalties. At the same time, in the elegant salons of Warsaw, members of the new elites — Polish haute bourgeoisie and Jewish industrialists — met on terms, if not of equality, then at least of mutual curiosity. Glamorous and mutually profitable marriages were occasionally contracted between the rich and the titled, and Polish literature began to offer stories of Polish-Jewish liaisons, with all the attendant psychological and social complications. The Jew, in this plot, was often portrayed as sensitive, carnal, anguished; the Jewess as beautiful, sensuous, neurasthenic, spoiled. To the Polish aristocracy and intelligentsia, the Jew was becoming, among other things, a figure of sexual interest and strange magnetism. Among the versions of Otherness, this was not the worst or the least flattering, and fascination sometimes at least led to intimacy and deeper reciprocal knowledge.

But the negative stereotypes of Jewishness were exacerbated in the last decades of the nineteenth century by the rise of a more assertive and exclusivist kind of nationalism. Ironically, as far as nationhood went, Poles and Jews had been in a similar position for a whole century: neither had an actually existing nation to go with their strong sense of collective identity, and both substituted a notional ideal for the real thing. It can be fairly said that for both, the substitution of fantasized ideas for solid realities strengthened, with rare exceptions, the drive to separatism.

On the Polish side, during the long period of the partitions, the visions of a reborn Poland became more abstract and more purist. To some extent, this can be understood as a reflex of self-preservation. If "Polishness" were to survive, it would have to be defined as a strong, distinct entity or quality. The prepartition Polish Republic accommodated all sorts of differences within it, but then its existence did not depend on a hypothetical notion of Polishness. In the absence of territory, or of sovereignty, the romancers of future nationhood began to envision a country that would somehow be clearly and wholly Polish. This potential "Polishness" was not yet equivalent to ethnicity, but it began to be associated with a kind of homogeneity. To qualify as Polish, members of the future nation had to declare unequivocal loyalty to the state and to a "Polish" system of values. To the nationalist thinkers, the prospect of a Jewish subculture in Poland, pursuing its own beliefs, education, and civic institutions, was becoming unacceptable, even intolerable. In their view, if Jews wanted to belong to Poland, they would have to assimilate completely; they would have to become Polish. Herein the source of true intolerance — of hostility toward the very existence and presence of Otherness — could be discerned.

In the meantime, among Jews there was renewed debate on just how Polish they wished to become. The question began to be posed more sharply with the rise of Zionism in Europe. From its inception, this movement had a number of adherents in Poland, who felt that emigration to Palestine was the only solution to the problems of perpetual alienation and insecurity. Even short of such an ambition, the majority of Jews in Polish territories continued to believe that remaining separate and nurturing a strong, distinct identity was the only guarantee of Jewish "nationhood," or even collective survival.

As at many junctures before, a small progressive contingent of Poles and Jews espoused very different principles. They argued that by then the two "nations" were historically linked together, and that their goal should be to forge a new Poland in the spirit of cooperation and common cause. The Polish thinkers in this camp believed that the relatively advanced economic position of the Jews would be a great advantage in the new nation, and that the Polish populace had much to learn

from its Jewish neighbors about the virtues of entrepreneur-
ship, hard work, and frugality.

In the meantime, an increasing number of educated secular
Jews were intent on entering Polish society and modeled themselves on Polish — or, as they might have preferred to think,
European — cultural lines. Some of the wealthy Jewish families
in Warsaw, for example, brought in private tutors for their
daughters, to give them lessons in music, painting, French — all
hallmarks of feminine cultivation in bourgeois circles. Interestingly, such urbane polish was not made available to the sons,
who continued to attend Jewish schools. Since women were
excluded from the traditional system of Jewish education, they
could, paradoxically, leapfrog to modernization — or, in some
cases, assimilation — more easily than young men. This was a
trend that to some extent continued in the twentieth century.

Reports of such changes no longer reached Brańsk only in
vague and deflected ways; the shtetl was becoming positively
receptive to them. Even from the terse vignettes of life described
in the Yizkor Book, one can sense stirrings of a new consciousness and a new openness. By the end of the 1880s, monthly
journals and newspapers, such as the St. Petersburg paper
Hacofe (The Observer), began to reach Brańsk regularly. By the
1890s, there were a few individual subscribers to Jewish publications. Sometime around then, a traveling bookseller made his
appearance in Brańsk. He was a "tall, thin Jew with a short
beard," who came to town every few weeks and displayed his
wares in front of the synagogue. First he took out the books of
the Torah and commentaries. Only later, half in secret, did he
exhibit his secular wares — the novels for which he "already
had his customers." Fiction in Hebrew was still forbidden fruit,
as Hebrew was the sacred language, and using it for secular
writing was seen as a profanation.

The nature of Jewish schooling also began to change. Both the Jewish intelligentsia and sympathetic Polish commentators had been calling for reform of the *cheder* system for some time. "The first and absolute condition of achieving a higher degree of prosperity and morality in the Jewish communities," wrote Eliza Orzeszkowa, a well-known Polish writer, in 1882, "seems to be the abolishing of the denominational schools, or *cheders* — those columns supporting the fatal edifice of alienness, those seas of legends mixed with drops of truly religious teaching. Nobody can or should demand that Jewish children should be brought up in ignorance of their ancestors' faith. But let them learn it on par with children of other denominations, in a secular school, offering them many-sided instruction, from the lips of a teacher whose enlightenment and morality would be guaranteed by communal and governmental representatives."

In Brańsk, the first whiff of educational reform came around 1900, when a teacher offering instruction not only in Hebrew and Yiddish, but also in Russian and mathematics, arrived in the shtetl. It is hard to tell whether the choice of Russian rather than Polish was part of the Russification policy or simple happenstance. In any case, other secular teachers followed, and in the less Orthodox families it became fashionable to send sons and daughters to these modern pedagogues rather than to the traditional *melameds*. The Yizkor Book begins to mention "intelligent," "worldly," and "enlightened" youths, as if these were becoming desirable values.

As soon as opportunities for a fuller education opened up, the shtetl children responded with astonishing vigor. Among the first generation of the educated young, several achieved a high degree of success and distinction. The Yizkor Book speaks with particular fondness about Józef Chaim Heftman, "famous poet and belle-lettrist," who contributed to major Jewish journals in Poland and went on, after emigrating, to become the chairman of the journalists' union in Israel. The future writer apparently showed his talents early, although his proclivity for versifying caused consternation among the respectable citizens of Brańsk. There were attempts to stop the budding poet from indulging in such frivolous and morally dubious pursuits; luckily, one of the community elders wisely assured everyone that the boy "had written nothing that was a lie."

Amazingly, Brańsk at the turn of the century harbored even more radical personages. The Yizkor Book mentions one Judel, a secular teacher who was known to address secret meetings in the forest, during which he "explained world events to the workers in the light of the socialist spirit." It seems that Judel's discourses met with the disapproval of Chaim Beker, a Brańsker who thought that young people and workers should be taught "the theories of Marx about surplus value," and that only this hard-core knowledge was important. This exchange seems to have been part of a conflict between socialists and Communists, which, on a wider scale, was turning into a heated battle during that period. In the end, Judel was tactfully reproached by the rabbi, who thought it wasn't suitable for a teacher "to keep company with such a clique."

Secret meetings similar to the ones in Brańsk forests were taking place throughout the Polish territories and in Russia. The socialist movement was growing in power, and immediately fractioning as well. In Poland there was a Jewish socialist party called the Bund, founded in 1897 in Vilno, and a Polish Socialist Party, also begun in Vilno, in 1892, which attracted many Jewish members. The Polish-Jewish alliance in the socialist movement, vexed as it often proved to be, was the heir of the earlier Haskala-Enlightenment affiliation, and it was once again viewed with opprobrium by traditionalists of both groups.

The disaffections and sense of injustice that were the source of socialism's strength exploded in the Russian Revolution of 1905. In the Polish lands, the rebellion was steered largely by socialist parties. The first shots of the revolution were in fact fired close to Brańsk — in Białystok, in 1904. We do not know how many people took part in the fighting near Brańsk, but in Łódź, a textile manufacturing center, for which figures are available, 79 Jews, 55 Poles, and 17 Germans were killed during the first week of clashes — indicating the extent of multiethnic comradeship-in-arms possible at that moment.

In 1906, in an attempt to appease the revolutionaries, the tsar quickly issued a new constitution and established a parliament, the Duma. For Brańsk, this had one immediate and exotic effect: the introduction of universal male suffrage. Under the legislation, 60 Brańsk Jews were eligible to register to vote at the district post in Bielsk. Only 54 decided to take advantage of this new right, although the ride to Bielsk was free. The rest, the Yizkor Book speculates, were probably afraid to step forward, and therefore developed sudden, very bothersome colds.

One can sympathize with these half-dozen timid souls. In a time of upheaval, voting was yet another strange innovation thought up by fearsome officials. How would it be used? For what purposes? For one thing, voting was a delicate skill. In the Yizkor Book's recounting of the revolutionary events, there is a rare and irritable mention of Warsaw, where, according to the authors, Jewish voters unwisely chose an anti-Semitic candidate for the Duma, which "later led to the boycotts, and Jews already felt that they would be victims, on account of politics."

The failure of the 1905 revolution was, as usual, followed by fierce reprisals. Józef Chaim Heftman wrote a poem to express his unquenched sympathy for the imprisoned and the persecuted:

The canons murmur and rumble,
The holy pyre burns,
Forward, standard-bearing masses,
Brothers, do not spare your blood.

In Brańsk, one Jew gave his life to the cause, a delicate youth who showed great promise as a scholar until he was recruited to fight in Warsaw. Sent to Siberia in the aftermath of defeat, he returned to town years later but could not recover from his terrible experiences, and died soon afterward.

"And so the Jews of Brańsk," the Yizkor Book concludes, "learned what politics means." But 1905, of course, was only one stage of the lesson. With the coming of the twentieth century, the layers of religious, cultural, and social insulation protecting the shtetl from the outside world had been punctured. From then on, the history of the shtetl was a story of its increasing penetration by that world. Between 1905 and 1914, change was peaceful but subtly decisive: those were the years of the shtetl's meeting with modernity.

In the Jewish parts of Brańsk, public life gained new variety and stimulation. The Yizkor Book records, around that time, the creation of a library. This modest institution, located in the attic of a private house, was used by people of most classes and backgrounds. The clientele for novels was mostly female, and the works of Sholem Aleichem, who depicted shtetl life with vivid spontaneity and humor, were especially popular. Readers probably also came across the stories and essays of Y. L. Peretz, the dean of Yiddish writers in Warsaw, in whose later writing the shtetl already appears in a nostalgic and sentimental light, as a pastoral world of innocent goodness and piety.

There were other exciting developments. "From theaters they didn't know in Brańsk," the Yizkor Book observes. Still, in 1910 a group of youths "dared" to stage a Yiddish play, expressively entitled *Shmendryks* (Smart Alecks). Apparently the performance was a great success. A more permanent feature of the cultural scene was the phonograph, emitting its music through an enormous horn. During the summer, on their twilight walks, people stopped in front of the open window behind which this magical contraption stood, and listened to fashionable Yiddish songs. Occasionally, a mother whose son had emigrated discreetly wiped away a tear with her apron on hearing "Do Not Be Late with Mama's Letter."

But openness to the wide world had more profound effects: it shaped new kinds of lives — lives with enough movement, choices, and intersections with larger events to acquire the outlines of biography. In the Yizkor Book, one of the longest biographical sketches comes from the beginning of the century. It is the story of Lejb Jakub Freind, the son of a cantor and clearly a man of many parts and talents. Around 1900, Lejb Jakub studied in both well-known yeshivas and secular schools. He attended the Royal Conservatory of Music in Vilno, where he learned "the theory of singing," and started writing for Hebrew journals. He was also fascinated by astronomy, and so impressed important scientists in his field that they nominated him for membership in the Royal Astronomical Society. Freind received a diploma in engineering, but when World War I broke out he made his way to Shanghai, where his life took yet more unexpected turns. He was befriended by a community of Sephardic Jews, organized a *kahal* along Ashkenazic lines, started the first Jewish choir in Shanghai, opened two synagogues, and expedited the publication of Russian and Hebrew dictionaries. At the same time, he continued writing scientific articles, and in 1923 he had the singular experience of spending three days with Albert Einstein.

The culmination of Freind's social activism came during World War II, when he became involved with a most interesting personage: Chiune Sugihara, who has recently been rediscovered and hailed as the Japanese Oskar Schindler. During the war, Sugihara was the Japanese consul in the Russian town of Kovno. According to the Yizkor Book, it was none other than Lejb Jakub Freind who, with the help of the Japanese consul in Shanghai, first persuaded Sugihara to give transit visas to Russian Jews, which enabled them to escape territories occupied by Hitler. As a result, thousands of Jewish refugees flocked to Shanghai. Sugihara has long been a legendary figure among survivors from Kovno and elsewhere, whose lives were saved by his daring ploy — although in postwar Japan he became persona non grata for his deeds, and was rehabilitated only in the late 1980s. As for his Brańsk-born assistant, he did not escape wartime suffering after all. During a business trip to Manila, Freind was taken prisoner and interned in a Japanese concentration camp. He survived, and in 1947 emigrated once more, this time to the United States, where presumably he ended his days in a more peaceful fashion.

There were others like Lejb Jakub Freind, people who, on leaving the shtetl, plunged into the world with a hungry curiosity and appetite for experience, and who made startling leaps from their narrow backgrounds to great achievements. The collision of traditionalism with modernity can liberate great energy and perception. It would be misleading, however, to suggest that the shtetl in the first decades of the twentieth century was suddenly becoming a modern metropolis, or that everyone in it was embarking on worldly adventure. According to a Russian census of 1897, Brańsk at that time had more than four thousand inhabitants, of whom 58 percent were Jewish. Only about half of the Jews were registered as literate — a surprisingly low percentage, which perhaps did not take into account literacy in Hebrew or Yiddish. For most of the ordinary folk, the texture of life remained fundamentally religious and embedded in tradition, convention, and routine. The social divisions that mattered were still between the *sheyne Yidn* (the "pretty," or upper-class Jews), the *balebatim* (respectable, well-off Jews), the *balmelokhes* (artisans), and the *proste* — a word borrowed from Polish, meaning simple or primitive.

For these conventional members of the community, the significant events had less to do with socialist revolutions than, say, with the arrival, in 1907, of a new rabbi. This rabbi, Yehuda Szkop, was the first important Talmudic scholar to lead the Brańsk community, and he was to play a key role in the town's life. He also put Brańsk on the Jewish map by bringing in an entourage of talented young scholars and founding a yeshiva, which attracted students from far and wide.

The Yizkor Book notes the addition of another element to the community: the Hasidim. By the time a small cluster of these distinctively observant Jews arrived in Brańsk, Hasidism had become an integral part of most Eastern European shtetls. This movement, which eventually expanded into a worldwide phenomenon, originated as a schismatic sect at the end of the eighteenth century, at about the same time and in the same Polish province that saw the birth of Frankism. Hasidism, too, was founded by a prophetic, charismatic figure known as the Baal Shem Tov. His teachings, conveyed through simple parables and stories, combined mystical elements with an emphasis on the personal nature of belief. He assured his followers that everyone was capable of direct contact with God, and that layers of doctrine and years of study were unnecessary to achieving a holy state. Like many prophetic sects, Hasidism had ecstatic elements. It taught that God was to be worshiped not by self-abnegation but in joy and praise. The human needs for food, drink, pleasure, were to be honored and satisfied rather than denied or suppressed.

In the first part of the nineteenth century, Hasidism spread like wildfire through Eastern Europe. For obvious reasons, it appealed to the poor, the disaffected, the unlearned — the people who felt left out of the *kahal* hierarchies or who rebelled against the severities of traditional Jewish theology. For reasons just as obvious, Hasidism was condemned as heretical and fought tooth and claw by the *mitnagdim*, the learned Orthodox Jews.

However, by the time they came to Brańsk, the Hasidim had become, in an ironic reversal, the keepers of the Jewish tradition, of the fervent piety that was waning elsewhere. It was partly because of this that their arrival in Brańsk met with as much ambivalence as the coming of the Litvaks. Even today, former Brańsk Jews say that "nobody liked the Hasidim," for they were seen then as fanatical and old-fashioned even by shtetl standards. They prayed incessantly, and they wore the black caftans abandoned by other Jews for more modern dress. The Hasidim were also exceedingly poor: the Yizkor Book mentions that in their threadbare and much mended coats, they found winter weather hard to bear. There were probably no more than twenty of them, but even this small group included followers of several *tzaddiks*, or teachers. On holidays and special occasions, the Hasids traveled — sometimes great distances — to visit their teachers, whom they considered holy men. Many of these religious leaders had become rich from their followers' donations, and held court in imposing residences or compounds. The Hasids' relationship to their teachers was much like the relationship of some modern cultists to their gurus — worshipful, ecstatic, entranced. The *tzaddiks*, following the Baal Shem Tov's example, tended to speak in parables, and their acolytes hung on their every word, analyzed their exempla, and disseminated their wisdom among those who did not have the privilege of hearing the sage sayings directly. Sometimes during special feasts or in the transports of dance and prayer, men lifted the *tzaddik* onto their shoulders and carried him in processions through the streets.

In Brańsk, the Hasidim congregated in prayer houses of their own, where, according to their Yizkor Book, they listened to "fabulous tales" of "good Jews" that seemed never to run out. On the High Holy Days, the "inner joy" of Hasidic rituals was "impossible to describe"; perhaps the spirit that moved these ardent worshipers reminded the other Jews of Brańsk, despite all their aloofness, of some dimension of belief they had come to miss.

⤳   ⤳   ⤳

This was the shtetl on the eve of World War I: amphibious, divided between settled old ways and the challenging promise of the new. The war itself was heralded in Brańsk by mobilization notices from the Russian authorities. There followed, in rapid succession, "sad scenes," as women said goodbye to sons and husbands; news from the front, of the dead, the wounded, the soldiers taken prisoner; and the press of refugees from towns closer to the front.

For Jews, these events were abrupt and confusing enough, but for Poles the situation was, if anything, even more uncertain. As the powers that had partitioned Poland declared war on each other, the Poles recognized that this was their best chance in over a century to win independence — if they played their cards right. What that meant was a matter of dispute, and two contending leaders — the rightist nationalist Roman Dmowski and the socialist Józef Piłsudski — pursued opposing and hostile aims. Piłsudski's strategy was to try to tilt the balance of power, initially against the Russians, by forming Polish legions in Galicia on the side of the Central Powers, which included Austria and Germany. He also tried to form a Jewish fighting force, but this attempt failed. Piłsudski demanded maximum concessions from the Central Powers, but sabotaged the creation of a Polish army under their sponsorship. After the conflicts between these tactical allies grew more acute, Piłsudski was imprisoned by the Germans in 1917, and his legions were disbanded and partly interned in camps and prisons.

In Brańsk, the Russian army arrived first, bringing with it Cossacks and Jewish soldiers — "Jews with beards," the Yizkor Book notes, to highlight the novelty and the incongruity. Alter Trus (clearly the author of this part of the text) recounts how the community organized a kosher kitchen for these guests. The Russian army was ostensibly friendly, but civilian Jews nevertheless felt threatened. The commandant was a "real pogromist," and warned the Jewish townspeople against betrayals to the Germans. This must have seemed quite sinister, for everyone had heard that "unfounded accusations" of such betrayals were common in the regions closer to the German sphere. Soon enough, a group of homeless Jewish refugees traveling to Brańsk on a peasant's cart were intercepted by Russian soldiers and accused of sabotage. They were about to be given a hasty trial when Rabbi Szkop intervened and managed to gain a reprieve for them. He did not succeed in doing so in the case of a man who "went mad" and actually cut telephone wires.

In fact, in the privacy of their own community, the Jewish population was divided into two camps: those who supported the Russians and those who cheered German victories. Moreover, this was an exceptional moment when the Poles were similarly divided, and were loath to support either of their warring enemies.

As the Germans gained the upper hand in the area, the Cossack soldiers got ready to set fire to Brańsk before retreating. Again Rabbi Szkop intervened. He instantly collected money to distribute among the Cossacks and, in a crucial gesture, offered his own watch to an officer who had taken a fancy to it. Clearly, the Cossack officer was a man of rather childish impulses, but by reacting quickly, Rabbi Szkop saved Brańsk from yet another conflagration.

This was in September 1915, and here the Yizkor Book comes close to something like dramatic irony. Within hours of the Russian retreat, a woman's cry of *"Mazel tov!"* was heard in the street. Only minutes later, the town was overrun by "Germans with murderous eyes and red, overfed faces." It is quite evident where Alter Trus's sympathies lay.

The Germans remained in Brańsk for thirty-eight months, and their occupation was brutal. They rounded up people for forced labor outside of town, and those who could not keep up with the pace of work were severely beaten. The army requisitioned flour and other food supplies from merchants, making and dispensing its own bread — which apparently made people ill, and may have caused several deaths. In addition, scarlet fever and typhoid epidemics broke out, striking a double fear in people's hearts and causing those who fell sick to conceal their condition. The rumor was that the unfortunates who were discovered by the Germans were taken to the hospital and poisoned.

In the meantime, the German command appointed its own "communal" representatives, who helped select people for forced labor. Alter Trus bitterly but plausibly asserts that, as usual, the poor were the first to go. When men became scarce, women were sent off. Some of these young recruits deserted and returned to Brańsk, often in sorry physical shape. Trus proudly admits to having been a deserter himself no less than five times!

As shortages of food became more severe, smuggling flourished. Alter Trus suspects that this was mostly perpetrated by wealthy Jews, some of whom had the protection of the German officers. Murmurs of dissatisfaction at the unfair distribution of wartime burdens rose to the level of protests. However, as 1917 approached, and with it the rumblings of revolution in Russia, the occupying army became less bold. The selections for forced labor stopped; Jewish political parties started up before the war were revived; the library books were brought out of hiding places. On November 11, 1918, the Germans abruptly packed up and left the reduced and impoverished town.

This was clearly a response to news from Warsaw, and to the war's strange denouement. Toward the end, the Austrian and German armies occupying Poland, perhaps knowing that their defeat on the western front was near, seemed simply to give up and walk away from the battlefields. In the meantime, Józef Piłsudski, newly released from his German prison, walked into Warsaw, where he did not so much seize power as step into a power vacuum. On November 11 a government was formed in Lublin, with Piłsudski as the chief of the still half-wishful Polish state. The rebirth of an independent Poland was declared by fiat, while the three imperial powers were busy with more urgent affairs.

For Jews living in the Polish territories, these events meant that they would once again have to adjust to an altered social and political landscape. The Yizkor Book concludes the chapter on the Great War with an almost reflexively pessimistic coda: "New sufferings are coming for the Brańsk Jews under Poland's governments." But the fatalism is surely too formulaic. Although the interval between the two world wars was destined to be full of turbulence for Polish Jewry, it was also a time of great expansion and development, of bold political activism and cultural efflorescence, of almost inexplicable acceleration of change. It was as if the Spirit of the Time floated above Poland, murmuring, *This is a new epoch* — and the dormant Jewish folk responded by shaking itself into an entirely new wakefulness. The streets of Brańsk were still unpaved, indoor plumbing was rare, and electricity had come to only a few selected streets, but even the most remote little towns suddenly turned into hotbeds of discussion, creativity, organization, impassioned conflict. On more levels than one, an era had come to an end, and a new one had begun.

4

Shtetl:
Between the Wars

"Yes, I grew up on this street," Irena Jabłonowska says. "But all the houses were burned down during the war. Mostly Jews lived here — there were only a few Polish families. When I walk down the street, I remember exactly who lived where. The Shapiros, the Gottliebs, Menda Goldwasser, Tykocki, and in the next house, that man . . . what was his name, the one who did business with Dad."

With the interwar decades we enter the region of living, if distant, memory. And precisely because it is distant, I am touched by the exactness of Irena Jabłonowska's recall. One does not remember the names of people and the houses they lived in for this long unless they registered deeply on one's consciousness, unless they mattered.

"We grew up together," she says. "I knew Yiddish. Not well, but enough. When they wanted to say something in Yiddish to each other in the shops, someone would say, 'She understands everything.' I grew up here, after all."

Irena Jabłonowska lives in a modest rural house that belonged to her family before World War II. Her father was one of the more prosperous Poles in town, the owner of a business that combined a carpet warehouse, a butcher shop, and a tobacco shop. But wealth, in the period of later Communist ascendancy in Brańsk, turned out to be a dubious advantage. Today Irena Jabłonowska is a small woman in her seventies, with a mild oval face and warm eyes, soft-spoken and soft-moving. She is serving tea and cookies to Zbigniew Romaniuk and me, and reminiscing. Zbyszek, as so often, is taking notes. Now and then, one says something that startles the other. Zbyszek discreetly hints at a mésalliance between a Jewish man and a Polish woman which took place in Brańsk some seventy years ago. "No, no, no," Jabłonowska protests, inhaling with surprise. "Yes," Zbyszek says. "And do you know who that lady's grandchild is?" "What are you saying? It's the first I've heard of this!" Jabłonowska says. To them, this is live gossip, as current as if it had happened yesterday. They are both remarkably at home in Brańsk's vanished world.

An affair between a Pole and a Jew before the war was so rare as to have shock value even today. As rare as marriages between the *szlachta* and the peasantry, cross-caste alliances were still surrounded by a taboo. In Warsaw at that time, Polish-Jewish unions were becoming almost acceptable in some circles, but in the shtetl they were seen as utterly scandalous.

But other kinds of contacts were becoming possible, much more so than before. Irena Jabłonowska went to school with Jewish girls — although not boys. The boys still attended *cheder*, and so were often behind in their knowledge of Polish. Under Polish laws enacted after World War I, everyone had to go to school of some kind, although peasant kids usually did not last beyond the fourth grade; they were needed on the farms. Irena's sister attended a Jewish high school in Białystok named Seligman's Academy because places in other schools were scarce. Irena remembers her sister's Jewish friends, and recalls the students' nervousness when they all traveled together to take their exams. Surely at other times as well — on the way to school and over lunch — the young girls gossiped, exchanged stories about their families, perhaps shared their romantic dreams. Surely, while discussing the same books and life at school, they were becoming somewhat understandable to each other.

Yet the barriers between them were still strong. Jewish people came to Irena's family's house on business errands, or to have drinks with her father. Her school friends dropped by too, but these visits posed delicate problems. The girls, she remembers, would not touch food that wasn't kosher — although the boys, more rebellious, sometimes asked her mother for a slice of ham. But the girls, no, never. And they knew so little about each other's faith. In school there were two sets of religion classes, one for the Catholics and one for the Jews. They never entered each other's houses of worship, and Irena did not like to discuss religion or other troublesome topics with her Jewish friends. "After all, one grew up here," she says. "And Daddy said one should be polite to everyone. The boys fought with each other — you know how it is when people live together." But the girls kept their good manners and their discretion.

And so they knew each other through proximity and familiarity, but not through frank exchanges or intimacy. Irena Jabłonowska saw Jewish weddings in back yards of people's houses, but she was never invited to one. She remembers how tender Jewish families were if one of their members fell ill. And they dressed so well. She thinks that Jewish people somehow "had it easier" than the Poles, that they worked less hard. But then she recalls Jews who did heavy physical labor after all. When I ask if she thinks that Jews were richer, she says, pensively, "I'm not sure . . . They also had their poor ones, oy, they did."

Does anyone in Bransk miss their presence? "One gets accustomed to people," she says simply. "I feel their absence." Of course there are others who feel something very different, although they may not say so — the forgetfulness of indifference, or even relief.

ॐ   ॐ   ॐ

In Brańsk, the call of independence was taken up as soon as it was sounded. During the night of November 11, 1918, immediately following the installation of a temporary Polish government, a meeting was held during which a transitional civil citizens' committee and a citizens' militia were established. Both bodies included Jewish members. Alter Trus must have been among the militia appointed to guard a valuable food warehouse, because he recalls a Jewish woman — undoubtedly unaccustomed to such sights — who kept pleading with him, "Alter, be careful with your gun."

On November 12, two prominent Poles from the district rode into Brańsk on horseback to make a concise announcement: "Gentlemen, we now have our own Poland." For the Poles, this must have been a thrilling sentence. The restoration of independence after 125 years of statelessness was a most momentous event which elicited outbursts of unparalleled patriotic enthusiasm. For the minority groups, the unexpected turn of history had more problematic implications. Indeed, independence was ushered in in a climate of sublimated ethnic tensions.

Although the first impulse in Brańsk was apparently to include Jews in the fledgling new order, the Jewish population viewed the unfolding developments with wariness and fear. There were good reasons for this — if only the total confusion of the next several months. The Podlasie area was part of a buffer zone negotiated by the Germans for their retreat, and as their army made its slow trek back to Germany, Brańsk was again the site of skirmishes, killings, and arson. For a while, banditry and robbery were rife and country roads dangerous to pass. Several Jews were captured and beaten on suspicion of loyalty to the Germans. A Jewish tailor in town was assaulted by Polish youths who were about to subject him to the humiliation of cutting off his beard. However, two bystanders — one Jewish, one Polish — set upon the attackers, giving them a beating instead. From then on, there were no beard-cutting incidents in Brańsk. But such episodes, and worse excesses as well, were occurring throughout eastern Poland, perpetrated by the Hallerczyki — soldiers who had fought in Polish legions on the side of the Allies, under the leadership of the ultraconservative General Haller.

The brother of Alter Trus was arrested for possession of a Bundist archive; however, in exchange for two liters of vodka, he was freed. For five liters of vodka, the town's socialists received permission to open a Bundist club. This kind of impulsive governance was not uncharacteristic of the Polish temperament, or of the new Polish officials, who were hardly used to doing things by the book. Particularly in small towns like Brańsk, much depended on personal caprice.

On the larger scale, the breakup of three empires left Eastern Europe in a geopolitical shambles, with dozens of nationalities, ethnic groups, and their self-appointed representatives making competing territorial and historical claims. In 1919, the international community convened the Paris Conference, whose unenviable task was to forge the geographical shape of new states, contain incipient conflicts in the splintered region, and establish ground rules for the treatment of minorities. The resolutions and agreements reached at the conference were ratified in Versailles in June 1919.

In the months before the Paris Conference, tensions among potentially affected groups began to rise throughout the ethnically mixed territories. In Białystok, representatives of the Jewish community proposed that the city and the surrounding region should become part of Lithuania rather than Poland, because this would put Jews in a better numerical position. The suggestion was met with outrage by Polish politicians. In the same year, all the Jewish congregations in Poland gathered for a meeting in Białystok, to discuss such issues and arrive at a concerted view. In Brańsk, five parties had participated in the election to choose candidates to the meeting; the Bund won.

At the Paris Conference itself, the international arbiters were confronted with a mind-boggling number of delegations, positions, claims, and counterclaims as groups and nations jockeyed for territory, rights, and redress of historical injustices. Among the Jews, one interesting division arose between Eastern European representatives and Western European advisers. The Eastern European delegations were made up mostly of Zionists who, besides the aim of obtaining a Jewish state, wanted a large measure of political and cultural autonomy within the new countries. The Western European Jews — whose fate was not, admittedly, immediately at stake — encouraged the Eastern European delegates to adopt a more limited agenda of civil rather than minority rights, modeled on their own accommodations with the countries in which they lived.

The Polish delegation was also split, between an uncompromisingly nationalist faction led by Dmowski and the Piłsudski camp, with its socialist origins, its liberal stance on many issues, and its acceptance of far-reaching autonomy for various ethnic groups. The Piłsudski contingent was recognized as legitimate, and ultimately Poland, like all the new Eastern European countries, signed the Minorities Treaty, which guaranteed full rights and freedoms, as well as cultural autonomy, to all the nationalities within its boundaries.

The new Poland was not destined to remain peaceful for long. In the spring of 1920, Bolshevik armies started to amass on the eastern frontier. Foreseeing clear danger, Piłsudski — in alliance with a Ukrainian leader, Petlyura, who had been defeated by Lenin — launched a preventive strike on the Russians by marching into Kiev. This was the beginning of another politically intricate embroilment, which came to be known as the Polish-Soviet War. In Brańsk, which had been part of Russia until very recently, the position of the Jewish community was still ambiguous. According to the Yizkor Book, views were divided between those who sided unequivocally with the Polish cause, and others who felt that Brańsk did not really belong to Poland, and therefore should not be required to supply soldiers to the Polish army. In the first glimpse of real public conversation between Poles and Jews, the text quotes "Catholics" who argued, "Your Itzhak and Moshe were born in the same year as my Staszek and Franek, so they should all serve together in the army." A simple point, but one that indicates a human recognition that both Polish and Jewish families had sons who might have to share the same fate. In the army itself, however, Polish-Jewish relations sometimes turned sour. In an infamous incident of the Polish-Soviet War, Jewish officers were interned at Jabłonna Camp in the summer of 1920 because of a general suspicion of Jewish disloyalty. The episode caused a great scandal and was protested by Jewish deputies in the Sejm. The officers were released in September.

At first Piłsudski was unsuccessful in his foray, and the Russian army launched a counteroffensive into Poland. The front passed through Brańsk in the late days of July, causing total havoc. The Polish authorities fled Brańsk; a people's militia was formed in which Jews were "properly represented"; the "Red soldiers" proceeded with their work of rape and robbery. A battle followed, which the Polish side lost and in which one Jewish man was lightly wounded. The Poles once again fled, leaving their fallen comrades on the streets of Brańsk. The Russian army occupied the town, and a Soviet commissar was placed in charge. The relationship of the Bolsheviks to Brańsk's population was not clear. Certainly, they would have considered the Poles their first enemy. They appointed a Jewish man as the head of their militia, and as was their time-honored practice, they commandeered informers who "checked in bakers' stoves to see what's baking" — that is, snooped around in order to report any irregularities to the new rulers. The authors of the Yizkor Book speak of such people with distaste.

It was the Red Army's progress through shtetls like Brańsk that gave rise to the stories of Isaac Babel — stories that record, with a restrained lyricism, the powerful, mercurial emotionalism of Cossack soldiers, their casual violence, their utter habituation to bloodshed and death, and the dignity and fatalism of shtetl Jews. In the Yizkor Book account of the first Russian occupation, one can discern some of the Isaac Babel atmosphere, and also hints of a shared Polish and Jewish plight. The commissar was a man with a sarcastic sense of humor, and at meetings Jews and Poles alike were targets of his jokes. The Yizkor Book's authors remember a "Catholic man" who questioned the commissar about selling food to the army for worthless money, which in turn would lead to shortages. "We'll bring you everything, including harsh troubles," the commissar replied. In response to young Jewish women who asked whether it was fair for them to have no cows while the peasants had two, the commissar retorted, "Have you ever had a cow? No? Good, then you'll still have no cow." In these crude quips we can hear the sound of a new kind of power — cheerfully brazen, populist, carelessly capricious. It is the sound of Soviet-style Communism, its signal tone, which was destined to become so familiar to everyone in Eastern Europe in later decades.

Within a few months, luck dramatically turned for the Poles. In their counteroffensive march, the Red Army managed to advance as far as Warsaw, but there, in an episode known in Polish history as the Miracle on the Vistula, the heavily outnumbered Polish troops (some of them still armed with scythes) managed to encircle and rout the enemy. This astonished everybody, including Lenin. In Brańsk, as the Red soldiers beat a hasty retreat, a number of Jews decided to join them in their flight. A handful of Jews later returned to Brańsk, but most remained in the Soviet Union for the rest of their lives.

The reentry of the Polish army into Brańsk was accompanied by more chaos. Jewish men were once again collared into hard labor. Two brothers from a nearby village and their sister's fiancé were murdered by Polish soldiers. It is not clear whether these were acts of anti-Semitic violence, political vengefulness, or sheer criminality.

It was only after the signing of the Treaty of Riga with the Bolsheviks in March 1921, ending hostilities, that something like normality returned. On March 17 a new constitution was announced. This document was modeled on the constitution of France's Third Republic, although it went further in providing a social "safety net." Among its surprising clauses were provisions to abolish hereditary and class privileges and titles and to ensure protection against abuses of children and women. The minorities were entitled to retain their religion, language, and cultural character, and were guaranteed equal citizenship rights.

Such were the principles, and the best intentions. But in Poland, as throughout Europe, the Spirit of the Time was called,

above all, nationalism. Polish politics in the interwar era to a
large extent revolved around the issue of nationality — and of
nationalities. Like almost all the new states created from the dis-
integrating empires, the new Poland was a patchwork of ethnic
groups. According to a 1921 census, ethnic Poles comprised
only 69.2 percent of the population. Ukrainians, at 14.3 percent, were the largest minority; Jews, who constituted less
than 8 percent of the population, were the second in size,
but undoubtedly the first in impact and importance. There were
also sizable groups of Germans and Belarusians.

At the same time, after more than a century of partitions, one
of the first questions of Polish politics was the question of identity. Just what was this new Poland? What kind of a state,
nation, country, culture should it become? Was Polishness
defined by citizenship and allegiance to the state or by inherited
ethnicity? The main axis of conflict on such questions — as in
Polish life altogether — ran between the main political groups
that were already present at the creation: the ideologically
hybrid centrist movement called Sanacja (Restoration), led by
Marshal Piłsudski, who remained the head of state until 1922;
the conservative faction, which included the National Democracy Party, or Endecja, with its later, radically rightist off-
shoots; and the Christian Democracy Party. In addition, there
was an important left wing, with the socialists playing the most
significant role and exercising great influence over the trade
unions. The socialists supported Piłsudski until the late 1920s.

All of these camps had definite views about the role of
minority groups in Polish life and identity. So did the minorities themselves. Alongside the Polish parties, there was a plethora
of minority parties, also divided into left, right, and center. For
a while, at the initiative of a Zionist leader, the minority parties
formed a national minorities bloc in parliament, but the coali-

tion was short-lived. In the new Poland, neither the preoccupation with ethnic identity nor the conflicts caused by clashing aspirations was limited to the Jews. Ukrainians, for example, had a strong separatist movement, which sometimes resorted to acts of sabotage and terrorism, and which was the target of harsh reprisals. In southeastern Poland, where the Ukrainian population was concentrated, violent encounters with Poles were not uncommon.

There is no doubt, however, that in the interwar period Polish politics became increasingly obsessed with the "Jewish question." The nature of that question was perceived differently than before; the imagery, the very formulation, of Jewishness changed in a fundamental way. Jews were still the main Other, the Polish alter ego, but this Otherness was no longer primarily religious or caste-based or even cultural. Instead, it had become political and ideological. In the new Polish nation, the Jews began to be seen as another nation, one whose character was utterly distinct from Polish identity. Jews were becoming, then, not so much a part — no matter how loved or denigrated — of the symbolic and social entity that was Poland, but an entity unto themselves, which was experienced as somehow foreign, and which could be mentally detached or expelled from the symbolic universe of a self-contained Polish state.

Even given this reinscription of Jewishness in modern terms, there was still a spectrum of attitudes toward the Jews in Polish society. In the formal political arena, Piłsudski's approach to the presence of a distinct Jewish subculture continued to be basically liberal and open-minded. He was not averse to a multicultural conception of the state, in which the minorities could retain a considerable degree of cultural and institutional autonomy. Indeed, he initially wanted to create a Commonwealth of Three Nations, which would hark back to the first Polish Commonwealth and include Polish, Ukrainian, and Lithuanian sectors in a federation. His attempts to do this failed, but Piłsudski was considered friendly enough to the Jews to be affectionately nicknamed "the Jewish Grandpa." He supposedly said that he would be ashamed to be a Pole if pogroms ever occurred in his country.

The dyed-in-the-wool socialists, who increasingly distanced themselves from Piłsudski, were the inheritors of universalist Enlightenment notions about the state. While they did not think there was anything intrinsically non-Polish about Jewishness, they deplored Jewish aspirations to a separate national identity and demanded a commitment to class, rather than ethnic, solidarity. This had its ironies, since Polish socialists were not immune to patriotic impulses themselves.

It was the Endecja that espoused an officially anti-Semitic agenda. As it happened, this movement was strongly anti-German as well, but anti-Semitism became the more salient element of its philosophy. The Endeks, as the adherents of the movement were called, were not only vehemently patriotic but ethnically chauvinistic — that is, they thought Poland was defined by something like an essential Polish character or spirit. Jewishness, in their belief system, was seen not only as alien but as intrinsically inimical to that spirit. In the 1920s these were marginal views, but during the thirties the Endecja became more vocally and virulently anti-Semitic.

Unfortunately, it was the Endecja, rather than the other political groups, that in the second decade of independence gained ascendancy in Poland and captured the popular imagination. The increasing dominance of this rightist movement can be traced to several causes. There was the instability of Poland's borders in both west and east, which led to a hardening of defensive nationalism. But the most important reason was a severe economic crisis, which deepened with the Great Depression. As everywhere in Europe, widespread joblessness and poverty stoked extremist and fanatical tendencies. In Poland these tendencies were given additional impetus by old prejudices and new statistical realities. In the twenties and thirties, the preponderant part of Poland's industrial economy was owned and managed by German and Jewish entrepreneurs — who of course also came in for a disproportionate amount of resentment.

ꝛ   ꝛ   ꝛ

Still, the beginnings were promising. Life in Brańsk returned to stability after the Polish-Soviet War, despite continuing episodes of highway banditry. The town had once again been devastated by looting and burning, but now the rebuilding began. For the Jewish neighborhoods, that meant reviving the traditional trades and crafts and reopening shops and stalls, many of which were operated by women. Jews reaped the first fruits of emigration, as the Brańsk associations in New York, set up at the end of the nineteenth century, came to the aid of their distressed relatives, helping greatly in the new start-up phase.

Jack Rubin was a young boy then, and he remembers the times as not bad, not at all bad. I meet Jack in his house in Baltimore, where he has lived for several decades. There is a group of Jewish survivors from Brańsk in that city, carrying on some of their old ways in their big, comfortable suburban homes, in their comfortable lives, with sufficient money, American fashions, and cars. Most of them have done very well in the new country after the terrible years of their tribulations, and so has Jack. He is retired now, but the successful wholesale business in inexpensive clothing he ran for many years can be seen, with some stretch of the imagination, as a kind of transposition of his

old family business in Brańsk, which involved raising and selling large quantities of geese.

Jack is a short, sturdily built man in his early eighties who
still moves with energetic briskness. He speaks, in Polish and in
English, with about the same degree of accent and quirky into-
nation. "By us, it was at least ten to twelve thousand geese," he
remembers proudly. "The fatter they are, the more you can
make on it." After all these years and all his experiences, Jack
still comes into a kind of focus when he talks about the family
goose farm. He recalls details of sixty-five-year-old transactions, the journeys he made to sell the fowl, the secrets of
poultry farming. There is relish and pleasure in remembering,
but also the sense that it was absolutely real. That was life, it
was Jack's life.

Jack's ancestors had lived in Brańsk for many generations;
one of his grandfathers was a cloth dyer. They were nicknamed
"Shimshuki" by the Poles, probably because of an early Shimon
in the family. Jack's mother was very religious, his father less so
— he put on *tefillin* for a few minutes a day, but that was about
it. Jack had a brother and a sister; four other children had died
in the scarlet fever epidemic during World War I.

The business itself had a complicated history of rivalries,
takeovers, and buyouts, but when Jack, who was born in 1913,
was growing up, it was thriving. By then, Jews were allowed to
own land, and his parents had bought "quite a few acres," which
they signed over to Jack and his brother when they came of age.
On their land the Rubins also raised other poultry, and their
fowl were shipped as far as Warsaw, and to Germany as well.
Jack made regular trips to the capital, where he had his connections and used a few tricks of the trade in order to get favorable
gradings for his geese. He smoked impressive cigarettes, which
raised his stature in the eyes of his prospective clients.

Jack went to a *cheder* and had a private tutor who taught him Polish. His parents spoke Polish in public and Yiddish at home, although a lot of older people "didn't know a word of Polish." He remembers relations with the Poles as unstrained. "By us, it was not hatred," he says. "With the people from our shtetl, we didn't see hatred." The Rubins employed several Poles in their business, and Jack played with Polish children on the street. He was a physically active boy, one of three Jewish kids to make the town's volleyball team, which also had adult players on it, including a priest. He took part in the bicycle races during Independence Day celebrations. One year, he came in second. The next year, he is convinced he came in first but was given second prize. He still remembers how hurt he was. Was he cheated of the first prize because he was Jewish? He thinks so. But still, physical prowess in teenage boys' society was the surest ticket to acceptance.

After he finished his *cheder* schooling, the family business became the center of young Jack's life. But there were also other activities. The family had a phonograph. Plays and movies started coming to town. Jack remembers a Ukrainian troupe of midget actors who brought a play to Brańsk called *The Converted Jewess*. Jack himself took part in an amateur production of a play called *Gott, Mensch, Teivel*, in which, he remembers smilingly, he played the Devil. His sister was part of a musical group that performed at parties and weddings and accompanied silent movies. She played the violin, and some Polish boys played mandolins.

The Yizkor Book, too, records the burgeoning of cultural life in Brańsk: performances of such plays as *The Dybbuk* and *The Village Boy*, which took place in a hall near the mill by the river; numerous talks, lectures, and courses in various subjects. There was a species of religious orators who were extremely popular among Jewish communities and often visited Brańsk — although one such preacher was cold-shouldered out of town after he gave a sermon condescending to the "ordinary masses." Less controversial were orchestral performances and cantors' concerts; both Jack Rubin and Irena Jabłonowska remember that the cantors' performances were wonderful, and were attended by Poles as well as Jews.

And on that miraculous record player, listeners could hear songs that were a demonstration of subliminal mingling of cultures — all-Yiddish songs permeated by the pastoral imagery and melancholy moods typical of Polish Romantic poetry. Shtetl crooners may have sung along with verses like these, from "Zu Majn Gelibter":

> Do you want me, oh my darling,
> To declare my love today?
> Come with me, then, to the field,
> To the field please come!
> In the field we won't be hindered,
> In the field on the hill's mount,
> There I'll confess all my secrets,
> Secrets of the heart.

Or a strophe from "Di Sun Is Fargangen," by the renowned self-taught composer Mordecai Gebirtig:

> Twilight falls, the sun is waning,
> I lie in the meadow, alone and sad,
> And remember my youth — those happy years —
> And my thoughts return to that.

Popular culture was one sign of modernity. But even people's personal styles were getting revamped. All of a sudden, Jewish women sloughed off their wigs and black dresses and started following the latest fashion trends in Warsaw — or even Berlin! In photographs from that time, young women strike sexy poses, with cocked heads and flirtatious eyes — quite a change from the demure and matronly image cultivated before. People took to furnishing their houses in the modern style and cleaning them once every few weeks instead of once a year. The center of town got covered with paving, and a tiled *mikvah* was built. Something like progress had come to Brańsk.

Progress — and politics. While Polish politics was developing its trends and conflicts, Jewish political life in the 1920s presented a spectacle of bewildering abundance and variety. Parties covering every inch of the political spectrum, clubs, organizations, and other formations — all of them represented in the smallest shtetls — sprouted on the Polish-Jewish landscape with lush prodigality. There was a very large Zionist movement, itself splintered into dozens of subparties, from the Left Poalei Zion to the Right Poalei Zion, the Zeirei Zion and Dror, not to speak of Betar, which was the military wing of revisionist Zionism. Then there were the big religious parties: the mainstream Mizrahi and the conservative Agudah Israel, which emerged from the Hasidic dynasties. There were leftist groups, from the Mapai workers' movement to the Jewish Communist Party and the socialist Bund, which continued to play a significant role in Jewish political life and consciousness. In addition, all of the major parties worked hard to gain the loyalty of young people and prepare them for their version of the future. There were organizations of *chalutzim*, or pioneers, who had their world headquarters in Warsaw, numerous sports and exercise clubs, and youth clubs of all sorts.

The extravagant pluralism can be viewed as a sign of healthful vitality or fragmentation, but either way, it bespoke the ebul-

lient self-confidence of Polish Jewry, even in the face of growing anti-Semitism. Whatever their long-term insecurities and
immediate fears, Polish Jews were certainly not driven to cam-
ouflage or silence. If political behavior is any gauge, they were
not timid about proclaiming their views or projecting their
presence in the public arena. Neither were they afraid to expose
their difference from the majority culture, or to air the differences among themselves.

The proliferation of political parties is often a phenomenon
of new countries — post-Franco Spain or, for that matter, post-
1989 Eastern Europe — in which the alignment of interests, and
even the categories of political thinking, have not yet crystal-
lized. For Polish Jewry, newly sprung into political participation, the creation of multiple parties was partly a way of explor-
ing new forms of public identity, and identification. Who were
Jews going to be in this new era, and how were they were going
to define their interests? How were they going to balance allegiance to the tribe with loyalty to the state, and where did they
fit in — if at all — on the national map? If religious faith was no
longer an absolute, what constituted Jewishness — as opposed
to, for example, Polishness? What did it mean, in other words,
to be a Jew in Poland, or a Polish Jew?

The dozens of parties and subparties were, in effect, the collective expressions of different proposals and postures vis-à-vis
such questions. There is no doubt that the main thrust of Jewish
thinking in the interwar years was culturally separatist. Aside
from a small group of assimilated or converted Jews, and the
convinced Communists, who wanted to dissolve all national
attachments, the great majority of Polish Jews were intent on
preserving a specific, separate identity and on retaining a fair
degree of institutional autonomy. This position was not without its quandaries. On the autonomous model, what were the

ties that bound Jews to the new Polish polity? Were Jewish obligations only formal — taxes, obedience to the law, military service — or were they a matter of deeper affinities or common interests? Now that they were fully enfranchised, in what sense were Jews living in Polish lands going to become citizens of the new state?

The major fissure on such issues ran between the Zionists, who believed that emigration to Palestine was the only noble and logical option for Jews who wanted to achieve full freedom and selfhood, and all the parties that believed Jews could best attain their true identity in the Diaspora. The revisionist Zionist movement, led by the charismatic Vladimir Jabotinsky, gained hundreds of thousands of adherents in Poland in the late twenties and thirties, especially among the young. It systematically prepared its members for life in Palestine by organizing experimental *kibbutzim* in Poland; its Betar branch trained people in military skills, in anticipation of the possible need for self-defense. Over the years, thousands of Polish Zionists emigrated to Palestine in successive *aliyahs*.

The Diaspora nonassimilationists included the major religious parties, which wanted to maintain the traditional Jewish way of life in Poland — where, after all, it had found fertile soil. At the other end of the spectrum, the socialist Bund also believed in solving problems *du,* or "right here," where Diaspora Jewry had its authentic existence and its problems. The Bund's ideology was, of course, anti-traditionalist and secular, but the party was intent on preserving Jewish culture and institutions, and supported the use of Yiddish in schools, in the press, and in literature.

The multiplicity of views may have mirrored actual needs, but one also has the irresistible impression that the fineness of ideological hair-splitting reflected the legacy of Talmudic thought, in which every shade of belief, every slant of interpretation, had to be accounted for and defended. The disputatiousness of it all, the heat and the argumentative energy, constituted a dynamic political education. Much of the future leadership of Israel was first tried and tested in the Polish political fires. Menachem Begin began his political career in Betar, Ben-Gurion in the Mapai. Shimon Peres and Itzhak Shamir came from Poland as well. But the diversity also had its price: it led to divisiveness and sometimes to acute animosities within the Jewish community. The factions quarreled, splintered, accused each other of betrayal and Jewish anti-Semitism. Not infrequently, members of competing parties disrupted each other's meetings and got into bloody street brawls.

Such skirmishes were reenacted, although in a more subdued fashion, in the central forum of the Polish Sejm. There were enough Jewish deputies in this body to form the Jewish Parliamentary Circle. Some of these representatives gained fame as diplomats and orators, and they spoke about their constituents' concerns with passion and directness. But the members of the circle included deputies of many parties, who were divided on the proposals they wanted the Sejm to adopt and the tactics they thought appropriate in dealing with Polish politicians. The powerful Agudah preferred a strategy of polite negotiation and of trying to gain concessions through personal contacts and compromise. In contrast with other parties, Agudah declared its loyalty to the Polish state openly. The Zionists and the Bundists, however, accused the religious Agudah deputies of compromising "Jewish honor" and referred to them as *shtadlanim* — the old term for the lobbyists at pre-partition Polish Sejms, but in this derogatory usage meaning, roughly, Uncle Toms. The Agudah, in turn, retorted that the role of the *shtadlanim* had been perfectly honorable. Not surprisingly, the Polish government preferred to deal with these less adversarial deputies and, for example, supported schools managed under Agudah auspices more readily than those run by other parties. But within the Jewish Parliamentary Circle, the question of how much allegiance was owed to the state was a perpetually rankling one, pitting, in one instance, Zionists from the former Russian territories against those from Galicia. The constant set-tos may not have been all that productive, but they indicate that, despite the undoubted strains of anti-Semitism in the Sejm, the Jewish deputies did not feel obligated to present a united front, and felt free to bring forth their demands in bold and sometimes radical terms.

In Brańsk alone, in the 1920s, there were no less than fifteen Jewish political groups: six major parties, several youth organizations under party sponsorship, and some small-fry splinter groups. The Zionists and the Agudah predominated, but the Bund was also influential. In addition, there were a number of Communists and a Komsomol cell for young people. The Communist Party was illegal in Poland at the time, on the grounds that it presented a danger to Polish sovereignty because of its close contacts with the Russian state. However, for understandable reasons, Communism, with its internationalist slogans, attracted Jewish followers. This was true in Brańsk, where the total number of Jewish Communists was small, but larger than among the Poles. The rest of the Jewish community kept their distance from these radical idealists, and even today Brańsk survivors speak of them brusquely, and in a sort of undertone, remembering that several of them served long prison sentences.

All of the parties, with the exception of the Communists, participated in Bransk's general elections, in which members of the town council were chosen by universal suffrage. A new

convention was quickly established whereby the mayor of
Brańsk would be Polish and the vice mayor Jewish. This was
well and good, but the one place where Poles and Jews cooperated really happily was the Firemen's Association. It is unclear
whether the Jewish councilors spoke Polish in their official
capacity. In Białystok immediately after independence, some
Jewish deputies spoke Yiddish at meetings, but after strenuous
objections from other politicians, competence in Polish became
a prerequisite for holding administrative office.

In the 1920s, the local Jewish government — heir to the old
kahal — regained some of its powers under the new Polish laws
and instituted its own elections, conducted on the basis of male,
rather than universal, suffrage. Young Jack Rubin signed up for
membership in the militant Betar, and applied several times for
a visa to Palestine, although his application was turned down
every time. He still remembers hearing the great Jabotinsky at a
rally in Białystok. Thousands of people attended such meetings,
and audience excitement ran high. Jabotinsky was introduced
by none other than Menachem Begin, whom "nobody liked."
In Jack's memory, people threw tomatoes at the young politician during his speech. Jabotinsky, on the other hand, "was the
finest speaker in the world" in Jack's view, an appraisal shared
by just about everyone who had heard the fiery orator.

Brańsk, too, saw famous political speakers, as well as rallies,
processions, speeches, demonstrations. Oddly enough, the Yizkor Book's authors regard all this "agitation" with prim disapproval. "The question is, what did all these parties do in Brańsk,
what constituted their main activity?" they rhetorically ask,
and answer: "Only one thing: to tear each other apart. If that
was their main goal, they accomplished it wonderfully." In
their memory, "there was no Saturday or holiday that passed
without a party fight." In Brańsk, as elsewhere, party meetings

were disrupted by the acolytes of all the other parties, and resulted in "bloody fights" that spilled into the streets. A tone of Jewish shame — the shame of a minority group that does not want to see its weaknesses exposed to the outside world — enters the text. "If non-Jewish passers-by asked what are they killing each other for here," the authors write, "there would have been no answer. Really, what were they killing each other for?"

The disapprobation may be retrospective, an aftereffect of faded sound and fury, but possibly distrust of politics was a matter of generational predilections. After World War I, something like a generation gap became observable in the shtetl. The pace of change had become so rapid that the stately continuity of Jewish life was irrevocably sundered, and the paths followed by the young took them a long, sometimes unbridgeable distance from their parents. Jewish politics was conducted mostly by the younger generation, for whom fervent ideological conviction had replaced religious belief. In Brańsk, older folk usually stayed out of the party melees, and when parents interfered, the Yizkor Book tells us, "it came to real scandals," as they rose to the defense of their insulted progeny. But politics could cause dissension even within traditionally cohesive and patriarchal families. The Yizkor Book tells of a father "blessed" with four sons, each of whom belonged to a different party. The poor man's Sabbath evenings were totally ruined, and the sons, after spending a day together, were often seen "with bandaged heads."

This may seem like a high pitch of passion to bring to politics, but the parties of that time were in the business not only of winning votes and solving problems but of transforming consciousness. As a means to this goal, each Jewish party sponsored schools in which it hoped to mold the young according to its vision. In Brańsk, a girls' school named Beth Jacob was established by the Agudah; larger cities like Białystok also had Bundist and Zionist schools, and schools offering curriculums in Yiddish and Hebrew, as well as in Polish.

In the Yizkor Book, intergenerational strife comes across mostly as comedy. But we have glimpses of how serious it could become from other sources — for example, the rich writings of Julian Stryjkowski, a Polish Jew who, after World War II, wrote several novels based on memories of his shtetl youth. In his fiction, the rift between generations is often extreme and leads to genuine family tragedies. The old are portrayed as disoriented by the changes around them and frightened of any contacts with the Gentile world. The young are beginning to make incursions into that world, which seduces and all too often abandons them. Sons stand condemned by their fathers for transgressions against religious law; daughters are cursed by mothers when they fall in love with Polish men. Many of Stryjkowski's characters are caught between the parental world that has rejected them and the Gentile society that ultimately does not accept them. And all the while the shtetl seethes with political contention, fragile alliances, realignments, disillusionments. There are glimmers of hope and possibility: among the more interesting passages of Stryjkowski's novels are the renditions of socialist meetings and debates, in which Poles and Jews try to discuss their interests as comrades and equals — and sometimes nearly succeed.

In the shtetl Stryjkowski retrospectively describes, literature itself was one of the chief vehicles of changing mentality, and the younger generation showed a positively voracious appetite for it. In Brańsk, aside from small libraries maintained by the political parties (whose collections were highly and tendentiously selective), there was a general library, a proud institution offering a cornucopia of classics and the latest publications. Gone was the time when secular books were thought to be slightly sinful. The interwar years were a period of fabulous flowering for Jewish literature, written in Hebrew, Yiddish, and Polish — a trilingual "polysystem" that made for fecund imaginative and verbal soil. There was a circle of Yiddish writers in Warsaw who consciously set out to preserve and nurture Yiddish culture. The brothers Singer — Joseph and Isaac Bashevis — were beginning to publish. And countless others, now forgotten, delivered volume after volume to a readership eager to see its lives and changing world reflected, and reflected upon. In the popular novels, one could find naturalistic, almost reportorial descriptions of Jewish life and of relations between Jews and Poles. Just as Jewish figures were often stereotyped in Polish fiction, so were Polish characters seen in simplified outlines by the less sophisticated Jewish authors. Poles were usually represented by several recurring types: the peasant, who was either a drunken simpleton or a good, honest soul; the nobleman, or *porets*, who was either reckless and improvident or full of largesse and goodwill toward Jews; often an educated priest given to friendly dialogue with Jews appeared as well. It was an indication of the linguistic intermingling prevalent in Poland that the pages of Yiddish novels were sprinkled with Polish words, and sometimes with whole passages transliterated from Polish.

Shtetl readers by that time regularly ventured beyond the territory of Jewish themes. Jack Rubin remembers devouring all of Jules Verne in Yiddish. Classics from many languages were translated into that language. But young people, especially girls who attended Polish schools, also read Polish classics in the original. If they had more contemporary tastes, these readers might have discovered numerous authors of "Jewish background" who wrote in Polish — such as Bruno Schulz, whose surreal stories, with their sensuous metaphysical vision of the shtetl, were admired by discerning Polish and Jewish audiences. It was a perhaps fortuitous but fascinating phenomenon of the interwar period that five of the most important Polish poets were Jewish — including Julian Tuwim, the most famous and popular of them all. These poets were completely integrated into Polish literary circles. They edited and wrote for serious avant-garde magazines and were generally recognized as leading literary lights. There were also Jewish prose writers who placed themselves squarely in the Polish or European tradition, and a few who managed to straddle both worlds. Indeed, the Polish intelligentsia contained a high proportion of prominent Jewish figures, people who neither emphasized nor hid their Jewish origins. Yet other authors used the Polish language to adumbrate Jewish themes, including Zionist writers who expressed in Polish their dreams of reaching Palestine.

The Jewish press, in the meantime, was burgeoning into a regular and powerful estate, with 130 publications appearing in the interwar years. Every major city had several Jewish newspapers — most in Yiddish, a few in Polish. Jack Rubin read *Der Tag* and *Der Forverts*. In the pages of the dailies, weeklies, and monthlies, writers and journalists conversed with each other, with the Poles, and with various segments of the Jewish community.

In Yiddish literature, as in the press, the shtetl was becoming a special topos — the site of the "Jewish soul," about whose state of health polemicists wrangled and poets rhapsodized. For the rationalist, leftist intellectuals, the shtetl was still a place without charm or merit, the breeding ground of superstition and passivity — a kind of collective Jewish embarrassment. This was, in a sense, nothing new. Like their Haskalic forebears, these modernists thought that the sooner the traditional Jewish masses shook off the shackles of Orthodoxy, the better it would be for everyone. What was new, however, was a species of modern Jewish intellectuals who were becoming nostalgic about the shtetl and saw it as the remote country of their origin, to which they may not have wanted to return, but whose passing they would have regretted, and whose specific culture — rituals, practices, personality types — they ardently wanted to preserve.

Some writers possessed of such feelings tried to save the shtetl from change and time by fictionalizing it. But in the 1890s, a more practical preservation movement was launched at the instigation of Simon Dubnow, a Russian-Jewish intellectual, who went on to found the YIVO Institute in Vilno in 1925. Dubnow realized that, amazingly enough, no history of Eastern European Jewish culture existed, and that troves of documents and artifacts — from communal *pinkas* books to locally crafted Hanukah candles — were in danger of crumbling in attics or being thrown away by people unaware of their historical worth. His call to salvage and document Jewish culture met with an enormous response, and a veritable craze of collection and "archaeological" investigation overtook Eastern European Jews. Poland was the largest center of unassimilated Jewish culture, and from the early twentieth century to the interwar decades, amateur ethnographers and anthropologists went to the shtetls to record songs and proverbs and collect embroidered cloths, dusty registry books, and, of course, photographs. In the eyes of secular modern Jewry, the shtetl and Orthodox Jews were becoming imaginatively distant: the homegrown exotic, the internal, primitive Other.

᧤　　᧤　　᧤

Clearly, consciousness was changing, and so were life's conditions. In the Yizkor Book, the place of honor is given not to the vehicles of spiritual change, but to the pragmatic organizations and associations that addressed the material needs of Brańsk's inhabitants. The associations were the descendants of the older shtetl brotherhoods, but they also reflected new social structures and divisions. They were formed because the ordinary folk, the small shopkeepers and artisans, felt that under the new system of taxation they were once again exploited by the rich. This was an old grievance, but this time the disaffected poor decided to take matters into their own hands, and in the summer of 1923 they established the Merchants' Association. A few months later the craftsmen, such as tailors, carpenters, butchers, bakers, and blacksmiths, broke off to create their own association.

In the Yizkor Book, the craftsmen's guild is referred to with evident affection. It gave its members the dignity of knowing that they, too, had the right to fair and respectful treatment. Their taxes were now determined by their peers, on the basis of income. And another new note enters into the description of this organization: pride in work. This was an attitude promoted by several Jewish parties — especially the Bund and the Zionists — which tried to counteract the traditional Jewish denigration of physical labor and to assert the dignity of the working person. The Jewish craftsmen of Brańsk soon began to partake of this novel feeling. In 1927, Poland adopted regulations for industry and crafts which required every worker to have a diploma or a certificate. The Brańsk craftsmen did so well on their exams that they gained the right to examine and certify new workers.

In addition to the craftsmen's guild, three workers' unions arose in Brańsk: the tailors' union, the carpenters' union, and the leatherworkers' union. Again, it is indicative of the fault lines in the community that the authors of the Yizkor Book consider the political parties' influence on these bodies as pernicious. The Bund "had the advantage" in the tailors' union, the Zionists dominated the carpenters, and the Communists reigned among the leatherworkers. In the Yizkor Book's odd slant, it wasn't until the unions threw off the parties' yoke that they won the right to an eight-hour day and better wages and raises. It is unclear whether everyone in Brańsk was required to cease working on Sunday. The issue of Sunday rest was a rankling one in the cities, since the compulsory Sunday off meant that observant Jewish employees lost two days of work a week. When, in 1919, the Sejm passed the Sunday law, the Jewish parties deplored the legislation. But Polish workers, who were now assured one free day a week, applauded the move as progressive. However, in unruly Poland, the law was never fully implemented, and it is likely that in the small workshops of provincial Brańsk such directives from above were simply ignored.

Undoubtedly, the most important accomplishment of grassroots activism was the creation of two financial institutions in the 1920s. The first was a "people's bank," which guaranteed credit for small merchants and laborers. For a while the bank operated fairly and to everyone's satisfaction, but after five years the management apparently fell into "party hands" and started giving credit on the principle of *protekcja*, or favoritism. Fortunately, the resourceful craftsmen started up their own interest-free loan society, or *kase*, modeled on the earlier associations for mutual help. As economic conditions worsened, the new lending society was in danger of going under, but in 1928 a *landsman* who had emigrated from Brańsk to Chicago thirty-five years earlier came to the rescue. The loyal emigrant was one David Fein, and the institution he saved came to be known as "Fein's Percentless Kase." In the United States, the Joint Distribution Committee, which was becoming involved in helping Jewish communities throughout Eastern Europe, pitched in as well.

Although a lending bank is rarely the object of personal sentiment, the writers of the Yizkor Book clearly loved Fein's Percentless and what it did for the poor folk of Brańsk. They call it the "lovely, pretty institution," and refer to its "good, marvelous work." They are effusive about their "beloved, respected friend" David Fein and his "magnanimous deeds." This may be the portraitist's flattery of the patron, but borrowers who benefited from the informal bank's services showed their gratitude by repaying the loans with exemplary timeliness.

Each year during Slichot (the prayers of forgiveness before the Jewish New Year), the craftsmen's guild celebrated the anniversary of its founding, and the description of the fifth anniversary is revealing of the interethnic atmosphere in Brańsk at its best. The celebration took place in a private house that was "electrically lit." Polish and Jewish flags were raised side by side, along with a craftsmen's banner bearing the motto "By the labor of your hands you shall eat, gain happiness, and prosper." The firemen's orchestra played the Polish national anthem and "Hatikva," which was the Zionist anthem of the dream homeland. All the political parties of Brańsk sent their greetings. During the speeches there were tears in people's eyes, and the festivities lasted till morning. For the moment at least, optimism was in the air.

ॐ   ॐ   ॐ

The interval of quiet and relative stability in Poland was made possible, ironically, by a demagogic move: in 1926 Piłsudski, frustrated by the ineffectuality of the government, executed a coup, which was shortly legalized by an election, and then installed his Sanacja camp in the Sejm. The coup was preceded by great political tensions and disarray, and Piłsudski was seen by many, including the Polish left and the Jews, as the only person capable of saving the moment. Despite this undemocratic means of seizing power, Piłsudski refrained from authoritarian measures, and his stance toward the Jews continued to be liberal. The first premier in the new government, Kazimierz Bartel, officially condemned economic anti-Semitism in 1926, in a speech lauded by Jews as a watershed event.

The halcyon period did not last very long. By the late 1920s, the leftist parties, including the Bund, were becoming disillusioned with the new government, which failed to stem the worst tendencies of Polish life. In the 1930s, the general atmosphere began to darken. The Great Depression had hit Poland extremely hard, and much of the population sank into dire poverty. It is difficult to evaluate where the Jews stood in the hierarchy of deprivation. The masses of small artisans and tradespeople were reduced to minimal livelihoods, but they were probably still better off than the peasants. At the same time, many major industries continued to be controlled by Jewish entrepreneurs, who hired — and fired — a large proportion of Polish and Jewish workers (even on the eve of World War II, Jewish firms employed more than 40 percent of the Polish labor force). In the interwar years, Jews were also prominent in several professions. In 1931, more than half the doctors in private practice and one-third of the lawyers in Poland were Jewish. But among the less privileged, the times weren't cheerful for any group, and economic competition became more dogged and desperate.

We have a picture of Brańsk at that time, as it looked to a visitor not used to its conditions. The sketch was left in the charming reminiscences of Grace Goldman, an American descendant of Brańsk Jews who went to the shtetl to meet her relatives in the summer of 1932. Writing much later, she remembered her visit in graphic detail. On her brief foray in Warsaw, she was impressed by the city's gaiety and elegance and the animation of its Jewish life. But once she reached the "muddy village" of Brańsk, she found endless potato fields, "unspeakable" roads, and poverty. Her uncle's family lived "in the most inconceivable and primitive surroundings imaginable," in a house that was "little more than a two-room shack," with no indoor plumbing or even a regular outhouse, no chairs, and only wooden "sleeping benches" to serve as seating by day and beds at night. Incongruously, in the midst of this penury, people wore fashionable clothes, castoffs sent to them by American relatives — that summer, the muddy streets of the shtetl sparkled with beaded dresses!

Another incongruity went deeper. Despite all the material discomforts, Grace Goldman writes, "my uncle's house was sanctified — a holy tabernacle. They were learned people. The days were filled with a succession of prayers. . . . Worship, study, history, world events, the synagogue was their stronghold. On a Sabbath, the mean houses and streets took on a still, ethereal light, a strange silence, as though holy." The children, she discovered, all had talents and aspirations: the eldest was a self-taught violinist, a daughter participated in amateur dramatics, the youngest was a fledgling scholar.

Grace Goldman was shocked by the "pauperization" of her fellow Jews, but she ends her brief memoir on a note of comparative anthropology, which places what she saw in a somewhat different perspective. Shortly after her visit to Poland, she spent a summer in the Ozark Mountains and found the conditions "among the natives" there just as primitive as in Brańsk — in some respects more so. "They were enveloped in the mental darkness of illiteracy and fanaticism," she says of the hillbillies. "Therein lay the contrast between the two worlds. The Jews . . . were never without meaningful and moral guidance. After the backwardness of Arkansas," she concludes, "I stopped speaking about Poland."

What a visitor from abroad could not discern from empirical local observation were the larger social trends and their gradual impact on daily life. The most unfortunate of these, from the Jewish perspective, was the increasing popularity of the Endecja and its radical wing, the ONR (Obóz Narodowo-Radykalny, the National-Radical Camp), established in 1934. The Endeks were becoming more fiercely nationalist and, as time went on, aggressively anti-Semitic. They reviled "Jewish nationalism," claimed that Jews were undermining Polish interests, and asserted that short of cultural assimilation and full identification with the Polish state — of which, they believed, Jews were congenitally incapable — the Jewish population should be encouraged to emigrate. Paradoxically, in this the Endecja was in essential agreement with the Zionists, although for different reasons and with very different moral credibility. Nevertheless, these two parties, so opposed in every other premise and aim, often supported each other in the Sejm on this issue.

After the death of Piłsudski in 1935, the Endecja's anti-Semitism became more rabid and gained adherents among large sectors of the population, including parts of the governing elite. The Catholic Church contributed to the reactionary climate by tolerating anti-Jewish sermons. Anti-Semitic literature, produced within the Church and by other sources, began to proliferate. Extremist pamphlets portrayed Jews as harmful to the economic interests of Poland, as a corrupting element threatening the people's moral health, and as the agents of

Communism. The term "Judeo-Commune" became common. In other words, for the self-professed anti-Semites, the Jew was no longer only the Other, but the internal enemy, the serpent within. In a book called *The Talmud about the Goys*, which became a "classic" of anti-Semitic literature, Father Stanisław Trzeciak argued that the Talmud provided the imprimatur for exploitation of "the goys" — and then went on to spin fantastic theories of conspiracy among Jews, Communists, and the Masons.

These were clearly hateful notions. It should be noted, however, that in contrast with German anti-Semitic writings, the element of biological racism — the claim that Jews were intrinsically, biologically inferior — was almost entirely absent from the Polish material. (An exception was the writing produced by the extremist fringe of the ONR, which became briefly fascinated by German fascism, until the Germans invaded Poland.) In most of the anti-Semitic literature, Jews were depicted as at once powerful and insidious, but they were not seen as quintessentially subhuman.

Nevertheless, the nationalist brand of anti-Semitism was quite enough to sanction unpleasant tactics against the Jews, aimed at displacing them from their economic positions, and other areas of Polish life. The economic conflict was played out with increasing acrimony, and eventually violence. But even today, in the memories of Poles and Jews, the events of that period are viewed from squarely opposing sides. The Jewish community felt impoverished and threatened. Government policies, such as new monopoly laws that placed several branches of industry and commerce in state hands, seemed to be designed to push Jews out of their successful businesses. In Brańsk such laws had modest repercussions, giving one Polish businessman the exclusive right to own a tobacco warehouse —

although not to sell cigarettes — and giving one Pole and one Jew liquor concessions. At the same time, Poles started moving into areas that had previously been Jewish domains. The Yizkor Book notes the appearance, from 1935 onward, of Polish shops and market stalls, of "Catholic" tailors, carpenters, and hat makers, who drew customers away from similar Jewish businesses. In the eyes of Jewish tradesmen, this was calculated to deprive them of their livelihoods, and they tried to resist Polish encroachments with such strategies as they had at their disposal. In 1936, for example, a Polish cooperative submitted a proposal to build a covered market hall in Brańsk's central square (which was surrounded by Jewish shops), with the understanding that the businesses opening there would be Polish. The project needed the unanimous approval of the town councilors. The Jewish representatives voted against it, blocking construction of the hall. In response, the Yizkor Book claims, a Polish politician met secretly with the Jewish councilors, threatening them with arson if they failed to approve the project. They changed their votes, and the market hall, consisting of twelve small shops, was built in 1938. The Yizkor Book notes, however, that the new Polish merchants had little success in selling their wares; apparently, most of the customers remained loyal to the familiar Jewish shopkeepers.

From the Polish point of view — one that Zbyszek, among others, is willing to uphold — the Poles were only trying to claim their rightful share against a virtual Jewish monopoly on trade and commerce. "Until then, Poles didn't defend themselves," he says, suggesting a disadvantaged Polish population passively accepting its position. In fact, the Jews in Brańsk did, for historical reasons, have a strong competitive edge in commercial fields. In 1926, out of 300 craft certificates purchased in Brańsk, 275 were issued to Jewish workers. In 1938, there were

315 Jewish craftsmen. Naturally, the town's Polish citizens, themselves struggling for basic existence, were not going to give great notice to the fact that Jews were practically absent from clerical and administrative posts, or that their entry into various professions was made increasingly difficult. At the same time, the Jews were not going to yield their traditional sources of income easily. In one incident, people in Brańsk claim, Jewish merchants overturned and set afire a truck belonging to Polish competitors.

As long as the Polish economy remained almost wholly agricultural, the division of labor between Polish farmers and Jewish merchants made for a complementary relationship. But as the nature of the economy changed, that balance was disturbed. The Poles still gave credence to the myth of hidden Jewish wealth. Zbyszek explains that this was because "Jews always kept something for a black hour. They knew their fate. That was how tales about fabulous sums of gold sprang up. Jews valued gold currency, while the peasants preferred paper. The peasants had a saying: 'Rubles tear through your pockets.' "

Old habits, old myths. To some extent, there developed a genuine conflict of interest between the two groups, as often happens when economies move into a new phase — although the majority, for all its subjective perceptions, had a simple, intrinsic advantage. Given the ideological climate of the time, however, the country's sinking economy became fodder for an obsession with Jewish power, and there seemed to be no one in the political sphere who had a large enough vision of Polish society to include everyone in it and find a way of resolving conflicts for the common good.

After 1935, the ideology of chauvinist nationalism moved closer to the center of political and social life. In response to Endecja's growing popularity, the formerly moderate Sanacja faction began to favor anti-Semitic legislation, including the policy of encouraging (although not forcing) Jewish emigration. It began to be difficult for Jews to find jobs in certain professions. The fiercest battles, though, were waged at the universities, where the radical Endecja and ONR youth engaged in an ugly and protracted fight to limit the number of Jewish students.

At the beginning of Polish independence, the faculties with genuinely open admissions, such as law and philosophy, attracted very high proportions of Jewish students. In the "polytechnics," which offered practical subjects, an informal quota was often imposed. If the new generation of Jews, newly sprung from Orthodoxy, flocked to the universities, it was because the Jewish system of values placed great emphasis on learning, and because, in the absence of inherited privilege or access to power, young Jews saw education as one of the few avenues of advancement available to them. However, the nationalist students took the presence of Jewish students as an attack on the "Polish character" of the universities. When their attempts to introduce a *numerus clausus* through parliamentary legislation failed, the rightist youth groups turned to thuggish direct action on university campuses. During registration, uniformed bullies beat up Jewish students and assaulted them with razors. At some universities, the nationalists managed to introduce the infamous "ghetto bench" — segregated seating for Jewish students in the classroom.

These intimidation tactics did not go unresisted. The Bundists and Zionists made a point of being on campuses at times of unrest, and came to the aid of endangered students. In the classroom, Jewish students stood during lectures rather than submit to the humiliation of the ghetto bench. From the Polish side there were protests too. Individual Polish professors and students stood through lectures in solidarity with Jewish students. Leftist student groups fought the Endek and ONR strategies, especially since they were themselves their targets. Well-known Polish intellectuals and academics made statements deploring the violations of academic freedom; a number of professors resigned their posts. The rector of the University of Lvov offered his resignation, and when a new rector more sympathetic to Endecja was appointed, the vice rector resigned also. Universities were shut down for weeks at a time in order to calm the situation. But none of these honorable responses succeeded, and the enrollment of Jewish students at universities dropped dramatically in the late thirties, as talented people chose to study abroad, or emigrated.

The Yizkor Book alludes to these unhappy trends, but for Brańsk it was the economic policies that continued to have the most painful relevance. In 1936, a new prime minister came out with the motto "Economic struggle by all means; to do harm, no." In March 1938, the first genuinely anti-Semitic law, restricting ritual slaughter, was passed in the Sejm, although it was never really enforced.

The infamous "by all means" (owszem) policy, although it was meant to restrain violent tactics, in fact had the opposite effect. In villages near Brańsk, "brutal guys" appeared at weekly markets, preventing peasants from approaching Jewish stands and roughing up Jewish tradesmen and their wares. The police were sent in to keep order, with uneven success. On one occasion, when plans for a major Endek attack on a village were discovered, a Jewish committee in Brańsk notified the mayor of Białystok, who sent in a team of policemen. In a clash with the police, several Endeks were wounded and killed. Still, the Jews of the village felt they had no choice but to relocate to Brańsk.

In Brańsk itself the boycotts started later, but they also led to ugly confrontations. Jack Rubin remembers that he first noticed signs of danger in Warsaw, where he began avoiding places known to be Endecja outposts. Then the boycotts reached Brańsk. He thinks that no one from Brańsk participated in them. They were conducted by "hooligans" from other towns, and at first they consisted mostly of intimidation tactics, intended to prevent Jews from displaying their products and Poles from approaching their stalls. The police were sent in, and the Bund attempted revenge actions after each disturbance. Nevertheless, the excesses continued.

Irena Jabłonowska remembers the escalating tensions and competitiveness, the Polish signs proclaiming "Ours to Ours," but also an incident in which Jews refused to rent a shop in the central square area to a Pole. "As for fighting, no, they didn't fight, but there was a lot of pressure," she says about the early stage of the boycotts.

Was Jack Rubin surprised at this change of mood? "Oh, we always knew the Poles were anti-Semites," he replies, as if there were no contradiction with what he had said before, that "there was no hatred." Perhaps he is expressing a conviction so unshakable as to be itself a form of prejudice. But perhaps the contradiction was so persistent as to have become a kind of unified truth — the simultaneous existence of benign, even warm acceptance and a gap that could at any time widen into a gulf.

Early in 1937, the market day excesses started turning violent. Jewish merchants were attacked despite police presence. Jack Rubin remembers seeing a Graf (Count) Potocki, who "grabbed" anyone attacking Jews and handed the miscreants over to the police. The peasants mostly tried to stay out of the troubles.

One day that summer, the boycotters diverted the police by setting off a false fire alarm in another part of town, then proceeded to overturn and rob the Jewish stalls. A few weeks later,

sensing perhaps that the police would not confront them, the
Endeks launched another attack, without any diversionary tactics. This time the brawling escalated into a full-scale riot.
Marauding youths broke windows in Jewish shops, wrecked
people's houses, and beat people up with impunity. According
to the Yizkor Book, several people were wounded and had to
be taken to a hospital in Białystok.

Irena Jabłonowska remembers her father herding her and her
sister indoors when it all started, saying, "Into the house, this
isn't ours." *Not ours:* another variant of the broader motto, a
phrase used instinctively when trouble erupted, even by people
with the best intentions. After all these years, Irena Jabłonowska remembers shouts, screams, the noise of windows being
smashed. "Maybe they wanted to show off," she says about the
thugs, not really acknowledging the nub of their intent. She
thinks that one or two people from Brańsk may have been
involved in that episode, but on the whole, Brańskers agree that
the violence was perpetrated by "imported" hooligans — as if
the Endecja understood that neighbor would not turn physically against neighbor, that the fabric of familiarity still held.

In the following days, news of the incident reached the Western press, and telegrams from American relatives started pour-
ing in. Two Jewish parliamentary deputies went to Brańsk to
see the damage, and registered a protest in the Sejm. A case was
brought in the district court against the rioters. No one was
punished.

The Endeks were responsible for one more attack before the
war, this time on the town government. This was in keeping
with the more fanatical elements of Endecja's right wing, who
believed that the government was too friendly toward the Jews.
On that occasion, shots were fired by the police, and the boycotts from then on were declared illegal. Actually, they had

never been too successful in the first place. In Brańsk, the Poles who were kept away from Jewish businesses on market days went back to them the very next day. "The people, they really wanted to buy by the Jewish shops," Jack Rubin says. "Because it was cheaper." The pattern was repeated elsewhere in Poland.

Throughout 1937 and 1938, the economic situation in Poland only got worse. The Jewish community of Brańsk suffered badly and had to turn for help to the Brańsk associations in New York. In the last months before World War II, anti-Jewish propaganda subsided, as Poles turned their minds to the more real danger coming from Germany. Interestingly, at that late date the main peasant party, which had supported "economic struggle" against the Jews, came out with a statement propounding that Jews were not the cause of the peasants' problems, and that peasant ire would be better directed toward the gentry and the government.

Such was the state of Polish-Jewish relations on the eve of World War II — probably as tense as at any time in Polish history, seething with difficulties that might or might not have resolved themselves into a new equilibrium. Still, no one expected or predicted or wanted what came next. Even in the late thirties, Jewish institutions, theaters, schools, and newspapers flourished. Daily life for Polish Jews much of the time retained its ordinariness, and was not as consistently dire as the bleakest episodes might suggest.

In the spring of 1939, Jack Rubin was trying to figure out what to do about his call-up notice from the Polish army. He had already arranged for two deferments before, and this summons seemed to be the same routine kind, which could be evaded by routine means. "Jewish people didn't want to go to the army," Jack says, unself-consciously echoing Polish criticisms. For one thing, the army had a reputation for anti-

Semitism, and besides, his father needed him in the business. So with the help of a Polish *macher*, or fixer — a Polish organist who knew the elder of Bielsk — Jack arranged for a shortened, five-month period of basic training. Once he got to his army camp, Jack didn't mind it so much. Some of the Jewish boys serving with him — weaklings, in his opinion — met with petty harassments, but Jack wasn't given any guff. He was strong, and a good shot, and those were the values that counted. "Some Jewish boys came to me saying, 'Make them stop picking on me.' And they stopped. They didn't pick on me, oh no." Jack palled around with some of the Polish recruits, especially a boy who had worked for his family's goose farm.

In August, Jack was released and went back home. Seven days later, Germany invaded Poland without declaring war.

5

Shtetl:
The Shoah

IN EACH of my conversations with the farmers of Brańsk, the inevitable question falls: What do you remember from that time — from the war? The robust peasant who has expressed relief at the absence of Jews in Brańsk says he remembers all kinds of things. He was about twenty when the war started. After the Germans came in, his brother was soon deported to a labor camp; he somehow managed to avoid a similar fate. How? I ask. "If a prick has a head, a prick can use it," he replies with relish. Then he adds, "Pani, you will forgive me for talking like this."

And did he know what happened to the Jews here? Ah yes, he answers eagerly, his eyes twinkling. All kinds of things happened. One time during the German occupation, on a morning after a night of shooting, there were many Jewish bodies in the street. The Germans had piled all the bodies in one place and, as he was passing on his cart, they ordered him to haul the corpses to a mass grave.

"Well, if that's what they say, you can't do anything," he remembers. "So I said, 'But sir, for so many bodies, I need someone to help.'" Then, with someone's assistance, he took the bodies to the other side of the river and threw them into a big open grave. Many of them had their clothes ripped at the seams, because the Germans were looking for gold.

"Well, we did what we had to, and we turned back."

"And that was it?" I ask.

"That was it. We went home — but through the river. Because you can imagine the state the cart was in."

No sentiment, no softening of the horrid tale, no pity or regret. Is it due to a hardening of the mnemonic or of the moral arteries? It is too late — I've come too late — to know. Zbyszek, who is with me, points out that it has been fifty years since the event, that the farmer has probably told the story many times before. To him, by now, it is just a story. But I sense something more than neutral distance, and as he goes on, the farmer peels away layers of hostility toward the Jews, and deep resentments. He recalls the Jews who, at the beginning of the war, welcomed the Soviet army that had invaded from the east. Some of them were rewarded with a small measure of very temporary power, and undoubtedly on occasion flaunted it. "The Jews treated the Poles very odiously under the Soviets," the farmer says. "I met my friend Shmulko once, in his new uniform and with his gun, and said, 'Shmulko, how are you?' And Shmulko showed me his backside and said, 'Sniff it.'

"Yes, yes," the farmer assures me when I look at him dubiously, "that's how it was."

Possibly. But was Shmulko's gesture an act of gratuitous vulgarity, an abuse of his short-lived and rather pathetic privilege? Or was it a repayment, a petty if nasty revenge, for insults addressed to him in the past? Was the farmer, harboring even now a rankling belief in Jewish exploitation, one of those who stood in front of Jewish stores, preventing customers from going in? Surely, he would have approved of the boycotts.

Impossible to know, impossible to unravel the coils of conflict, injustices, and injuries that had preceded the moment when the farmer's Jewish acquaintance turned away from him

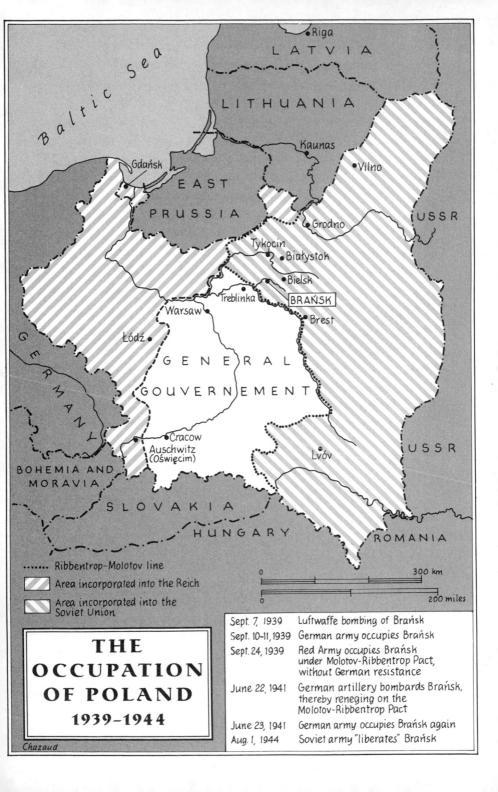

THE
OCCUPATION
OF POLAND
1939-1944

Chazaud

..... Ribbentrop-Molotov line

Area incorporated into the Reich

Area incorporated into the
Soviet Union

Sept. 7, 1939	Luftwaffe bombing of Brańsk
Sept. 10-11, 1939	German army occupies Brańsk
Sept. 24, 1939	Red Army occupies Brańsk under Molotov-Ribbentrop Pact, without German resistance
June 22, 1941	German artillery bombards Brańsk, thereby reneging on the Molotov-Ribbentrop Pact
June 23, 1941	German army occupies Brańsk again
Aug. 1, 1944	Soviet army "liberates" Brańsk

0   300 km

0   200 miles

so unceremoniously. As he reaches further back in his memory, the farmer reveals more strands of preconceptions and fragments of stereotypes. In times of peace, such prejudices might simmer in his breast, creating perhaps an air of cockiness or aggression about him at the market, but not wreaking any enormous harm. But in times of war? This man probably did nothing terrible. By now, such things are known in Brańsk, and he is too cheerful, too open, to have anything concrete to hide.

What of others like him? I can imagine how, with the incitements of Nazi rhetoric ringing in his ears, with the imagery of anti-Semitic posters before his eyes, with the repeated warnings that helping Jews was punishable by death, and with the orders, shouted in German, to turn Jews in to the authorities or else; with the sight, above all, of Jews being publicly hounded, humiliated, killed — how, with all that, a farmer might turn his murky notions and muddy aversions into the clear knowledge that, as far as Jews were concerned, anything was permitted, anything at all. I can see such a man, in such a time, slipping into the kind of darkness in which a fatal betrayal might be perpetrated, or a murder committed, quite casually, in the light of day.

⚬   ⚬   ⚬

In the evening, I go with Zbyszek to meet a person of quite a different ilk: one of those who helped. She is Janina Woińska, a small, elderly woman with a heart-shaped face and a sweet, mild manner. She is a retired pharmacist, and was already working at the pharmacy when the war started, although she had moved to Brańsk only shortly before. She has reasons to remember that time very clearly. Her brother was taken to Auschwitz, and then to Buchenwald, as a member of the Polish resistance. She was a young woman then, in her early twenties, but she marshaled all her resources to help him. She raised a big sum of money in a scheme to get him out which did not succeed; she mailed packages to him at Buchenwald. She still marvels that in a carton of 120 eggs she sent him, only four arrived broken.

Almost by accident, she found herself helping others as well. When the ghetto was established in Brańsk in 1941, the pharmacy building sat in the middle of it, fenced off arbitrarily from the designated Jewish area. She could see from her window what was going on in the ghetto, and at first it was not horrifying. People could easily sneak in and out; Poles went in to trade food, and Jews smuggled goods to and from Białystok. But then, in November 1942, everything changed. One night early that month, someone jumped over the ghetto fence and ran into the pharmacy. It was Lejb Shapiro, the pharmacy's prewar owner. He told Woińska that the ghetto was surrounded, and nobody knew what was going to happen. He wanted to hide with his wife, his two sons, and his brother's fiancée in the basement of the pharmacy. Woińska, and two other women living in the building, decided that this was a suicidal plan: the pharmacy was right in the ghetto, and frequented by Germans and Poles. Instead, it was agreed that the Shapiros should go to another building, close by but outside the ghetto area. There, Woińska made a hiding place behind piles of lumber. Together with the two other women, she brought the fugitives food for the next few days.

"Did you know what the danger was?" I ask. "Maybe not palpably," she answers. "I was so naive." The penalty for a deed like hers was death — but perhaps she could not allow herself to know this with full clarity when she took her risk, any more than a person trying to survive can afford to feel the imminence of death.

Her sense of danger was sharpened, however, after a close

call with the Gestapo, who came to the pharmacy a few days later and ordered a search. By that time, with the help of a young priest, the Shapiros had gone on to another, safer place outside Brańsk. The Gestapo found their suitcases, left behind in the pharmacy's attic. "Someone has been here," one of the Germans said. "How can I vouch that someone has or has not been here?" Woińska responded.

"I spoke logically," she now says, "although I was very afraid. You should see the Gestapo man. He had those high boots, and he didn't talk — he shouted." As it happened, the whole "aristocracy" of Brańsk had gathered in the pharmacy, including a doctor, a priest, and a teacher. They all knew about the hiding place. No one said a word.

During the search, another Gestapo man started hitting a peasant quite viciously. He wasn't one of the truly brutal Gestapo men — he was Brańsk's "good German," and tried to spare Jews from the worst — but he had to react. He ordered the pharmacy cordoned off more securely from the ghetto.

"It's a miracle we survived," Woińska says. This must have been brought home to her all too vividly by the sights and sounds she witnessed on the days and nights following the Shapiros' appearance: screams, shots, people falling dead in the streets. The ghetto was being liquidated. At night she could make out silhouettes of people trying to escape through the pharmacy's courtyard. Once she watched as two Poles ("this is a shameful thing to talk about," she says) pointed out to the Gestapo a hole in the fence through which people could flee. One afternoon she saw people being herded onto horse-drawn carts, which were to take them on their deadly journey to Treblinka.

Then there was the curious incident that took place a few days after the liquidation of the ghetto was complete. A Jewish man named Isaiah Cukier entered the pharmacy with a Gestapo escort, saying he had a message for the Shapiros from their relatives. As a former member of the Judenrat, the Jewish Council set up by the Germans, he would have known people's hiding places, and he was sure that the Shapiros were still at the pharmacy. She knew nothing about their whereabouts, Woińska said. But Cukier insisted they must be there, and that they would be safe if they came out. Their relatives, he said, wanted the Shapiros to join them in Bielsk. Woińska felt confused. In an attempt to play for time, she turned to an older woman, a teacher, who had been staying in the building. "Do you know of any Jewish people who've been here?" Woińska asked, and the teacher categorically denied it. Woińska followed her lead and reiterated she had not seen the Shapiros. Cukier never found the Shapiros, and their lives were spared, unlike the lives of others, whose fate he sealed.

Janina Woińska was an inadvertent witness, forced to look at terrible things that, in a way, had nothing to do with her — although, by accident of proximity, they implicated her in life-and-death choices. Almost inadvertently, she made the decision to help save lives rather than turn away.

But why? Why did she act as she did, briefly and impulsively perhaps, but in disregard of her own safety? "A human being is a human being," she answers. "I was helping human beings."

That must have been true, because in the abstract she was hardly a philo-Semite. Before the war, she had a close Jewish friend at school, but as for Jews in general, her views are hardly pure. She thinks they "had money in their hands, and exploited others' dependence on them." She speaks of the attempts to impose *numerus clausus* in the universities with naive and mild-voiced approbation — to her, this seemed simply right. "Eighty percent of the professions were in Jewish hands," she says with considerable exaggeration, but undoubtedly repeating inflated propaganda figures. "Students were fighting for their places." (Here, Zbyszek interposes to say that he emphatically disagrees, and condemns the quota system out of hand. He is in favor of free competition.)

"But how did you feel," I ask again, "when the Shapiros came to ask for help?" I want to plumb the mystery of motive. "When a person needs help, you have to help them," Woińska says. "Those are our feelings. Anyway, that's our faith as well, that you help those in need." Signs of Catholic piety are displayed in her apartment: religious pictures on the walls, a photograph of herself with the pope.

The young priest who arranged for the Shapiros' second hiding place, and who escorted them on their short but hazardous journey, was Vicar Józef Chwalko. His superior, Rector Bolesław Czarkowski, reiterated in his sermons that "one must help people" who were in need. A priestly word, a priestly example, carried enormous moral authority in a congregation such as Brańsk's — perhaps enough weight to tip the scales of conscience for people like Woińska. As I keep probing her memories and reasons, she says that somewhere inside her was the thought that someone else might one day help her brother. Perhaps through her altruistic gestures she was propitiating fate, making sure she was not tipping the scales of justice, or of mercy, to the wrong side.

ॐ   ॐ   ॐ

During World War II, borderliness once again proved fateful. For Brańsk, it meant that the war was marked by not one but two invasions: the Soviet one from the east and the Nazi onslaught from the west.

Before these main acts there was a kind of ghastly prelude. In

Above: In the square before the church, Brańsk, 1910. *(J. Moczulski; courtesy of Zbigniew Romaniuk)*

Below: Representatives of the Jewish community in Dęblin greet Józef Piłsudski, the head of the Polish state, with bread and salt, 1920. *(Jewish Historical Institute, Warsaw; photo by Marjan Fuks)*

Top: A group of Jewish girls celebrate Lag b'Omer, when traditionally children go to the countryside and play with bows and arrows to commemorate the Bar Kokhba war against the Romans. *(Courtesy of Rubin Roy Cobb)*

Bottom: Judging by the names of the newspapers they are holding — *Befreiung* (Freedom), *Arbayter Vort* (Workers' Word), *Heint* (Today), all in Yiddish — these teenagers were probably associated with the socialist movement, possibly the Bund, which advocated the use of Yiddish. *(Courtesy of Rubin Roy Cobb)*

Above: Students of the Beth Jacob girls' school, Brańsk, 1920s. *(Courtesy of Evelyn Iteld Silverboard)*

Below: Volunteer fire brigade, Brańsk, 1926. This was probably the social institution in which Poles and Jews cooperated most fully, and without conflict. *(Courtesy of Zbigniew Romaniuk)*

Above: A sewing and embroidery class, Brańsk, 1927. The classes, offered for free by Singer, were primarily for Jewish women, but Polish women participated as well. *(D. Zeifman; courtesy of Zbigniew Romaniuk)*

Left: Jack Rubin, second from left, with his family in Brańsk in the 1920s. *(Courtesy of Jack Rubin)*

Above: A procession in Brańsk celebrating a Polish patriotic holiday, "Days of the Sea," 1935. The shop sign says "Hairdresser, D. Izakowicz," indicating a Jewish owner. *(Antoni Kaleszuk; courtesy of Zbigniew Romaniuk)*

Below: Seventh-graders and their teachers in the Brańsk elementary school, 1935. The man seated at the far right taught Jewish religion. Some of the teachers wear black arm bands as a sign of mourning for the death of Józef Piłsudski. *(Courtesy of Zbigniew Romaniuk)*

ANTI-SEMITIC
CARTOONS
OF THE 1930S.

A Jewish Bolshevik brings
death to Poland.

A Jewish factory owner
turns away Poles imploring
him for work. From the
pamphlet "The Nation's
Self-Defense." (*Jewish
Historical Institute,
Warsaw*)

Overfed Jews confront
downtrodden Poles.
The ironic caption says
"Compatriots!" From
"The Nation's Self-
Defense."

The Jewish area of Brańsk after the Luftwaffe bombing of September 7, 1939. *(Courtesy of Zbigniew Romaniuk)*

Right: Jewish partisans in the forest near Brańsk, probably in 1943. *(Courtesy of Zbigniew Romaniuk)*

Below: A forced labor camp set up by the Nazis on the site of the liquidated Brańsk ghetto, 1943. At center is an SS officer nicknamed "Knut," who was later assassinated by a partisan unit. *(Courtesy of Zbigniew Romaniuk)*

Above: Before the Crematorium in Stutthof, 1945 by Marek Włodarski (1903–1960). *(Jewish Historical Institute, Warsaw)*

Below: Zbigniew Romaniuk and Marian Marzynski in the memorial cemetery in Brańsk, which Romaniuk has created from the gravestones he restored and carried there. *(© Frontline/Slawomir Grunberg)*

the dawn hours of September 1, 1939, the loud drone of air-
planes was heard over Brańsk. At nine o'clock that day, a radio
announcement informed the town's inhabitants that the Germans had marched into Poland. The news aroused rage and disbelief in everyone, but the Jewish population knew it had more
reasons to be afraid. Rumors of the Nazis' anti-Semitic policies
in Germany had probably seemed disquieting, but remote.
Now the knowledge of German attitudes contributed to the
feeling of general terror.

On September 7, squadrons of planes appeared in the sky
again. For no apparent reason, the Luftwaffe was bombing
Brańsk. The Jewish neighborhoods were hit hardest, and the
destruction there was instant: fires, crumbling houses, burned
corpses in the street.

On September 10, German ground forces started moving
into the Podlasie region. There were several hopelessly unequal
battles with the Polish army, in which Polish cavalry confronted German tanks. The outcome, of course, was predeter-
mined. Afterward, the Germans executed twenty-three civilians
and thirty soldiers in one village and burned another village
down. In the areas already occupied by the Germans, farther
west, executions of Polish civilians were rampant.

On September 14, German tanks rolled into Brańsk. Anti-
Jewish policies went immediately into effect, and three hundred
people were herded into a church and shipped to Germany. On
the twenty-third, the Germans set the Old Synagogue on fire,
pushing the caretaker and his family into the burning building.

On September 24, the German army left Brańsk under the
arrangement of the Ribbentrop-Molotov pact, in which Germany and the Soviet Union carved up Poland between them.
Under the terms of this secret nonaggression pact, Brańsk fell
within the Soviet sphere. As the Germans made their exit west,

the Soviet army entered from the east to claim a town that "belonged" to them. The prelude was over; the first act now began.

The advent of the Soviets was greeted very differently by the two parts of Brańsk's population. To the Poles, the Russians were a traditional enemy, hated nearly as much as the Germans. To the Jews, the Red Army was seen, first and foremost, as an army of liberation from the much worse German menace. In addition, a segment of the Jewish population felt an ideological affinity with the Soviets. There was a handful of Communist believers in the shtetl, but for others as well, the slogans of internationalism, of full equality for all classes and ethnic groups, were highly attractive. The Robin Hood promises of taking away from the rich and empowering the proletariat appealed to the poor and the disaffected. But above all, the Russians were not the Germans.

A sizable portion of the Jewish community therefore welcomed the Soviet soldiers with flowers, banners, and expressions of joy. To the Poles, this was a distressing and an alienating spectacle. The villages just east of Brańsk were inhabited mostly by Belorussians, who viewed the Russians as their natural allies. As a result, Brańsk saw itself as a beleaguered bastion of Polishness in the region, the last line of patriotic defense. At least at the beginning of the Soviet occupation, the interests of Jews and Poles seemed, once again, utterly divergent, and this historical episode continues to be one of the more discomfiting and delicate subjects in the Polish-Jewish dialogue.

The Soviets quickly installed their new order, in which Jewish inhabitants were favored. Polish administrative offices and other institutions were dismantled and new ones created, and most of the high positions were given to Jews, especially those with Communist affiliations. As the Yizkor Book puts it, "A new privileged class sprang up" in Brańsk. Its members did not always resist the temptation to flex their muscles in a show of power: when a rabbi's son went to apply for a work permit, for example, he was told by a young Jewish woman that he had to declare himself a "freethinker" before she could do anything for him.

Soon, however, the disadvantages of the new dispensation began to be felt by Poles and Jews alike. The Soviets "nationalized" all the businesses and confiscated all "bourgeois" property — an action that hurt Jewish merchants inordinately. In keeping with time-honored traditions of conquest, the occupiers began an instant Russification — or, this time, Sovietization — campaign: names of streets were changed, Russian became the obligatory language in public offices, and religious institutions, such as the *cheder* and the *mikvah* as well as the church parish house, were abolished. The peasants were forced to join cooperatives and collective farms, or *kolkhozes*. Placards showing Stalin and Hitler embracing each other were affixed to fences and walls.

In the middle of November came the deportations to Siberia. In Poland as a whole, deportations were conducted on a massive scale, and entire classes of people were targeted, such as the intelligentsia, the aristocrats, and the foresters — the latter because they knew how to use arms. Altogether, hundreds of thousands of Poles — in some estimates, well over a million — were deported to Siberia during the war. In Brańsk, 113 people were taken away, among them 94 Poles, 14 Jews, and 5 Russians. Alter Trus was among the first wave of deportees. According to the Yizkor Book, the Jews singled out for this punishment were mostly the old association activists, so favored through the agitations of the newly privileged Jews. Zbyszek confirms that informing at that time was commonplace, even "fashionable," and that in some cases depositions naming "anti-Communist" foes of the cause were signed by a member of the suspect's own family. The encouragement of such behavior was, of course, another Soviet specialty, designed to destroy the fabric of basic human trust — to turn friend against friend and relative against relative. But in an unforeseen twist of fate, banishment proved to be a stroke of luck for the Jewish exiles, for it removed them from the reach of the Nazi death machine. Among those deported from Brańsk, sixteen people did not survive; others, for varying reasons, did not return.

Irena Jabłonowska also spent five years in Siberia with her family, who were classified as "undesirable bourgeois elements." She thinks that perhaps the new Jewish elite could have helped her family avoid deportation, but she dismisses the conjecture with a resigned, "so it was" flick of the wrist. She thinks that only "rubbishy" people joined the Soviet regime anyway, not the decent Jewish neighbors and families whom she knew. After the war ended, her brother was among those who were afraid to come back to Poland, because they knew they would immediately face reprisals from the new Communist government; he emigrated to England instead.

For Jack Rubin, the twenty-one months of Soviet occupation were not the worst of times. Jack's instincts, from the beginning, were those of a survivor — someone who used all his agility and alertness to sense and outwit danger. As soon as the Germans approached Brańsk, he and his brother made their way to a village farther east. What he knew about the Germans at that time was "only rumors," but those were enough to prompt his instincts to escape. It was only when they saw phalanxes of the Red Army walking toward Brańsk that the brothers decided it was safe to return.

The Russians' first move regarding the Rubins was to confiscate all the geese as well as other parts of the business. "They took everything. We were clean," Jack says. In addition, the Rubins' house had been destroyed in the Luftwaffe fire.

Jack and his brother were undaunted. They immediately started to "manipulate," as he calls it, freely transporting the word from Polish. "From the beginning, the Russians didn't bother you much," he asserts, and although this may seem like a strange thing to say, the Russians didn't exactly run the tightest of ships, and in the cracks people could go on with their lives more or less unobserved. They were known for their drunkenness, these occupiers, and also for being easily, childishly bribable — especially with watches, for which they seemed to have a passion, even though they couldn't always read them. Some of the soldiers, Zbyszek has been told, wore several watches on each arm, showing them off like wondrous ornaments.

Jack and his brother got into the thriving illicit food market. They smuggled barley, flour, and meat to Białystok, and made so much money that within a few months they built themselves a brand-new house. At one point, Jack was arrested and jailed for twelve days, and once again he "manipulated" his way out of jail. But after that he stopped smuggling. Luckily, he was given a job with the Russians, in a concern producing army supplies. "It was so funny with the Russians," Jack says, marveling at their arbitrary ways. Once they ordered him to haul in wood from fifty kilometers away, even though wood was plentiful right near town. When Jack pointed out that this was very expensive, and asked why he should go so far, his superior said, "It's an order." Jack simply disobeyed it and acquired the wood closer to home. In time, Jack impressed his boss so much that he attained the rank of a Stakhanovite — a model worker. When the Polish "turfmeister" was sent to Siberia, Jack got the man's job. Jack's boss said, "Tovarish Rubin, you'll be the turfmeister." "But I don't know what to do," Jack said. That, apparently, didn't matter. Such were the irrational ways of Soviet power — still preferable, as it turned out, to the later, rational ones.

I ask Jack whether he thought the Poles resented him and other Jews for their privileged positions. Again Jack responds with the first of his two paradoxical views: "It was not so much hatred in our town."

Gradually, as the occupation continued, a kind of uneasy calm settled over Brańsk. New educational courses and diversions were organized. There were dance parties, often held outdoors, on a platform built for the purpose. On the night of June 21, 1941, the dance went on till the small hours of the morning. Józef Broida, who would join a partisan unit in the nearby forest and later wrote a memoir about the experience, remembers that dance in lyrical terms. He was still in his teens then, and on that night, life seemed full of possibility, and the faces around him radiant and filled with pleasure.

In the early morning hours of June 22, booming artillery explosions were heard in Brańsk. This caused complete disorientation; even the Soviet soldiers were confused, thinking that the shelling was part of their own army's maneuvers. In fact, it was the boom of Hitler's betrayal. In an abrupt turnabout, he broke the nonaggression pact and launched an attack on the Soviet Union. By nightfall, the German army was once again marching into Brańsk. There was no great battle this time, but in the forest, civilians caught between the two armies were massacred, and escaping Soviet soldiers killed one family in bestial ways, cutting off women's breasts and gouging out eyes. Irena Jabłonowska's father was among forty people being readied for deportation to Siberia; they were immediately murdered. About one hundred Jewish people fled with the Soviet army, knowing this was their best gamble for survival.

On June 25, the Nazis began their reign with the murder of ten Poles, who at the time were burying the bodies of the family massacred by the Soviets. Once again a changeover of power was effected, as the Germans put in their set of "representatives": a Pole named Władysław Dąbrowski, identified as a "known pogromchik" in the Yizkor Book and described by Zbyszek as a man of openly anti-Semitic views, was appointed as mayor; he was soon replaced, however, by a *Volksdeutsch*, a German of Polish nationality. A Nazi garrison was stationed in town. In 1943, this force was strengthened by the addition of a group of Ukrainian fascists.

At the outset, Polish and Jewish police units were formed. At the same time, the Germans appointed a Judenrat, whose task was to carry out all Nazi directives concerning the Jewish population. It was the Judenrat, for example, that assigned people to forced labor details and collected "taxes" for payments and bribes to the Germans. On one level, in creating the Judenrat the Nazis were following their old habits of conquest; but now this administrative body was maneuvered into making utterly untenable choices and executing the Nazis' diabolical demands.

On July 12, a directive written under German auspices but signed by the new mayor was posted in Brańsk, setting a curfew for the entire population and ordering all Jews over ten years old to wear a yellow star or disk on their arm. The measurements and specifications of this badge of humiliation were meticulously detailed. Ritual slaughter of cattle was prohibited.

The directive also included points like the following, which pertained to all inhabitants: "Whoever is suffering from sexual disease, with the danger of infecting others, and who knows of this condition, or should know of the circumstances giving rise to it, has the duty of remaining under medical supervision until complete cure. . . . Until complete cure, all contacts that might cause infection . . . are forbidden." Violations of these orders were going to be severely punished, and "if a German will be infected through contacts, the Commandant of the German Town Command may pronounce the penalty of death."

This was the specific tone of Nazi fanaticism — the tone not only of hostility, or even hatred, but of repulsion, and also of the cold intent to make the colonized population appear repulsive, to portray them as socially leprous. In the Nazi imagery, Poles and Jews were likely to be infected with sexually transmitted diseases. Contact with them was contaminating, and if they inflicted themselves on the clean and healthy race, their presence should simply be eliminated.

But the Jews were being thrust even further out, beyond the borders of common respect and concern. In a seemingly small but vicious directive, Jews were forbidden to greet Germans. Greeting, after all, assumes some human parity, and Jews were supposed to be below humanity, and below notice. The policy of humiliation was sometimes carried out in inventively perverse ways. For example, Jewish elders in Brańsk were forced to give a full funeral to a statue of Lenin erected under the Soviets — an idea aimed purely at exposing Jews to mockery. The object of such orders and such sadistic whimsy was truly the imaginary Jew — no longer only the Jew whose economic power was feared, or whose beliefs were disapproved of, but the ridiculed, the subhuman, the totally repellent and repelled part of human nature.

Jack Rubin remembers the first time the Judenrat ordered all Jewish men to report to the market with their rakes, shovels, and brooms. People had heard from other towns that if you worked for the Germans, you would remain safe. At the same time, the orders said that failure to register for work was punishable by death. "You don't know what to do," Jack says. "You stand there and you shake like a leaf." But the Germans struck a reassuring tone: "If you work for us, you'll be all right."

It was hard to appraise the level of menace at that point. Jack remembers a young boy who came to Brańsk earlier from the German-occupied territory near Warsaw. He had just lost his father, and he told terrible stories of German atrocities in a matter-of-fact, toneless voice. Jack did not believe him. "He don't cry," he recalls. "He tells it like a story. I must say — although I'm ashamed — I thought, His father died only yesterday, how come he don't cry?" Later, Jack found out for himself that there is a certain level of terror that causes the stoppage of all tears. But at the time, he disregarded the boy's tale; undoubtedly, no one wanted to credit such gloomy, dreadful news.

The Judenrat had the onerous task of making work selections and choosing who would be sent to the toughest of the labor encampments, in the village of Łapy, near Brańsk. Alter Trus was in Siberia during the period of the Nazi occupation, but in his reading of events, it was, as always, the poorest people who got the short end of the stick. Writing on the basis of information he collected later, he is critical of the Judenrat. In his eyes, this Nazi-appointed body was yet another form of power, and if there is any underlying moral lesson in the Yizkor Book, it is that power corrupts. He singles out one member, Moshe Tykocki, for praise as a man who refused to hand over Jewish fugitives or denounce fellow Jews, even at the risk of endangering his own life. But in general, Trus describes the Judenrat as cynically self-serving, and details all kinds of abuses of privilege by its members.

Other survivors from Brańsk are more understanding of that unhappy institution's predicament. Jack Rubin remembers a small but telling incident when a Judenrat member went around collecting items like leather gloves and watches at the Germans' behest. Jack's father willingly gave up everything that was asked for. But a woman neighbor resisted the order, vociferously protesting the injustice. "Why my daughter's watch?" she kept shouting. "Why not your own?"

Essentially, the Judenrat had been forced into a zero-sum game: they had a choice of placating their Nazi overseers and thereby becoming the instrument of their vile policies, or of ceasing cooperation and thereby possibly exposing the Jewish population to greater danger. Later, when the horror escalated, the Judenrats in small towns and big cities hoped that by delivering up the required quota of Jews to the Nazis, they could at least keep others from being sent to their deaths. But there were also individuals on these councils who believed that they could save their own lives, or better their own conditions, by remaining dutiful and compliant. On both counts, the people who served on the Judenrats were sadly, tragically wrong, but they did not know this in advance, even at the very approach of catastrophe.

The Yizkor Book is also unforgiving of both Polish and Jewish policemen. According to Alter Trus, the head of the Polish police, named Pietrzak, was a cruel bully who "enjoyed striking Jewish women." Zbyszek gives a different portrait of this man, who eventually deserted his post and formed a peasant battalion in the Brańsk forests. Altogether, the existence of the Polish police is a sore point for Zbyszek: only two of the policemen, he believes, committed actual crimes during the war; two entered the force as spies for the underground resistance movement, and others were recruited into resistance work. A few later escaped, unable to continue their awful work.

Alter Trus also goes to some lengths to demonstrate that the Jewish police "were recruited from the lowest element." The commander was Itzhak Wasser, known as "Tall" Wasser, who according to several testimonies was only too ready to ally himself with his employers. He started speaking German rather than Yiddish, and was eager in pointing out people who weren't wearing the yellow star. Other Jewish policemen took bribes, and punished people for disobeying Nazi regulations.

But regardless of the individual personalities, the social structure of the town was becoming gruesomely, grotesquely warped: the worst were given power and encouraged to do their worst. Cruelty was condoned, while decency was punished. The very notion of humanity — that of Jews in particular — was being willfully, methodically destroyed. In the imagery, vocabulary, and actions of the Nazis, Jews were being transmogrified into something close to animals or commodities. The Poles in Brańsk (as well as the Jews, for that matter) saw from routine daily occurrences that it was perfectly acceptable to hit a Jew.

The Nazi command in Brańsk was headed at first by a "good German," Lieutenant Sturman, who was apparently susceptible to bribes but who nevertheless showed enough kindness toward Jews to be dubbed "Grandfather" by them, in an odd echo of Piłsudski's nickname. The extent of his goodwill cannot be ascertained; what is certain is that even an individual in his position could not alter basic Nazi policy or avert its intended consequences. The structure of the situation was too powerfully determining. For a while, however, Sturman was able to avoid taking the harshest route. When the order to create a ghetto was given in the fall of 1941, he allowed Jews to choose the area in which it would be established, and endorsed the idea of a second, "little ghetto," thus making the conditions of life somewhat more bearable. About 2,400 people, among them Jews from the nearby villages, were herded into the two ghettos. The Poles living within these areas were relocated.

I try to imagine: families loading their belongings onto carts, the hasty leave-takings, the moment of indecision about whether to lock the house; most realized this would be a futile gesture. And the fear, the constriction of heart and nerves, the sense of unknown fatality hanging over it all. The journey to the ghetto wasn't long, but it involved the crossing of an irrevocable line. The Jews were now placed on the "other side," symbolically beyond the pale of society or solidarity. More than that, posters in the town warned the Poles that the penalty for helping Jews, taking food to them, or sheltering them was death. Acts of compassion were being criminalized, made nearly unaffordable.

In the ghetto, overcrowding led to a high rate of disease and mortality. Food was severely rationed. A boot factory was opened, and Jews had to supply the labor. Yet at first a kind of life, and a kind of coping, could go on. This was the period about which Jack Rubin can jokingly say that "with three or four women cooking in the kitchen, you can imagine what it was like." The ghettos were not yet closed off, although their inmates weren't allowed to leave their houses without good reason. Still, the absence of a physical barrier made movement on the sly fairly easy. Smuggling into and out of the ghetto was widespread. Occasionally, whole cows were brought in and slaughtered in the proper way; before Passover, matzo was made in secret. Amazingly, some people managed to spend whole days outside, working in Polish homes as cobblers, tailors, domestics. In the ghetto, anger occasionally erupted in gestures of rebellion. Józef Broida describes an episode in which the hated Tall Wasser beat up his brother for walking around without his yellow insignia. In revenge, Broida and other young men jumped Wasser and administered a cathartic beating.

There was also illegal traffic of goods from Brańsk to Bia-łystok, conducted by both Poles and Jews. Jack was among those who kept smuggling as long as he could, delivering food to the much larger Białystok ghetto. This could get extremely dangerous. Once, two buggies carrying Polish and Jewish smugglers, among them Jack and Józef Broida, were stopped by a German and a Polish policeman. Perhaps because nothing awful happened as a consequence of this, Jack remembers the episode as high drama: the German *Halt!* bringing them to a stop, the order for Christians to stand on one side, Jews on the other. Jack joined the Christians; no one gave him away. Suddenly a confused scuffle ensued in which Broida and the others overpowered the policemen. During the fight, Jack ran off, he knew not where. A few minutes later he found himself near some buildings, face to face with a German soldier. "What are you doing here?" the German asked, and Jack had the presence of mind to answer, "I'm the guard." He got away that time.

In the summer of 1942, the two ghettos were consolidated into one area, and the main ghetto was enclosed by a twelve-foot-high fence. Lieutenant Sturman was recalled, perhaps because he did not carry out his duties with sufficient enthusiasm. He was replaced by a *Volksdeutsch* named Barwinski, and later by someone named G. Schmidt, who apparently had the requisite commitment and temperament for the job.

The closing of the ghetto had one temporarily positive side effect: people could now walk freely on the ghetto's streets and exchange speculations, news, griefs. The news — sometimes hard to distinguish from rumor — was somber. People were beginning to learn of the roundups and deportations from other towns. They had heard about the construction of Treblinka, but were as yet unsure what it was intended for.

And still, a kind of life went on, and some niches for illicit activity remained. According to the Yizkor Book, Christians managed to come in, and even worked for Jewish artisans inside. Others continued to trade food for money. At the same time, premonitions of the worst must have been deepening. Religious feeling and observance increased. The Hasidim prayed in their own prayer house; others turned from "free-thinking" to God.

I try to imagine: a patch of town, almost a village, densely covered by low cottages, now interspersed with tinier huts and sheds, constructed when the inmates of the second ghetto moved in. It is all so small, so exposed, so transparent. How could anyone hope to hide, escape the vigilance of the guards who lit flares at night to monitor all movement in this wretched space?

On the night of November 1, 1942, a warning came from Białystok: the Brańsk ghetto was going to be liquidated the next day. Despair and pandemonium followed. Some people tried to escape before the action was carried out, others ran to hiding places in the ghetto, having prepared for this eventuality.

In the dawn hours of November 2, the roundups started. The Germans, as they had done in other towns, brought in special units of Lithuanian and Ukrainian guards to aid them. Poles were not forced to participate in these brutal procedures, perhaps because they were considered too anti-German or too unruly, or because they lacked the mettle for the job. Despite the sinister cordon surrounding the ghetto, a large number of people broke through the fence or fled through underground openings. Some were wounded or killed before they got out. Several hundred people escaped to the nearby forests or looked for shelter in farmers' houses. A few found refuge; others were turned away by Poles terrified by the murderous atmosphere and by the threat — reiterated constantly over loudspeakers —

of execution for helping Jews. In the next few days, many people returned to the ghetto, not knowing what else to do.

On November 6, the Gestapo gave the order to assemble in the center of the ghetto. At that point, people knew what was in store for them. They said goodbye to each other. Some said Kaddish in their houses. Others destroyed their possessions so as not to leave anything behind for their persecutors. The Yizkor Book records several instances in which Jews refused help offered to them by Poles, because they did not want to abandon the others. In one case, a "Christian shoemaker" prepared a shelter for a Jewish friend, who at the last moment walked back into the ghetto in order to share his family's fate.

As the Germans began to herd people into the five hundred wagons that would take them away, the community's rabbi, Itzhak Zaav Zuckerman, made his farewell to Brańsk — which had seen so many generations of Jews — and to the people before him. "This is a sentence passed in heaven," he is remembered to have said. "We have to die. But I hope that those who survive will tell others of our sufferings." This is a moral mandate that the Yizkor Book and other testimonies have fulfilled.

In the next three days, two thousand people were transported to Bielsk and then to Treblinka. On November 10, several hours after arriving at the concentration camp, they were all murdered in the gas chambers.

In the chaos of the ghetto's liquidation, there seemed to be a range of responses from the Polish population. There were examples of monstrous cruelty, such as a Polish policeman who gratuitously shot and killed Jewish children. Others delivered Jews to the Gestapo. In the village of Oleksin, the mayor, named Józef Adamczuk, forced some of the inhabitants to join a search for Jews, whose presence in the surrounding forests had become known. He was the cause of fourteen deaths. (In

1948, a Polish court gave him a life sentence, which was later commuted to ten years.)

But insofar as one can judge from scattered stories and memories, among the populace the impulse of ordinary compassion was still alive. In an incident described in the Yizkor Book, when a Gestapo officer caught several Jews trying to escape from the ghetto, a group of Poles, summoned by the distressing cries, gathered round and pleaded for their release. Józef Broida, who hardly glosses over Polish transgressions, remembers a Pole who wept as he described scenes of carnage in the ghetto.

In the following days, placards appeared declaring Brańsk to be *Judenfrei*. Nevertheless, the Nazis in their bureaucratic efficiency, realized that a sizable number had managed to escape their net. The actual figures are difficult to pin down; Zbyszek estimates that between 200 and 350 people were unaccounted for. In any case, the Nazis announced a hunt for the hidden Jews. The Catholic priest, to his credit, preached a sermon in which he told people to "wash their hands" of such murderous activity, and enjoined them to help those in need.

In the next few days many of those in hiding were caught. The stories of the two main captures and surrender are painful in the extreme. In one case, Isaiah Cukier came back from Bielsk with the Gestapo and led them to several hiding places. (He was the former Judenrat member who had gone to the pharmacy asking for the Shapiros, and whose curious behavior had been witnessed by Janina Woińska.) Altogether, he was responsible for giving away seventy people, among them two Poles who were evidently smuggling food to one of the hidden groups. The motives for his actions remain enigmatic. Woińska defends him, saying that when she saw him, he was clearly frightened and disoriented. Some of the Jewish survivors conjecture that he was tortured in Bielsk or was acting in the naive belief that Jews would only be taken to a labor camp. Others believe he was trying to save his own life by complying with the Gestapo. On the morning following the roundup, the seventy unfortunates were taken to the Jewish cemetery, where they were ordered to undress and were shot. The Yizkor Book says that many Poles were forced to witness the massacre.

There was still one major hiding place left in the ghetto, a bunker with about thirty people huddled inside. It was destroyed when a woman inadvertently started a fire while cooking. As the people emerged from the burning enclosure and tried to flee, they were shot by the Nazis, led by a soldier called Martin by the locals. Twenty-three of the people were killed, and buried by Christians in the Jewish cemetery.

This was the end of the Brańsk ghetto, and of the Jewish community. From then on, there were only remnants, human atoms scattered in the forests and in Polish houses. For them, there were two ways to survive: through solitary ingenuity or through attempts to join with others in similar danger.

Jack Rubin took the solitary road. On the night before the ghetto's liquidation, a Pole whom he knew knocked on his window and warned him of what was to come. That was the last moment when it was still relatively easy to escape. Jack and his family made their way to the house of farmers who used to work for the Rubins' geese business. Once there, they had to figure out what to do next. Jack's father asked him what was going to happen. Jack said that things looked very bad, and he would try to hide in the woods. His parents decided they were too old for that, and they would go back to the ghetto voluntarily. Jack's mother said that in that case, they should give Jack their remaining money; they would have no need for it anymore. Jack couldn't bring himself to take it. He tried to say that this might be a false alarm, that maybe nothing terrible would happen. But it was the last time he saw his parents. He cries now, sixty-four years later, when he recalls that moment. Then, there was no time and no space to cry.

There was only the urgent task of survival. The following day, Jack joined his brother, who with a few others was at the house of a farmer whom they trusted. This man, named Kozłowski, showed an almost self-abnegating magnanimity toward them later on, but at this point he was afraid. The atmosphere in Brańsk was ominous. The ghetto had been fortified with barbed wire and lit by searchlights. Everywhere there were German, Lithuanian, and Ukrainian guards with large dogs. So Kozłowski, after feeding everyone, asked the fugitives to leave. Otherwise, he was sure, they would all be discovered and killed.

Jack, his brother, and other relatives spent several weeks in the woods, coming across others who had retreated into this primitive refuge. After dark, they sneaked into Brańsk, entreating farmers for food and a night's shelter in barns or stables. They were lucky: they were not found or betrayed. But the countryside was turning deadly dangerous. The hunt for Jews was on, and aside from the vigilant Germans and their cohorts, there were enough Poles willing to inform to make evasion very difficult. In a forest near Brańsk, a group of people hiding in holes dug in the ground were discovered by someone who notified the Germans of his find. A few managed to escape, but most were murdered on the spot.

There are more accounts like this in the Yizkor Book, too many for anyone's comfort. It is no longer possible to know the motives of the informers or how many there were. It would have taken only a few to do untold damage. Some may have been frightened of failing to cooperate with the Germans. Some

were undoubtedly after the money they believed Jews had
with them or the meager reward — one-half kilo of sugar! —
received for bringing a Jew to the Gestapo. There were also
people for whom Jews and Communists were still inextricably
tangled, and for whom killing Jews was considered political
revenge. The notoriously cruel Rycz brothers, who relished
torturing Jews, are reported to have shouted "No Jew or Communist gets out of our hands alive!" as they attempted to kill
the brother of Alter Trus. People in Brańsk long remembered
Jewish corpses floating in the river with their throats slit and
the water running bloody. Under Nazi stimulation, brutality
was becoming normalized. One gains the impression that, as
Jewish lives were further devalued, as Jewish men and women
were reduced to hunted animals, it became easier for some
Poles to identify with the aggressor — to lengthen the emotional distance between themselves and the victims, and give
away Jewish lives as casually as one might slaughter a non-
human creature.

There may also have been, for some Poles, an awful element
of transferred aggression — rage deflected from its actual, unat-
tainable target to a much more vulnerable one. Attempts to take
armed action against the Germans were countered with wholesale carnage. In 1942, the village of Rajsk, near Brańsk, was
burned to the ground, and all 140 of its inhabitants murdered, in retaliation for the killing of four Germans. In 1943, the
village of Koszewo met the same fate, with 200 people massacred, this time for aiding the partisans. In September of that
year, when a resistance unit shot the German commandant of
Brańsk, someone apparently intervened on behalf of the local
population, and instead the Germans killed 118 people in a
Białystok prison.

Jack kept evading all danger. His will to live was enormous, and he thought that the worst would be over in a matter of weeks. In retrospect, he reflects that if people in hiding had known how long the war was going to last, their determination to survive would have flagged, and they would have given up. Jack did not, and after a while Kozłowski allowed three Jewish men — Jack, his brother, and a friend — to stay in his stable. However, when Jack's sister-in-law and the third man's girlfriend came to join them, Kozłowski got worried. No women, he insisted, and Jack pretended to go along with him. But the women stayed on in the stable without Kozłowski's knowledge.

Within a few days a crisis arose, which Jack remembers in every detail. Jack's sister-in-law had left her nine-month-old baby in the house of a Pole, who promised to take care of it. She now wanted to bring it to Kozłowski's stable. This was a time of terrible — of tragic — choices. Jack said that "with the child, we will all be dead." Without the child, there was a chance of survival. The hapless mother screamed at Jack, calling him a bandit and a murderer. Eventually she relented, and the group decided to send an intermediary — another Pole whom they trusted — to check on the child's welfare. He returned and reassured the mother that the child was being treated well. The messenger went to see the child every few days, bearing small offerings for its temporary guardian.

In the meantime, conditions in the stable were becoming awful. Jack's group were filthy, infested with lice, and bleeding from skin lesions. When a distant relative came to see them, he was shocked by their state and suggested that they make their way to the big Białystok ghetto, where getting through the winter would be easier. As Jack tells it, an "action" had just taken place there in which ten thousand people were removed; that meant things should be quiet for a while. In telling his story, he does not stop to reflect on the horror of such considerations. In those times, one could not pause for death; one had to find the niches of survival.

Jack and the others agreed that Białystok was a preferable alternative and prepared to leave. They agreed they would take the baby with them. When they went to retrieve it, they found that the farmer had panicked after Germans showed up at his house, and he dropped the infant on someone else's doorstep. Again it was ascertained that the child was well — although its presence had now been reported to the Germans. The group then formulated a risky plan: Jack's sister-in-law would go into the house where the child was now kept, snatch it, drop some money on the floor, and run out to a sled waiting for her. She executed this plan faultlessly. "And this wasn't a gangster with a gun," Jack says in an admiring tribute. "This was a mother. A mother who fought to get her child back."

Neither mother nor child was to live much longer. Of the fourteen people who set out for the Białystok ghetto, only Jack reached his destination. On the way there in their sled, in sub-zero weather, they were warned by a passer-by that a village they were about to enter was full of Germans looking for men to ship off to labor camps. Not knowing another route, Jack's group asked another Pole for directions. He showed them the way, but about two hours later, in the dark, as they stopped to rest and eat, they heard the sound of a sled approaching them. What happened next was instantaneous. As soon as Jack discerned that the sled was driven by two horses, his reflexes told him it was the Germans. He turned and ran. His brother, who was practically touching shoulders with him, did not follow. Neither did any of the others. As Jack ran blindly ahead, he heard machine-gun fire. A day or two later, he learned that thirteen people had been killed on the road to Białystok. He feels sure that the Pole whom they met on the road had given them away.

This is one of the points in the story where Jack has to pause, his face contorting with suppressed tears. "And now I blame myself for not warning my brother" is what comes out. "In the woods, I never cried. When others cried, I said we shouldn't cry because our families got killed, we should cry because we're still alive." But in fact, Jack wanted to live very much. On the night of the shootings he ran, and then walked for many miles; he stumbled and fell into a frozen river. Then he was too tired to continue. He had to ask someone for help. But who, how to know which house to choose? Curiously, it was a rule of thumb for people on the run that the poor-looking houses were safer. He chose one standing off by itself, away from any village, and knocked on the door. There was a brief exchange. The man went back into the house to consult with his wife, then he told Jack to come in. He gave Jack something to eat and let him stay overnight. In the morning, Jack offered his host some money, and the man led him all the way to Białystok, walking ahead so he could signal to Jack of approaching danger.

The man left him on the outskirts of Białystok. Now Jack was really on his own, and a sense of bleak solitude enters his narrative. Jack somehow inveigled himself into the Białystok ghetto, where he spent several months, using his talent for "manipulating" to make money again. Between raids by the Gestapo, a surreal semblance of normality prevailed. Some Poles were brought in to work; Jews were taken each morning to work outside. In addition, there was an underground convoy that smuggled things from Białystok to the Warsaw ghetto. Jack tried to join in this activity, but was warned away at gunpoint. There were people in the ghetto who had arms, later used in an uprising.

Jack lived through an "action" during which he hid with about seventy others in a concealed room on the fourth floor of a building. There the group sat huddled, listening fearfully to the terrifying sounds of the hunt for human beings. Somewhere in the dark, a baby got increasingly restless and unhappy. When its cries became too dangerous, it was taken from its mother to the other end of the hiding place. Soon its cries ceased; the mother understood that it had been strangled. When the group could finally emerge, Jack was handed the small body to carry. He remembers that it felt like a piece of wood.

The ghetto was being emptied out. It was time to go. Jack had acquired a partner named Ben in preparation for this moment. It was understood by everyone that to be totally alone was the worst condition. Jack was desirable as a survival companion: he was strong and resourceful, and he had already spent some time in the woods. With a handshake, he and Ben sealed an agreement that they would stay together and help each other whatever happened.

After returning to Brańsk, Jack decided to turn once again to Kozłowski, the farmer who had sheltered him before. Kozłowski was incredulous and moved to see Jack again; he thought Jack had died with the others on the road to Białystok. He unhesitatingly decided to give shelter to Jack and Ben, and soon afterward he built a concealed addition to the stable that made a relatively safe hiding place — at least as safe as anything could be in the flat countryside near Brańsk. There, Jack and his friend spent the remaining months of the war. In the winter it was very cold; in the summer, with the sun beating down on the roof of their stifling space, it was unbearably hot. But they were safe and in the hands of people who wished them well.

Jack speaks of Kozłowski as an "angel," a "gentleman," a man of decency but also of delicacy. The farmer not only saved

Jack's and Ben's lives but tried to soften the harshness of their lot as much as possible. When he began to feel more secure, he invited them into the house to eat with his family. If there was any troubling news, he waited until after they had eaten to tell them. He brought them newspapers. Once when the Germans were nearby, he got very nervous — Jack could tell, because he started picking at his teeth with a piece of straw. Kozłowski said he thought the two men should leave temporarily; it was his adolescent son who dissuaded him. From Kozłowski's point of view, all of his actions carried the ultimate risk. People knew that an old woman in Brańsk had been killed by the Nazis for sheltering Jews. Another Polish family narrowly escaped death when their property was burned down by the Germans, and remained in hiding for the rest of the war. Another person was sent to a concentration camp for offering minimal help. Yet others were sent to labor camps, including a man who was punished when a young Jewish boy was found to be huddling, without the man's knowledge, in his field. In what was perhaps the most shocking incident to the local populace, in July 1943 a priest named Henryk Opiatowski, who was a member of the Home Army, was executed for helping Jews and Soviet deserters from labor camps. Kozłowski and others like him knew they were risking not only their own but their families' lives.

At the very end, however, it was too dangerous for the two fugitives to remain where they were. The Germans were retreating from the Soviet Union, and the front was approaching Brańsk again. Skirmishes and fires erupted everywhere. The Kozłowski stable might well get caught in the middle. Jack and his friend made their way to a swamp outside town. There they constructed a sort of platform from tree branches, which kept them barely above the pestilent waters. They heard the Germans screaming. "How they screamed!" Jack recalls. One night, they saw a tank rolling eerily in the distance. There was a shootout. Then, "so quiet — you didn't hear nothing." They saw a convoy coming in their direction and listened intently for the sounds of speech. At last they heard: it was Russian. They emerged from the swamp with their hands up. *"Tovarishi, my Yevrei,"* Jack said. Comrades, we are Jewish. The *tovarish* facing them told them to relax and gave them cigarettes — American cigarettes!

It was August 1, 1944, and they were free. The two men walked back, in broad daylight and on the open road, to the place that had been their refuge. Kozłowski came out to meet them and walked toward Jack. "Nu, Pan Yankiel," he said, spreading his hands, "you survived." And that was when Jack broke down and cried.

⁓   ⁓   ⁓

During the twenty-one months of Jack Rubin's infernal journey, a group of Jews were trying to survive in a different way, by organizing a self-defense group in the forests against the longest odds. The two written accounts of these partisans' activities — in the Yizkor Book and in Józef Broida's memoir, *In the Forests of Brańsk* — do not tally with each other in every detail. The memoir was initially transcribed from oral reminiscences, and Brańsk survivors admit that its heroic and exciting tale contains elements of exaggeration and self-inflation. Still, the outlines of events are clearly discernible, and compelling enough even in their pared down version.

The idea of armed resistance was apparently engendered in the ghetto when seventeen-year-old Herszel Rubin (no relation to Jack) began buying weapons, possibly from a German soldier who was a closet Communist. After escaping from the ghetto, Herszel hid in the woods with his sister Dora, where they were joined by a few others, including Józef Broida. At first the most acute danger to the small group came from an unexpected quarter: clusters of escaped Soviet prisoners, who were also trying to weather the war in the forest, and who wanted to prevent Jewish fugitives from penetrating their terrain. The Jewish group debated whether to attack the Russian opponents or to persuade them to make common cause. They chose the latter alternative, and gradually the two small bands started acting in concert, as the Jews demonstrated the will and the ability to defend themselves.

It is striking that the instigators and main actors in the Jewish group were mostly very young. Of course, in part this was natural, given the strenuous physical demands of the task. Still, even Alter Trus observes that the young people at that time acted with admirable resourcefulness. It may be that the younger generation, schooled in political thinking and activism, could more easily conceive their awful situation in collective terms, and also that they were better prepared to take initiatives, even of a militant kind. To begin with, Herszel and Dora were the recognized leaders of the Jewish group. According to Broida's reminiscences, they undertook several extremely hazardous actions, such as staging an assault on a German training center for the infamous Gestapo dogs. The Yizkor Book and Józef Broida attribute to them heroic deaths; but this, alas, was not the reality. After an interval in the forest, they chose to go into hiding in a farmer's house, and in the summer of 1943, they were discovered by the Germans. Herszel apparently tried to shoot, but his pistol jammed. Both he and Dora were killed. The Yizkor Book tells us that Christian villagers buried brother and sister "with great respect and honor to their memory."

The forest partisans continued to function and even to grow, adding people who escaped from Białystok after the liquidation of the ghetto and even from the train transports to Treblinka. From 1943 on, there were more than eighty Jews trying to survive in this way. They organized themselves into a unit, consisting of a "family camp," which sheltered those who could not use weapons, and a defense camp. Their supply of arms was replenished by "intelligent Poles," who were sympathetic to their plight and who included schoolteachers and a priest. In addition, there was the Russian group, with which the Jews were now formally cooperating. In deference to the Russians' greater military experience, the entire unit was placed under Russian command.

It is a consistent element of all the testimonies by and about the Jewish fighters that, despite the devastating personal losses they sustained, their morale improved as soon as they got weapons and learned to use them. The arms, of course, literally made it possible for them to defend themselves, but the weapons also lessened their sense of humiliation and helplessness, of being turned into pure victims. Gradually the Jewish group gained enough confidence to come out of their bunkers and live aboveground. With arms, hunger became less of a problem. Given their conditions, they were not scrupulous about the methods of acquiring food. They conducted raids on farmers' stores, or "requisitioned" food at gunpoint. They also had contacts with Poles who were willing to deliver food voluntarily. The raids led to later acts of revenge, but the accounts stress that Poles grew much more respectful when they realized that the Jews who had come to negotiate with them were armed.

The unit was capable of military engagement. In December 1943, a group of Germans and Ukrainians led by Shumanski, a man notorious for his brutality, attacked the forest camps. Shumanski was killed by the partisans' Russian commander, and the Germans retreated. On two occasions, members of the group carried out executions of Poles who were known for anti-Jewish atrocities. In both cases, military protocol was observed: the sentences were read out to the men in the presence of witnesses before they were shot, and notices informing the surrounding villages of what had happened were posted. Grim as such scenes were, their descriptions in Józef Broida's memoirs and in the Yizkor Book brim over with feelings — surely justified — of relief and triumph.

At the beginning of 1944, the Brańsk group was contacted by a regular Soviet military unit that had penetrated the forest, bringing with it equipment, paratroopers, and fighting know-how. The disparate bands of fugitives in the surrounding forests were transformed into proper partisan units and brought under Soviet army command. There were four units; the Brańsk division was named the Zhukov group. The partisans were given missions: to cut telephone lines, to raid German food depots, to destroy tactically important bridges. They recruited Poles to inform them of any suspicious movements in the villages, and brought a Polish doctor to the forest to treat the wounded. The Poles also tipped them off to the presence of a spy, who was executed; later, a Russian woman was interrogated and shot for spying as well. In May 1944, the forest was surrounded by a battalion of Germans and Ukrainians. The partisans managed to fend off this force with minimal losses.

Another recurring theme in the Jewish accounts is the danger posed to the partisans by the Home Army, known as the AK (Armia Krajowa). The AK was the chief resistance force in Poland, aside from the rival Communist underground. The resistance movement in Poland embraced all segments of the population; it was proportionally the largest of any occupied country. In Brańsk, the AK units did not carry out many military operations, because they were afraid of reprisals against civilians. For the most part, the Home Army engaged in intelligence activities and in gathering arms for a potential large-scale encounter.

The Yizkor Book speaks bitterly of several incidents in which people who were perceived as members of the AK assaulted or killed Jews. Zbyszek, on the basis of his research, vehemently denies such allegations. He believes that such acts of violence were committed by bandits who used the AK as a cover. He points out that the AK executed two people who had stolen guns from it, and employed the weapons for "dirty work." When the AK was implicated directly, Zbyszek believes, it was for other reasons. He cites one episode in which the AK attacked a group of eight Soviets and four Jews, in retaliation for their violent behavior during food raids. One Jew was killed in that skirmish, and two Russians wounded. Zbyszek also notes that members of the AK did try to help Jews by warning them when their hiding places were discovered or reported to the Germans.

The relationship between the AK and the Jews in Poland as a whole was complex, and remains today a wrenchingly contested matter. The Jews blame the AK for its failure to do much — hardly anything — to help the most cruelly persecuted part of Poland's population. The Poles retort that the AK could barely help itself — that it was fighting for Poland's survival from a highly vulnerable position, with insufficient resources and arms and almost no help from the West. At the same time, it has often been pointed out in its defense that the AK did not remain entirely indifferent to Jewish fate. In the big cities, AK cells dispensed false papers that enabled Jews to pass for Gentiles. As a matter of policy, the resistance movement strongly condemned informers, and some of the AK's leftist units went so far as to execute Poles who were known to have denounced

Jews. In what was undoubtedly one of its proudest accomplish-
ments, in 1942 the AK created a Council for Providing Aid to
the Jews (known as Żegota), a body consisting of Catholics and
Jews which helped Jews escape from ghettos and conceal themselves on the "Aryan" side. When the Warsaw Ghetto Uprising
broke out in April 1943, the Home Army publicly declared its
solidarity with the fighters inside. The ghetto fighters, in turn,
used the old romantic slogan of Polish resistance in their
proclamations and appeals for support: "For your freedom, and
for ours." However, it has recently been revealed that some
murders of Jews were probably committed by AK members
who belonged to its extreme right-wing units.

In the eastern borderlands, the politics of Polish-Jewish relations continued to be further complicated by the proximity of
the Soviet Union. Although active hostilities were suspended in
1941, when Stalin entered into an alliance with Poland against
Germany, the nationalist resistance never ceased to view the
Soviets, or the Communist underground, with wary suspicion.
Toward the end of the war, as the Russian front neared Brańsk,
a meeting was held in the forest between the Soviet military
command and the AK. The Soviets demanded the surrender of
arms; the AK refused. On August 2, 1944, the day after the Red
Army liberated Brańsk, the Soviets attempted to take power.
They were unsuccessful.

The Poles, at this stage of the war, had renewed reasons to
feel impotent wrath toward the Soviets. People in Brańsk
would have been well aware of the events in Warsaw, where, at
the end of July, the AK called for a last-stand uprising against
the Nazis. As the population of the city turned all its resources
to wage a desperate battle, the supposedly friendly Red Army
stood on the other bank of the Vistula River, waiting while
Warsaw was razed to the ground, and its inhabitants slaugh-

tered. The uprising lasted sixty-three days, in the course of which 240,000 civilians lost their lives. When it was all over, the Red Army simply crossed the river and occupied the city. Some of the Polish leaders of the long battle referred to the Warsaw Ghetto Uprising as a precedent for their own heroic action, but both bids for survival and freedom were doomed from the start.

For Brańsk the war did not end in 1944, or even in 1945. The Soviet army remained in the town until January 1945. Between August and November 1944, a new wave of arrests and deportations to Siberia started in Brańsk and throughout Poland, aimed mainly at the AK and Polish elites. In a neighboring village, twenty members of the Home Army were killed. For the next three years, a state of virtual civil war prevailed in the Podlasie region, with murderous hostilities breaking out between Communists and the AK, between various armed partisan units and vigilante groups, between Poles and Belarusians, and, farther south, between Poles and Ukrainians, who slaughtered each other in impressive numbers. In addition, "common banditry," as Zbyszek calls it, was widespread. In one incident, a priest was killed during a failed robbery. There were other wanton killings and assaults. Some deserters from the AK, turned into bandits, were executed by the AK itself.

After the Jewish survivors emerged from their hiding places, they congregated in one house in Brańsk. There were sixty-four of them, although seventy-six survived altogether. They were painfully aware of the utter devastation of their community and their way of life. They were desolated; this was the first time they took the measure of their losses. They still did not feel secure in their hometown. They could see that Polish peasants, who had occupied Jewish homes, were afraid that the former owners would try to reclaim their properties and belongings. They were aware of the atmosphere of lawlessness and disarray.

In March 1945, two young Jewish women who were taking sewing lessons from a Polish seamstress were murdered for unknown reasons. The seamstress was killed as well. At that point, the cluster of survivors decided to move to Białystok. In 1947, a Jewish man who had come to the Brańsk market was shot dead in the middle of the day. It is rumored that he had stolen some money, and this was the lawless revenge. But from then on, no Jewish person came to Brańsk for a long time.

By 1948, most of the remaining Jews of Brańsk had emigrated to the United States and to Israel. Jack puts his reasons for leaving Poland succinctly: "How could I stay in a place where the land was soaked in blood?"

Epilogue ♨

AT NIGHT in Brańsk, I lie awake listening to a chorus of crows whose eerie, screeching cries all too fittingly disturb the dark. By any measure, the story of Brańsk's Jews, of Poles and Jews during the Holocaust, of Poland during the war, is an awful story. It induces awe, and it induces horror. To touch it is to risk moral vertigo, a sickness unto death. But if we choose not to fall silent before it (as we well might), if we choose to reflect and analyze, then what can we make of it, what can we understand?

There were those who helped and those who harmed. On one level, that is all we know. It is too late, in most cases, to know why people acted as they did, the state of their souls as they did so, their full considerations and motives. Perhaps it isn't even right to speak of motives. The war in Poland created circumstances so uniquely terrible that the usual patterns of cause, intention, and consequence were altered, as the behavior of molecules alters under extraordinary pressure. If we are to make an attempt at understanding, we have to take the psychological effects of this ethical warp into account in our criteria of judgment.

In relation to Jews in particular, the Nazi occupation created a world of monstrously inverted morality. It was a world in which the ordinary qualities of decency, responsibility toward others, concern, and compassion were criminalized, and in which rank brutality and sadism were normalized. We must imagine this: a pastoral town or village in which life looked, on the surface, almost normal, but which had actually been turned into a zone of legalized perversion — a zone in which the indigenous population, not very sophisticated or educated, was rewarded (albeit poorly) for selling the lives of its neighbors and killed for helping them, and in which the message of this law was reinforced by the pervasive presence of murderous occupiers, armed guards, and vicious police dogs.

In this atmosphere, there were some who took the new rules as permission to behave swinishly, and yet others who felt liberated by them into bestiality and violence. When criminality is rewarded, there will always be those who are pleased to take advantage of this incentive. When sadism is legitimized and unleashed, there will be those whose latent cruelty, released from the usual inhibitions, will emerge and flourish. Although the situation of Poles and Jews was not equivalent at that time, we must not too easily glide over the fact that, when pushed to extremes, there were Jews as well who did not behave according to the highest ethical standards. Among the Poles in Brańsk, in Zbyszek's reckoning, there were two groups of "catchers" who worked for the Germans in denouncing Jews. There were a few who undoubtedly delighted in murdering Jews personally. There were rough youths for whom spotting hiding places may have been in the nature of a game, particularly when the detachment from the humanity of those hidden had turned into entrenched indifference.

But there were others who found it in themselves to behave with common decency, at a time when such behavior required uncommon courage and selflessness. Even the motives of the rescuers cannot always be understood in ordinary moral terms. Sometimes the decision to help was made on the basis of considered principle, and renewed over time; all honor to those who had the largesse of spirit to sustain such acts. But often life-and-death choices had to be made in an instant, on the basis of lightning-quick calculation. Whether to open the door to a Jewish stranger in the middle of the night, whether to let someone in and offer bedding and food — the gestures made in such emergencies are often impulsive, a kind of condensation or crystallization of deeply ingrained values and instinctive reactions. Undoubtedly, the outcome of such situations depended on a person's previous attitudes toward Jews in general, but the answer to a plea for help could also be swayed by the state of someone's larder or the expression on the face of the person at the door. There were people who were willing to protect a Jewish neighbor from across the street, but who might have turned away a stranger from the other end of town. It was another feature of the distorted morality of the time that preferences and aversions that would normally have been insignificant and mundane carried ultimate and tragic consequences.

Poland did not have a policy toward the Jews during the war — it was not in the position to have one. The decisions about how to behave toward a population slated for extinction were wholly individual. For the survivors who felt so radically abandoned and for Poles who feel that their national character has been impugned, the question of proportions becomes important. Were there more Poles who helped, or more who harmed?

The attempt to reduce such matters to sums has its own presumptuousness, and requires tolerance for ambiguity, for keeping opposites in mind at the same time. And yet some things need to be pointed out. If one listens carefully to the stories of the survivors, or reads their accounts, one is struck by the number of people who were willing to take small or big risks to help them: in Jack Rubin's story, the farmers who let him sleep in their barns, the intermediary who checked on his sister-in-law's child, the man who led the way for him to Białystok — not to speak of the Kozłowski family, all of whom were implicated in hiding two Jewish men over many months. But (assuming that Jack's hunch about how his family died is correct): the single action of one man accidentally meeting a sled on the road at night, and making the possibly casual decision to inform the Gestapo of what he saw, ended the lives of thirteen people in one stroke. In the impossible calculus of that time, it took at least several people to save a Jewish life; it took only one person to cause the deaths of many. Moreover, the presence of a few who were willing to betray a Jewish presence was enough to paralyze many others. The fear of informers must have been as strong for the helpers as for those who were hidden.

If one listens less carefully, it is easy to let the shock of the atrocities overwhelm all other parts of the story and drown our capacity for understanding. For the survivors themselves, as they tried desperately to wrest a few lives from catastrophe, the Polish betrayals could well cover the landscape and suffuse their psyches with darkness. These acts of coldness and cruelty were gratuitously merciless, an unbearable addition to the policy of wholesale extermination. They were aimed at people who were already hounded, whose vulnerability was extreme. Hurtfully, Polish crimes of commission and omission happened in familiar places, and they were perpetrated by familiars, by people whose faces or characters were intelligible and known. After the war, much of the sorrow, fury, and moral outrage of survivors was directed at these personal perpetrators. Their actions were unforgivable, and they remain so. But in survivors' memories one can often discern, besides the fully justified hate, a kind of elision of hatred, a transference of it from the first-order cause of their suffering to the one nearer at hand. After all, it is hard to direct true, living hatred at an impersonal death machine, at the monolithic Nazis. The German soldiers in Brańsk had frightening, hard faces — everyone agrees on that — but they existed at such a remove of power and terror that they were hardly individual; they were embodiments of an abstract force. But the Polish behavior — the "catching," the informing, the trading in Jewish lives — had the nastiness of intimate betrayal. In addition to being deadly, such deeds were piercingly, consummately wounding. "Now you see why we hate the Polacks," one survivor concluded her account, in which she presented many instances of Poles' help. There was no word about hating the Germans. It is possible that the Nazis were beyond hate, transferred to the realm of psychological trauma, of numbing and wordlessness.

The land was indeed soaked in blood. But more than fifty years later, the task may be different from what it was then. Immediately after the war, it was necessary to bring transgressors to justice. It was necessary to mourn and to hate. Today the task of memory may be not to forgive those who were guilty but to put together the disparate parts of the picture, to understand the structure of the awful situation as a whole.

᧰   ᧰   ᧰

As I walk around Brańsk with Zbyszek and contemplate its lovely views — the angled slope of the riverbank, the gentle curve of the river — I now cannot help but imagine: that flat stretch of land leading away from the river was an escape route to ostensibly safer places. I can envision the dark silhouettes moving across that space at night, under a row of trees that provided a sort of cover. Not much of one. The parish house where the German command had its quarters stands right above these flatlands, overlooking the river and its other bank. A light turned on by a patrolling soldier could have caught anyone in its glare. It is all so naively rural, so exposed. And of course the exposure must have added to Polish fears. It wasn't easy to conceal anything or anyone from the vigilant eyes of potential killers or betrayers.

Zbyszek talks about the betrayers with reluctance. When I ask about statistics of survival in Brańsk, he hesitates before telling me about the damage caused by Poles. "Should I really talk about it?" he asks, looking troubled. But we agree that if we want to understand the truth, we must tell all of it. Zbyszek brings out the figures: by his count, Brańsk "bandits" were responsible for the deaths of thirty-two Jewish people. If one includes the surrounding villages, the number, by his count, rises to seventy.

Zbyszek is quick to add that nine Brańsk families, which would have included about forty persons, have been honored as Righteous Gentiles by the Yad Vashem memorial in Israel. He is proud of such people, and believes that they represent the Polish norm, and also the normal human instincts. In his view, the murderers and informers were the aberration, the inevitable marginal fringe of people all too easily prodded into crime in the climate of Nazi lawlessness. The survivors believe just the opposite. They think that anti-Semitic hatred was the Polish norm, and that during the war, the anti-Semitism lurking in every Pole came out and showed its true virulence. On this issue, as on many others, Polish memories and Jewish memories remain stubbornly, even unyieldingly, divided.

The divergence of views on this matter points to another, more structural question: Was the wartime situation so exceptional that it has to be viewed as an encapsulated period without any connections to the historical past, or was behavior during that period an outcome of previous relations between Poles and Jews? Ironically, one of the historical continuities between "before" and "after" can be discerned precisely in the difference of memories and views on such matters. There is still "them" and "us" in this quarrel, as there was "them" and "us" before the war. Jewish concerns are still "not ours" to the Poles, and vice versa.

The gap that still divides the two communities today is the most persistent fact of their common history, and perhaps it is in that gap that we should look for the continuities in Polish behavior. During the war, it was the sense of separateness that — whatever the nuances of personal attitude — had to be overcome by any Pole who made a conscious decision to help. Before the war, most Poles and Jews did not include each other within the sphere of mutual and natural obligations. A Pole who decided to risk his or her house, life, and family for a Jewish person was stretching his compassion beyond the bounds of absolute responsibility. And there are Jewish survivors honest enough to say that if the roles had been reversed, they cannot vouch for how they would have acted toward people whom they still call "the goyim."

It is quite possible that without the rifts separating the two groups, the proportion of inhumane to humane behavior, of callousness to kindness, would have been different; that more people would have felt the compelling ethical imperative to help. This would not have altered the situation substantially. The Nazi intention to eliminate the Jews was the first and last cause of the Final Solution, and short of massive international intervention, the intention would have been carried out. But some lives would have been saved instead of being wantonly eliminated, and what is just as important, inclusion in the circle of concern would have made the Jews of Poland — as of other countries, for that matter — feel less alone, less abandoned in their most tragic hour.

ॐ   ॐ   ॐ

Now the shtetl, the world of Polish Jews, is no more, and the two nations, the two peoples, confront each other with two sets of memories. In the confrontation, both have felt that their moral truth has been violated. Poland lost three million non-Jewish citizens during the war. It put up the most concerted resistance of any occupied country and had its independence wrested away by infuriatingly unjust means. The Poles have felt that none of this has been recognized as the world has asked — often much too righteously — why they failed to save more Jewish people from death.

The Jews have felt just as outraged and wounded when the Poles have emphasized their wartime heroism while giving scant attention to the genocide committed on their soil and to their own contributions to Jewish suffering and losses. When I was growing up in Poland, I gradually understood that there had been two cataclysms in the land, that although most of the adults I knew had suffered tragedies, my parents' war was horribly — for a long time unspeakably — different from the war experienced by our Polish neighbors.

But that other war — the Holocaust — came to be surrounded by secrecy and silence. Not entirely, and not immediately: right after the war, the Central Jewish Historical Committee set up branches in most towns and cities, to record the accounts of witnesses of wartime events and bring perpetrators of crimes to justice. A parallel Polish committee was also established. As a result, several Nazi leaders were put on trial. Among others, Rudolf Hess, the commandant of Auschwitz, was executed in 1947. At least some of the Poles found guilty of crimes against Jews were sentenced to prison or condemned to death. In another gesture of acknowledgment, on the fifth anniversary of the Warsaw Ghetto Uprising, a monument was erected on its site. The Warsaw Uprising — the desperate insurrection of Poles against the Nazis — was not honored with a comparable commemoration, to the considerable bitterness of many Poles. In a brazen inversion of the truth, the Home Army was portrayed by the Communists as pro-German, and public remembrance of Polish resistance was prohibited for several decades.

At the same time, the immediate postwar period saw ugly outbreaks of anti-Jewish violence, including the infamous Kielce pogrom of 1946, in which forty-two Jews were killed in a massacre possibly provoked by the Communist government. In the following decades, the country subsided into a moral miasma of official lies and private rancors and frustrations. By the time I was growing up, the subject of the Holocaust had become surrounded with an aura of taboo. The reasons for this were undoubtedly in part psychological. In most countries, and even among survivors themselves, a kind of latency period seemed necessary before the memories of the horror could begin to be confronted again, and assimilated into individual and collective consciousness.

That was true in Cracow, where until the mid-1950s there was still a sizable Jewish community. And it was even more true in small towns and villages that had been the shtetls, where there were no Jews at all, and probably little conscious thought was given to what had happened to them. In Brańsk itself, there may have been a few people, like the Rycz brothers, who felt — in the most repellent of the Polish sentiments expressed after the war — grateful to Hitler for solving the Jewish problem. There may have been others, like Irena Jabłonowska, who felt an odd sense of emptiness, or perhaps regret, at the eerie disappearance of more than half of her town's population. It is difficult for anyone of sensitivity and minimal goodwill to live in the proximity of wholesale murder, on a street filled with the spectral presence of vanished friends and neighbors, without some heaviness of the soul. But most inhabitants of Brańsk probably remained fairly oblivious of the dimensions of the catastrophe and indifferent to the fate of those Others. Perhaps occasionally a scrap of memory or bits of conversation might surface. Expressions including Yiddish words ("It's as noisy as a *cheder*") might be unself-consciously used. But in a daily way, people were occupied with their own considerable problems — trying to seize some semblance of freedom from the Communist powers and daily coping in the face of economic stagnation and regression. Communist reprisals against Brańsk included punitive economic measures. Brańsk and Poland were once again becoming exceedingly poor.

What happened happened to someone else, outside the sphere of full, articulated consciousness. Perhaps on the Polish side as well, the Holocaust had been relegated to the psychic realm of denial and numbing. Immediately after the war, both Jews who were hidden and those who hid them wanted anonymity. They were afraid to reveal their secret. Whether this was because they feared other Poles' disapproval or because of some strange sense of shamefulness about what had passed is difficult to know.

In the subsequent decades, Polish-Jewish relations in the country as a whole went through several twists and turns. Amazingly enough, despite their almost total annihilation, the Jews, in some popular imaginings, were once again conceived of as powerful. The Communist Party, and particularly the hated UB (internal security forces), was believed to be predominantly Jewish. In the more anti-Semitic theories, the Judeo-Communist cabal was seen as responsible for the oppression of Poland. This was, as so often in the past, a paranoid fantasy feeding on a measure of reality: Jews were indeed disproportionately represented in the Communist Party and the UB, although they were hardly a dominant faction. The limits of their influence were definitively demonstrated in 1968 when, as a result of internecine struggles, most Jews were expelled from the Party, and most of the remaining Jewish population in Poland was, in effect, forced to emigrate. The anti-Semitic policies fell on fertile ground among the general population, but because these were government policies — and because the government was hated and mistrusted — they induced, especially in dissident circles, a kind of pro-Semitic reaction, or at least the impulse of solidarity with Jews.

But in places like Brańsk — which could be called shtetls no longer — all was absence and a kind of forgetting. There had been sporadic communication between survivors who emigrated and their wartime rescuers: Jack Rubin, for example, wrote letters to the Kozłowski family and occasionally sent them gifts. These would have been private matters, probably not much discussed — although some tongues might have wagged about a cow someone bought with money from abroad, or later, even a car.

The seeming forgetfulness could coexist with a kind of quiescent memory — with subliminal stereotypes, stored somewhere in the psyche, ready to surface on appropriate occasions, and on the other hand, fond recollections of Jewish habits, folklore, music. People in Brańsk still remember snatches of Yiddish songs. In other villages, Jewish proverbs and bits of Jewish lore are a vivid part of the peasants' imaginative world even today. Sometimes villagers go to pray at the graves of *tzaddiks* and rabbis, in the belief that these places and their spirits possess magic powers.

In the 1970s, with the liberalization of Polish politics, Jewish visitors started coming to Brańsk, undoubtedly awakening more concrete memories. Irena Jabłonowska renewed her friendship with Józef Broida. The Shapiros visited, and so did Jack Rubin. But none of this revived a public consciousness or discussion of the "Jewish question."

So things remained until 1989, when everything abruptly and dramatically changed. The themes of the last eight years are difficult to summarize, as they are in a constant state of flux. But it has often seemed in Poland, and indeed in all of Eastern Europe, that with the lifting of the Communist lid, the contents of the repressed past have emerged again in perfectly preserved form. It is as if old attitudes, predilections, and antagonisms have been released from their historical deep freeze without being modulated by the passage of time. In relation to the Jews in Poland — or rather, to the abstract notion of Jewishness — this has meant a return of both anti-Semitic notions and an intense and sometimes nostalgic interest in Jewish history and culture.

Zbigniew Romaniuk represents the more positive trend. Zbyszek started on his strange journey into Brańsk's past as a solitary explorer. In the last few years, he has published a journal called *Brańsk*, which regularly features articles about the town's Jewish history. But he is hardly alone. Throughout Poland, scholars, archivists, and literary and art historians are researching and documenting the country's Jewish past. There are festivals of Jewish culture, university departments of Jewish history, institutes concerned with Jewish matters. Recently, in an attempt to improve Poland's relations with international Jewry, the government has appointed an official "ambassador" to Diaspora Jews. There are also growing numbers of Jewish scholars who study the history of Jews in Poland.

Unfortunately, one can also sense in today's Brańsk the presence of something much more disturbing. Zbyszek has been attacked as a lackey of the Jews for his preoccupations, and the staircase of his former home was regularly defaced with anti-Semitic graffiti — scrawled there, he thinks, by young "hooligans." Astonishingly, one can find lists in Brańsk, distributed through murky channels, of "Jews who are harmful to the interests of Poland." A stack of the lists is left in the church, among other places — the same church that played such an honorable role during the war. These paranoiac publications include many names of important non-Jewish politicians, for in the purely symbolic rhetoric of the new anti-Semitism, anyone whose influence or views seem objectionable can be called Jewish.

Lists like these, or anti-Semitic slogans, result in few repercussions in today's Poland — and have little effect on voting patterns, it appears — but they indicate the rooted persistence of old prejudices in their most unreal and unregenerate form. Such expressions of outmoded attitudes are of course damaging for Poland's international image, but also perhaps for the health of the Polish body politic. The Jews were Poland's paradigmatic Other, and anti-Semitism, in the Polish psyche, is the paradigm of all prejudice; it stands not only for itself but for the more unpleasant strains of chauvinistic arrogance and defensive exclusionism.

Still, such manifestations continue to be marginal in Polish life. More central, and much more hopeful, is the reopening of public discussion about Polish-Jewish history, including its most painful episodes. The discussions, conducted in the press and in other forums, often draw furious heat and ardent feelings, but they are also filled with self-examination, self-criticism, and thorough searching of personal and collective conscience.

Those are the internal Polish conversations, but they make

the conditions for a Polish-Jewish dialogue much better. The Jewish counterparts in that dialogue have often been defensive as well, assuming nothing but ill will on the other side, downplaying discomfiting aspects of their own history and demanding full moral reparations where no reparations are really possible or satisfactory. No wrath or regret can make up for what was lost. But the need for a conversation — for the juxtaposing and sharing of facts, perceptions, views — remains, since only a composite picture, a shared understanding, can come close to a complete vision.

For those who lived through this history, or who feel personally implicated in it, the need for a full record and full comprehension is of urgent and passionate import. But what kind of understanding can we derive from the study of the Polish-Jewish past, and what light can it throw on the present? One hesitates to speak of lessons or to derive conclusions in a terrain where pieties are easier to come by than wisdom. And yet, perhaps the long and fascinating narrative of Polish-Jewish coexistence has something relevant to tell us after all. The Holocaust was the most extreme imaginable result of the most extreme form of Nazi anti-Semitism. In a way, the conclusions to be drawn from that catastrophe are stark and clear: racist prejudice is an unacceptable form of feeling against which we must constantly guard and educate ourselves. The clarity of this historical lesson does not, of course, guarantee that it will be — or has been — learned. In recent decades, we have seen repeatedly how quickly and unexpectedly dormant ethnic tensions can be inflamed into hate and violence. Moral ideas about prejudice seem to evaporate in the heat of ideological passions.

And this is why the history of the Polish-Jewish experiment can be profitably studied — not for illustrations of worst-case scenarios, but for the subtler and more ambiguous suggestions:

about the possibilities and pitfalls of multicultural relations; about situations in which prejudices can be contained, and circumstances in which collective feelings turn ugly; about political stimuli that lead to eruptions of violence, and factors that may restrain hostility. It is only fair to be explicit about my own views — or prejudices, for none of us is without them — as I risk some summarizing remarks. The quandary faced by Poles and Jews was the dilemma of any long and close relationship: how to live together while remaining themselves. Both Poles and Jews were "nations" with forceful, proud, and touchy identities, with a sometimes overweening sense of their moral worthiness and, in certain periods, their martyrdom. They were each other's strong Other, and there is no doubt that both their cultures were enriched in the long centuries of what has often been called the Polish-Jewish marriage.

The marriage had its idyllic moments of union, but too often it was full of turbulence and discord. It seems to me that this was because the partners — the polities involved — repeatedly erred on the side of distance and self-containment. As it happened, there was less pressure for cultural assimilation in Poland than in any Western European country, and yet, neither Poles nor Jews came up with a satisfactory paradigm for combining respect for difference with a sense of mutual belonging. The Poles undoubtedly had the first responsibility for envisioning a more generous and inclusive model of their society, but the Jewish minority was hardly helpless or unimplicated in the conversation. Especially in the period between the two world wars, in an era of ascendant Polish nationalism, there was a dearth of conceptions that would transcend or incorporate various "nationalisms" and particular interests. Neither Poles nor Jews found, or even theorized, a sphere of commonality, in which they could think of themselves not as adversaries fighting for their corner but as members of one social body.

The failure was not necessary or inevitable, for what the better phases of the Polish-Jewish experiment demonstrate is that, given good enough conditions and a sufficient meeting of needs, the desire for peaceful coexistence and the capacity to accept others for what they are can outweigh the impulses of suspicion and even philosophical prejudice. During most periods, the streets of Poland's cities and the paths of its shtetls did not seethe with hatred. In some spheres, there was interaction between Jews and Poles, and moments of genuine fraternity. In a shtetl like Brańsk, people left each other alone in their customs and beliefs, but they also worked and joked together, negotiated with each other, got used to each other. The more hopeful lesson of Polish-Jewish history may be that when conflicts of interest are not exacerbated or extreme, when fanatical notions are not willfully fanned, the instinct of tolerance, surely as basic as that of prejudice, can find breathing space.

Why couldn't these phases of concord and comity be better sustained? Over the span of centuries, Poles and Jews did not construct an effective underpinning of shared structures and convictions, and it seems to me what the Polish-Jewish experiment suggests — to put it in the most general terms — is that "identity politics" may be inadequate without a sense of solidarity. If we are to live together in multicultural societies, then in addition to cultivating differences, we need a sense of a shared world. This does not preclude the possibility of preserving and even nurturing strong cultural, spiritual, and ethnic identities in the private realm, nor does it suggest collapsing such identities into a universal "human nature." But if multicultural societies are to remain societies — rather than collections of fragmented, embattled enclaves — then we need a public arena in which we can speak not only from and for our particular interests, but as members of a society, from the vantage point of the common good.

It is difficult to know what would have happened to the Polish shtetl had the thread of its history not been so peremptorily severed. On the eve of World War II, it was a world rife with new energies and potentials. Its descendants in Israel, the United States, and Western Europe have amply shown the vitality of the shtetl heritage. Given time and change, Poles and Jews of the small towns might yet have found a new accommodation, and the increasing interpenetration of their cultures, as well as the grafting of modernity onto traditional Judaism, might have once again resulted in something unique and rich.

✒   ✒   ✒

On my last day in Brańsk, Zbyszek takes me to see the memorial cemetery he has created from the gravestones he has restored and carried here. It is a somber enclosure, and yet it is also oddly solacing. Someone was willing to honor both the gravestones and the murdered people, to take care of what was not his own. Nothing can bring back what was lost; after the Holocaust, we are in an era of symbolic action. But symbolically, this is an act of synthesis and of reconciliation. It is time to pay attention, wherever possible, to such acts — to attend to each other's pasts. The absence of mercy during the war had consequences so dark that its shadow has covered the horizon of perception. For too long afterward, the two memories remained insulated, deepening old rifts and wounds. It is time for Poles and Jews to recover the memory of generosity and the generosity of memory, to take the risk of erring on the side of compassion. For ourselves, we need to stop splitting our own memories and perceptions in half, and pushing away those parts which are too distressing for owning or acknowledgment. As for those who perished, the time may have come to let them rest in our full remembrance, and in peace.

Notes on the Sources ❧

Unless otherwise indicated, translations from Polish are by the author. Place names in the text are given in standard Anglicized spellings whenever applicable; the spellings of Polish and Yiddish first names have been standardized as well.

Direct quotations in the text come from the following sources: P A G E 1: Antoni Słonimski, "Elegy for the Jewish Villages," quoted in *The Jews in Polish Culture* by Aleksander Hertz, translation probably by Aleksander Hertz, p. 6. P A G E S 30–31: Statute of Kalisz in *Dzieje Żydów w Polsce, XI–XVIII Wiek: Wybór Tekstów Żródłowych (History of Jews in Poland, XI–XVIII Century: A Selection of Primary Texts)*, pp. 15–19. P A G E 42: burgher writer cited in *Świat Panów Pasków* by Janusz Tazbir, p. 219. P A G E 48: Francesco Giovanni Commendoni quoted in *Dzieje: XI–XVIII Century*, pp. 69–70. P A G E 49: Pietro Duodo, ibid., p. 70. P A G E S 50–51: Itzhak of Troki, ibid., pp. 86–87. P A G E S 58–59: Meir of Szczebrzeszyn quoted in "A Minority Views the Majority," by M. J. Rosman, *Polin*, vol. 4, p. 32. P A G E 59: Natan Hannower quoted in *Dzieje: XI–XVIII Century*, pp. 89–90. P A G E S 59–60: Shabbetai HaKohen in M. J. Rosman, *Polin*, vol. 4, p. 32. P A G E 62: Rabbi Levi Itzhak, ibid., p. 35. P A G E S 64–65: Mateusz Butrymowicz in *Dzieje: XI–XVIII Century*, pp. 100–103.

PAGES 65–66: Herszel Józefowicz, ibid., pp. 103–106. PAGES 66–67: Salomon of Vilno, ibid., pp. 106–108. PAGE 69: Tadeusz Kościuszko quoted in *The Jewish Community in Poland* by Isaac Lewin, translated by Isaac Lewin, p. 23. PAGES 69-70: Berek Joselewicz, ibid., p. 25. PAGES 95-96: Ber of Bolechów quoted in "The Role of Jews in Polish Foreign Trade, 1648–1764," by Janina Bieniarzówna, *The Jews in Poland*, vol. 1, p. 105. PAGE 98: *Z jarmarku (From the Market)* by Sholem Aleichem, translated from Yiddish into Polish by Michał Friedman, pp. 135–36. PAGE 104: Sholem Aleichem, ibid., p. 200. PAGES 107–108: description of peasant beliefs from *Wizerunek Żyda w polskiej kulturze ludowej (The Image of the Jew in Polish Folk Culture)* by Alina Cała. PAGE 109: Solomon Maimon, *An Autobiography*, translated from German by J. J. Clark Murray, p. 7. PAGES 110–111: Statement of the State Council of the Polish Kingdom quoted in *Dzieje Żydów w Polsce, XIX Wiek: Wybór Tekstów Źródłowych (History of Jews in Poland, XIX Century: A Selection of Primary Texts)*, p. 34; Statement of the Warsaw District Synagogue Council, ibid., p. 36; Rabbi Ber Meisels, ibid., p. 89. PAGE 128: Samuel Zvi Peltyn, ibid., p. 93. PAGE 132: Ignacy Kraszewski quoted in "The Image of the Shtetl in Polish Literature," by Eugenia Prokopówna, *Polin*, vol. 4, p. 133. PAGE 146: Eliza Orzeszkowa quoted in *Dzieje: XIX Century*, p. 86. PAGE 149: Józef Chaim Heftman quoted in the Yizkor Book. PAGE 174: songs included in *Yiddish Songs: Andre Ochodło Sings Mordechaj Gebirtig and Ewa Kornecka*, pp. 36, 40. PAGES 189–191: *A Family Saga: A Gathering of Memories* by Grace Goldman, pp. 32–36.

Bibliography ✺

DOCUMENTS

Trus, Alter, and Julius Kohen. *Brańsk: Pomnik Poległym.* New York: New York Brańsk Relief Committee, 1948. Part 3 of this memoir, "The Destruction of Brańsk," was translated into English.

Archives of the Wojewódzka Żydowska Komisja Historyczna, Białystok:
MII/B294, Zeznanie Prybuta Arie-Lejba, Białystok, January 3, 1947.
MII/B329, Zeznanie Kamienia Mejsze, Białystok, January 26, 1947.
MII/B307, Podanie Trusa Altera, Białystok, January 22, 1947.
MII/B300, Zeznanie Rubina Jankiela, Białystok, January 9, 1947.
MII/304, Zeznanie Trusa Lejba, Białystok, January 13, 1947.

MEMOIRS

Broida, Józef. *W lasach Brańska. Pamiętniki partyzanta żydow-skiego.* Compiled by Icchak Alperowicz.

Goldman, Grace. *A Family Saga: A Gathering of Memories.* Unpublished work.

A History of the Horowitz and Trus Families from Brańsk, Poland. Compiled by Susan Horowitz Cartun, November 1992.

Kaplan, Nathan. *A Letter to the Unknown.* Unpublished work, including correspondence between the author and Zbigniew Romaniuk. A short fragment of the book was published in English in *Search* 11, no. 2 (1991), 12–16.

BOOKS

Adelson, Józef, et al. *Najnowsze Dzieje Żydów w Polsce.* Warszawa: Wydawnictwo Naukowe PWN, 1993.

Aleichem, Sholem. *Z jarmarku.* Wrocław: Wydawnictwo Dolnosląskie, 1989.

Aleichem, Sholem. *Dzieje Tewji Mleczarza.* Wrocław: Wydawnictwo Dolnosląskie, 1989.

Bauman, Zygmunt. *Modernity and the Holocaust.* Cambridge, England: Polity Press, 1989.

Ben-Cion, Pinchuk. *Shtetl Jews under Soviet Rule: Eastern Poland on the Eve of the Holocaust.* London: Basil Blackwell, 1990.

Borzymińska, Zofia. *Dzieje Żydów w Polsce, XIX Wiek: Wybór Tekstów Żródłowych.* Warszawa: Żydowski Instytut Historyczny, 1994.

Buber, Martin. *Opowieści Chasydów.* Poznań: W. Drodze, 1986.

Cohen, A. *Everyman's Talmud.* London: J. M. Dent, 1961.

Cohen, Chester G. *Shtetl Finder.* Bowie, Maryland: Heritage Books, 1989.

Davies, Norman. *God's Playground: A History of Poland*, vols. 1 and 2. Oxford: Clarendon Press, 1981.

Davies, Norman. *Heart of Europe: A Short History of Poland.* New York: Oxford University Press, 1986.

Dec, Dorota, et al. *Żydzi-Polscy: Czerwiec-Sierpień, 1989.* Kraków: Muzeum Narodowe w Krakowie, 1989.

Ficowski, Jerzy, ed. *Rodzyńki z migdałami: Antologia poezji ludowej Żydów polskich w przekładach.* Wrocław, Warszawa: Zakład Narodowy Im. Ossolińskich, 1988.

Fijałkowski, Paweł. *Dzieje Żydłow w Polsce, XI–XVIII Wiek: Wybór Tekstów Żródłówych.* Warszawa: Żydowski Instytut Historyczny, 1993.

Finkielkraut, Alain. *The Imaginary Jew.* Lincoln and London: University of Nebraska Press, 1994.

Fishman, David E. *Embers Plucked from the Fire: The Rescue of Jewish Cultural Treasures in Vilna.* New York: YIVO Institute for Jewish Research, 1996.

Fogelman Eva. *Conscience and Courage: Rescuers of Jews During the Holocaust.* London: Victor Gollancz, 1995.

Fuks, Marian. *Żydzi w Warszawie: Życie codzienne, wydarzenia, ludzie.* Poznań, Daszewice: Sorus, 1992.

Goldhagen, Daniel Jonah. *Hitler's Willing Executioners: Ordinary Germans and the Holocaust.* London: Little, Brown, 1996.

Grynberg, Henryk. *Dziedzictwo.* Londyn: Aneks, 1993.

Grynberg, Henryk. *Żydowska wojna.* Warszawa: Czytelnik, 1989.

Gutman, Israel, et al., eds. *The Jews of Poland Between Two World Wars.* Hanover, N.H., and London: University Press of New England, 1989.

Hertz, Aleksander. *The Jews in Polish Culture.* Evanston, Ill.: Northwestern University Press, 1988.

Horn, Maurycy. *Regesty dokumentów i ekscerpty z metryki koronnej do historii Żydów w Polsce 1697–1795*, vol. 2, part 1. Wrocław: Zakład Narodowy Im. Ossolińskich, 1984.

Kersten, Krystyna. *Polacy Żydzi Komunizm: Anatomia półprawd, 1939–1968*. Warszawa: Niezależna Oficyna Wydawnicza, 1992.

Kymlicka, Will, ed. *The Rights of Minority Cultures*. Oxford: Oxford University Press, 1955.

Kugelmass, Jack, and Jonathan Boyarin, eds. *From a Ruined Garden: The Memorial Books of Polish Jewry*. New York: Schocken Books, 1983.

Lewin, Isaac. *The Jewish Community in Poland*. New York, 1985.

Maimon, Solomon. *An Autobiography*. New York: Schocken Books, 1967.

Maurer, Jadwiga. *"Z Matki Obcej ..." Szkice o powiązaniach Mickiewicza ze Światem Żydów*. Londyn: Polska Fundacja Kulturalna, 1990.

Mścisławski, T. *Wojsko Polskie a Żydzi*. Warszawa: Rozwój, 1923.

Newman, Louis I. *Hasidic Anthology: Tales and Teaching of the Hasidim*. New York: Schocken Books, 1963.

Paluch, Andrzej K., ed. *The Jews in Poland*, vol. 1. Kraków: Jagiellonian University, 1992.

Polonsky, Antony, ed. *From Shtetl to Socialism: Studies from Polin*. London and Washington, D.C.: Littman Library of Jewish Civilization, 1993.

Richmond, Theo. *Konin: A Quest*. London: Jonathan Cape, 1995.

Roskies, David G. *Against the Apocalypse: Responses to Catastrophe in Modern Jewish Culture*. Cambridge, Mass.: Harvard University Press, 1984.

Scharf, Rafael F. *Co Mnie I Tobie Polsko . . . Eseje bez uprzedzeń.* Kraków: Fundacja Judaica, 1996.

Siedlecki, Jan. *Brańsk Bogusława Radziwiłła, 1653–1669.* Białystok, 1991.

Singer, Isaac Bashevis. *Sztukmistrz z Lublina.* Warszawa: Państwowy Instytut Wydawniczy, 1990.

Singer, Isaac Bashevis. *The Seance and Other Stories.* Middlesex, England: Penguin Books, 1974.

Steinlauf, Michael C. *Bondage to the Dead: Poland and the Memory of the Holocaust.* Syracuse, N.Y.: Syracuse University Press, 1996.

Stryjkowski, Julian. *Austeria.* Warszawa: Czytelnik, 1979.

Stryjkowski, Julian. *Echo.* Warszawa: Czytelnik, 1988.

Tazbir, Janusz. *Świat Panów Pasków.* Łódź, 1986.

Todorov, Tzvetan. *Facing the Extreme: Moral Life in the Concentration Camps.* New York: Metropolitan Books, 1996.

Trzeciak, Stanisław. *Talmud o Gojach a Kwestia Żydowska.* Druk Braci Albertów, 1939.

Weinryb, Bernard D. *The Jews of Poland: A Social and Economic History of the Jewish Community in Poland from 1100 to 1800.* Philadelphia, 1973.

Wiśniewski, Tomasz. *Bóżnice Białostocczyzny. Heartland of the Jewish Life: Synagogues and Jewish Communities in the Bialystok Region.* Białystok: David, 1992.

Wisse, Ruth R., ed. *The I. L. Peretz Reader.* New York: Schocken Books, 1990.

Yiddish Songs: Andre Ochodło Sings Mordechaj Gebirtig and Ewa Kornecka. Sopot: Fundacja ART 2000.

Zamoyski, Adam. *The Polish Way: A Thousand-Year History of the Poles and Their Culture.* New York and Toronto: Franklin Watts, 1988.

Zawisza, M. C. *Jak Żydzi Rujnowali Polskę.* Warszawa: Rozwój, 1928.

266 ᴐᴎ BIBLIOGRAPHY

Zborowski, Mark, and Elizabeth Herzog. *Life Is with People: The Culture of the Shtetl.* New York: Schocken Books, 1971.
Żebrowski, Rafał. *Dzieje Żydów w Polsce. Wybór Tekstów Źródłowych, 1918–1939.* Warszawa: Żydowski Instytut Historyczny, 1993.

JOURNAL

Ziemia Brańska. Edited by Zbigniew Romaniuk. Vol. 1, 1989; vols. 2 and 3, 1990–91; vol. 4, 1993; vol. 5, 1994; vol. 6, 1995.

ARTICLES

Bartal, Israel. "Loyalty to the Crown or Polish Patriotism? The Metamorphoses of an Anti-Polish Story of the 1863 Insurrection." *Polin* 1, 1986.
Bartal, Israel. "Non-Jews and Gentile Society in East European Hebrew and Yiddish Literature, 1856–1914." *Polin* 4, 1989.
Bartoszewski, Władysław T. "Some Thoughts on Polish-Jewish Relations." *Polin* 1, 1986.
Bartoszewski, Władysław T. "Poles and Jews as the 'Other.' " *Polin* 4, 1989.
Berberysz, Ewa. "Guilt by Neglect." In Antony Polonsky, ed. *My Brother's Keeper?* Oxford: Routledge, 1990, 69–71.
Biale, David. "Love Against Marriage in the East European Jewish Enlightenment." *Polin* 1, 1986.
Bryk, Andrzej. "The Hidden Complex of the Polish Mind: Polish-Jewish Relations During the Holocaust." In Antony Polonsky, ed. *My Brother's Keeper?* 161–183.
Cała, Alina. "The Question of the Assimilation of Jews in the

Polish Kingdom (1864–1897): An Interpretive Essay." *Polin* 1, 1986.

Cichy, Michał, and Adam Michnik. "Polacy-Żydzi: Czarne Karty Powstania." *Gazeta Wyborcza*, January 29–30, 1994. A debate on this subject continued in the following issues of *Gazeta Wyborcza*: February 12–13 and April 16–17, 1994.

Eisenbach, Artur. "Sejm Czteroletni a Żydzi." In *Żydzi w Dawnej Rzeczypospolitej. Materiały z Konferencji "Autonomia Żydow w Rzeczypospolitej."* Wrocław, Warszawa: Zakład Narodowy Im. Ossolińskich, 1991, 180–192.

Ettinger, Shmuel. "Sejm Czterech Ziem." In *Żydzi w Dawnej Rzeczypospolitej. Materiały z Konferencji "Autonomia Żydow w Rzeczypospolitej,* 34–44.

Gieysztor, Aleksander. "The Beginnings of Jewish Settlement in Poland." In Chimen Abramsky, Maciej Jachimczyk, and Antony Polonsky, eds. *The Jews of Poland.* Oxford, 1986, 15–22.

Goldberg, Jacob. "The Changes in the Attitude of Polish Society Towards the Jews in the Eighteenth Century." *Polin* 1, 1986.

Hundert, Gershon David. "Some Basic Characteristics of the Jewish Experience in Poland." *Polin* 1, 1986.

Kersten, Krystyna, and Jerzy Szapiro. "The Contexts of the So-called Jewish Question in Poland after World War II." *Polin* 4, 1989.

Kieniewicz, Stefan. "Polish Society and the Jewish Problem in the Nineteenth Century." In Chimen Abramsky, Maciej Jachimczyk, and Antony Polonsky, eds. *The Jews of Poland.* 70–78.

Klier, John D. "The Polish Revolt of 1863 and the Birth of Russification: Bad for the Jews?" *Polin* 1, 1986.

Kołakowski, Leszek. "National Stereotypes." *Polin* 4, 1989.

Korzec, Paweł, and Jean-Charles Szurek. "Jews and Poles under Soviet Occupation (1939–1941): Conflicting Interests." *Polin* 4, 1989.

Mendelsohn, Ezra. "The Dilemma of Jewish Politics in Poland: Four Responses." In Bela Vago and George L. Mosse, eds. *Jews and Non-Jews in Eastern Europe, 1918–1945*. New York, 1974.

Mishinsky, Moshe. "A Turning Point in the History of Polish Socialism and Its Attitude Towards the Jewish Question." *Polin* 1, 1986.

Monkiewicz, Waldemar, and Józef Kowalczyk. "Pomoc Żydom w regionie białostockim podczas II wojny światowej."

Opalska, Magdalena. "Polish-Jewish Relations and the January Uprising: The Polish Perspective." *Polin* 1, 1986.

Polonsky, Antony. "Polish-Jewish Relations and the Holocaust." *Polin* 4, 1989.

Pritsak, Omeljan. "The Pre-Ashkenazic Jews of Eastern Europe in Relation to the Khazars, the Rus, and the Lithuanians." *Polin* 7, 1993, 3–21.

Prokopówna, Eugenia. "The Image of the Shtetl in Polish Literature." *Polin* 4, 1989.

Rosman, M. J. "Jewish Perceptions of Insecurity and Powerlessness in 16th–18th Century Poland." *Polin* 1, 1986.

Shmeruk, Chone. "Jews and Poles in Yiddish Literature in Poland Between the Two World Wars." *Polin* 1, 1986.

Siedlecki, Jan. "Sejmiki szlachty ziemi bielskiej w Brańsku w XVI–XVIII wieku." *Przegląd Historyczny,* 80, no. 2, 1989.

Tazbir, Janusz. "Images of the Jew in the Polish Commonwealth." *Polin* 4, 1989.

Tec, Nechama. "Of Help, Understanding, and Hope: Righteous Rescuers and Polish Jews." *Polin* 4, 1989.

Turniansky, Chava. "Yiddish 'Historical' Songs as Sources for the History of the Jews in Pre-Partition Poland." *Polin* 4, 1989.

Wexler, Paul. "The Reconstruction of Pre-Ashkenazic Jewish Settlements in the Slavic Lands in the Light of Linguistic Sources." *Polin* 1, 1986.

Wiślicki, Wacław. "Uwagi o sytuacji gospodarczej ludności żydowskiej w Polsce" (part 4). *Biuletyn ŻIH*, no. 1–2, 1988.

Wróbel, Piotr. "Żydzi Białegostoku w latach, 1918–1939." *Przegląd Historyczny* 79, no. 2, 1988.

Baltic Sea

Gdańsk •

• Szczecin

Bydgoszcz •

G E R M A N Y

• Berlin

Poznań •

Warta R.

Odra R.

Elbe R.

Dresden •

Wrocław •

C Z E C H   R E P U B L I C

Prague •

MODERN POLAND

Chazaud